A MIRROR
for
AMERICANS

COTTON PLANTATION

A MIRROR
for
AMERICANS

Life and Manners in the United States
1790-1870
as Recorded by American Travelers

II. THE COTTON KINGDOM

Compiled and Edited by
WARREN S. TRYON

THE UNIVERSITY OF CHICAGO PRESS

11-17-87

THE UNIVERSITY OF CHICAGO PRESS, CHICAGO 37

Cambridge University Press, London, N.W. 1, England

To
My Mother
LUCY TRYON

Contents

Volume II: THE COTTON KINGDOM

Contents

Part II

THE COTTON KINGDOM

The spreading territory below the Mason and Dixon Line and south of the Ohio River—in large part the areas which made up the Confederacy—was considered in the popular mind as a great Cotton Kingdom. That it was not all given over to the production of cotton, the tobacco plantations of Virginia and the rice and sugar plantations of South Carolina and Louisiana testify. But since nearly all the vast section was agrarian in economy, dominated by a planting aristocracy, and involved in the "peculiar institution" of slavery, it was natural enough that it should be conceived as a unit.

It was an area which, decade after decade, diverged continuously from the general patterns of American development. It set up a localistic states' rights *politique* in opposition to the rising nationalism of the North and West; it created a class system from planter aristocrat to Negro slave in contrast to the democratic spirit elsewhere in the nation; and it turned its back on the rising industrialism and urbanization of the North and East to maintain a persistent agricultural and rural way of life. Its unique position, and the contrast it afforded to the rest of the United States, excited a wide curiosity, and, accordingly, the South was much visited and described, especially by northerners.

In general, the observations and interests of travelers were absorbed in the spectacle of the planter and his slaves, sometimes to the neglect of other legitimate aspects of southern life. Because the subject was highly controversial, and became increasingly more so as the century advanced, it was natural that the observer's already preconceived notions colored his views. For that reason, if no other, a single account of the South is unsatisfactory; many accounts need to be compared before a balanced picture can be secured. Most travelers from the outside condemned slavery, and, certainly, very few unstintedly praised it. On the other hand, it should not be overlooked that there was a considerable number of northerners who, upon contact with the slave society, found it was not so bad as it had been painted and who mellowed their views about it. Perhaps because of the unusual amount of prejudice, for or against the system, there were many efforts to obtain "a record of the South as it really was." Of this type, Olmstead's narration is a classic.

Not all travelers were overwhelmed by the South's slave system. Occasionally there are observations about the poor whites and the mountain whites, though usually in their connection to the planter class, and such cities as the South possessed came under surveillance. Charleston and Savannah received due attention, and New Orleans, because of its exotic and almost foreign flavor, entranced the tourist. It is interesting to note, too, the distinction the travelers found between the older and settled Old South of the Atlantic Coast and the frontier, western character which survived in the newer plantations of the Gulf and Mississippi region.

Like New England, the South suffered in the quality of its observers once Reconstruction was over. The tendency was to emphasize the "quaint" or to embower in a nostalgic scent of magnolia blossoms, the virtues of the ante bellum South. By the close of the century few appeared to recognize either the economic and social changes or the needs of the Cotton Kingdom.

15

A Boston Brahmin Dines with
the Virginia Democracy, 1815

George Ticknor (1791–1871), in the great age of New England's "flowering," was one of the most brilliant members of Boston's literary circle. Born into a family of wealth, a graduate of Dartmouth College, he was endowed by nature with both physical and mental charm. Nor did anything in his life ever destroy the rich promise of his inheritance. He traveled widely and was as much at home in Europe as in his fine mansion on Park Street, Boston. Cultivated, urbane, and dignified, this Boston Brahmin was the very essence of enlightened aristocracy. Following an extended tour abroad, Ticknor in 1819 was inducted into the professorship of the French and Spanish languages at Harvard. He did much to promote a knowledge of European, and especially Romance, culture among his less enlightened fellow-Americans. He was a prime mover in the founding of the Boston Public Library and he was the author of the History of Spanish Literature *(1849), a work regarded highly by his contemporaries, and not without value today.*

When he was a youth of twenty-three, long before his later fame was achieved, he resolved to visit "at the South, to see the men the cities contain, and get some notion of the state of my own country." His observations were set down in letters to his father and contain a graphic as well as elegant grace characteristic of his later writing. The journey, well prepared for by introductory letters from ex-President John Adams, occurred at the conclusion of the War of 1812 as references to the burned capitol at Washington and the Battle of New Orleans make clear. Though bred in a deep-dyed Boston Federalism, he noted with little prejudice the two arch-leaders of Jeffersonian Democracy. It may well have been the unconscious reaction of one gentleman to another.

As we drew near to the metropolis of Washington I got out and rode forward with the driver, that I might see all that was strange and new. We were travelling on the very road by which the British had approached before us. We crossed the bridge at Bladensburg by which they had crossed, and saw on its right the little breastwork by which it was so faintly and fruitlessly defended. The degree and continuance of the resistance were plainly marked by the small mounds on the wayside, which served as scanty graves to the few British soldiers who fell; and the final struggle, which took place about a mile from the spot where the opposition commenced, was shown by the tomb of Barney's captain and sailors. These few mounds, which the winters' frosts and rains will quickly obliterate, are all the monuments that remain to us in proof of the defence of the capital of the country.

We drove forward three miles farther, and in the midst of a desolate-looking plain, over which teams were passing in whatever direction they chose, I inquired of the driver where we were. "In the Maryland Avenue, sir." He had hardly spoken when the hill of the Capitol rose before us. I had been told that it was an imperfect, unfinished work, and that it was somewhat unwieldy in its best estate. I knew that it was now a ruin, but I had formed no conception of what I was to see,—the desolate and forsaken greatness in which it stood, without a building near it, except a pile of bricks on its left more gloomy than itself,—no, not even a hill to soften the distant horizon behind it, or a fence or a smoke to give it the cheerful appearance of a human habitation.

Soon after my arrival in Washington I dined with President Madison. About half the company was assembled when I arrived. The President himself received me, as the Secretary was not on hand, and introduced me to Mrs. Madison, and Mrs. Madison introduced me to Miss Coles, her niece. This is the only introduction, I am told, that is given on these occasions. The company amounted to about twenty. There were two or three officers of the army with double epaulets and somewhat awkward manners, but the rest were members of Congress, who seemed little acquainted with each other.

The President, too, appeared not to know all his guests, even by name. For some time there was silence, or very few words. The President and Mrs. Madison made one or two commonplace remarks to me and others. After a few moments a servant came in and whispered to Mr. Madison, who went out, followed by his Secretary. It was mentioned about the room that the Southern mail had arrived, and a rather unseemly anxiety was expressed about the fate of New Orleans, of whose imminent danger we heard last night. The President soon returned, with added gravity, and said that there was no news! Silence ensued. No man seemed to know what to say at such a crisis, and, I suppose, from fear of saying what might not be acceptable, said nothing at all.

Just at dark, dinner was announced. Mr. Madison took in Miss Coles, General Winder folowed with Mrs. Madison. The Secretary invited me to go next; but I avoided it, and entered with him, the last. Mrs. Madison was of course at the head of the table; but, to my surprise, the President sat at her right hand, with a seat between them vacant. Secretary Coles was at the foot. As I was about to take my place by him, the President desired me to come round to him, and seeing me hesitate as to the place, spoke again, and fairly seated me between himself and Mrs. M. This was unquestionably the result of President Adams's introduction. I looked very much like a fool, I have no doubt, for I felt very awkwardly.

As in the drawing-room before dinner, no one was bold enough to venture conversation. The President did not apparently know the guest on his right, nor the one opposite to him. Mrs. Madison is a large, dignified lady, with excellent manners, obviously well practised in the ways of the world. Her conversation was somewhat formal, but on the whole appropriate to her position, and now and then amusing. I found the President more free and open than I expected, starting subjects of conversation and making remarks that sometimes savored of humor and levity. He sometimes laughed, and I was glad to hear it; but his face was always grave. He talked of religious sects and parties, and was curious to know how the cause of liberal Christianity stood with us, and if the Athanasian creed was well received by our Episcopalians. He pretty distinctly intimated to me his own regard for the Unitarian doctrines. The conversation, however, was not confined to religion; he talked of education and its prospects, of the progress of improvement among us, and once or twice he gave it a political aspect, though with great caution. He spoke to me of my visit to Monticello, and, when the party was separating, told me if I would go with him to the drawing-room and take coffee, his Secretary would give me the directions I desired. So I had another *tête-à-tête* with Mr. and Mrs. Madison, in the course of which Mr. M. gave amusing stories of early religious persecutions in Virginia, and Mrs. M. entered into a defence and panegyric of the Quakers, to whose sect she once belonged. At eight o'clock I took my leave.

I passed the whole of this morning in the Supreme Court. The room in which the Judges are compelled temporarily to sit is, like everything else that is official, uncomfortable, and unfit for the purposes for which it is used. They sat—I thought inconveniently—at the upper end; but, as they were all dressed in flowing black robes, and were fully powdered, they looked dignified. Judge Marshall is the Chief Justice of the United States, the first lawyer—if not, indeed, the first *man*—in the country. You must then imagine before you a man who is tall to awkwardness, with a large head of hair, which looked as if it had not been lately tied or combed, and with dirty boots. You must imagine him, too, with a strangeness in his manners, which arises neither from awkwardness nor from formality, but seems to be a curious compound of both; and then, perhaps, you will have before you a figure something like that of the Chief Justice. His style and tones in conversation are uncommonly mild, gentle, and conciliating; and soon I had forgotten the carelessness of his dress and person, and observed only the quick intelligence of his eye, and the open interest he discovered in the subjects on which he spoke, by the perpetual variations of his countenance. Judge Washington is a little, sharp-faced gentleman, with only one eye, and a profusion of snuff distributed over his face; and Judge Duval very like the late Vice-President, George Clinton. The Court was opened at half past eleven, and Judge Livingston and Judge Marshall read written opinions on two causes.

I dined at Mr. Robert Oliver's, with a large company of some of the more considerable men of Maryland; the most distinguished being Mr. Charles Carroll, the friend of Washington, one of the three surviving signers of the Declaration of Independence, at one time Senator of the United States, and the richest landholder, I suppose, in the country. At eighty he reads and enjoys his classical books more than most young men of the present generation. He is a specimen of the old *régime,* one of the few who remain to us as monuments of the best bred and best educated among our fathers. He wears large gold buckles in his shoes and broad lace ruffles over his hands and bosom, the fashion, I suppose, of the year 1760. His manner has a grave and stately politeness, and his tact and skill in conversation lead him to the subjects most familiar to his hearer; while he is so well read that he appears to have considered each himself.

We left Charlottesville on Saturday morning for Mr. Jefferson's. He lives on a mountain, which he has named Monticello, and which is a synonyme for Carter's mountain. The ascent of this steep, savage hill, was as pensive and slow as Satan's ascent to Paradise. We were obliged to wind two thirds round its sides before we reached the artificial lawn on which the house stands; and, when we had arrived there, we were about six hundred feet, I understand, above the stream which flows at its foot. It is an abrupt mountain. The fine growth of ancient forest-trees conceals its sides and shades part of its summit. The prospect is admirable. The lawn on the top, as I hinted, was artificially formed by cutting down the peak of the height. In its centre, and facing the southeast, Mr. Jefferson has placed his house, which is of brick, two stories high in the wings, with a piazza in front of a receding centre. It is built, I suppose, in the French style. You enter, by a glass folding-door, into a hall which reminds you of Fielding's "Man of the Mountain," by the strange furniture of its walls. On one side hang the head and horns of an elk, a deer, and a buffalo; another is covered with curiosities which Lewis and Clark found in their wild and perilous expedition. On the third, among many other striking matters, was the head of a mammoth, or, as Cuvier calls it, a mastodon, containing the only *os frontis,* Mr. Jefferson tells me, that has as yet been found. On the fourth side, in odd union with a fine painting of the Repentance of Saint Peter, is an Indian map on leather, of the southern waters of the Missouri, and an Indian representation of a bloody battle, handed down in their traditions.

Through this hall—or rather museum—we passed to the dining room, and sent our letters to Mr. Jefferson, who was of course in his study. Here again we found ourselves surrounded with paintings that seemed good.

We had hardly time to glance at the pictures before Mr. Jefferson entered; and if I was astonished to find Mr. Madison short and somewhat awkward, I was doubly astonished to find Mr. Jefferson, whom I had always supposed to be a small man, more than six feet high, with dignity in his appearance, and ease and graciousness in his manner. He rang, and sent to Charlottesville for our baggage, and, as dinner approached, took us to the drawing-room,— a large and rather elegant room, twenty or thirty feet high,—which, with the hall I have described, composed the whole centre of the house, from top to bottom. The floor of this room is tessellated. It is formed of alternate diamonds of cherry and beech, and kept polished as highly as if it were of fine mahogany.

Here are the best pictures of the collection. Over the fireplace is the Laughing and Weeping Philosophers, dividing the world between them; on its right, the earliest navigators to America,—Columbus, Americus Vespucius, Magellan, etc.,—copied, Mr. Jefferson said, from originals in the Florence Gallery. Farther round, Mr. Madison in the plain, Quaker-like dress of his youth, Lafayette in his Revolutionary uniform, and Franklin, in the dress in which we always see him. There were other pictures, and a copy of Raphael's Transfiguration.

We conversed on various subjects until dinner-time, and at dinner were introduced to the grown members of his family. These are his only remaining child, Mrs. Randolph, her husband, Colonel Randolph, and the two oldest of their unmarried children, Thomas Jefferson and Ellen; and I asssure you I have seldom met a pleasanter party.

The evening passed away pleasantly in general conversation, of which Mr. Jefferson was necessarily the leader. I shall probably surprise you by saying that, in conversation, he reminded me of Dr. Freeman. He has the same discursive manner and love of paradox, with the same appearance of sobriety and cool reason. He seems equally fond of American antiquities, and especially the antiquities of his native State, and talks of them with freedom and, I suppose, accuracy. He has, too, the appearance of that fairness and simplicity which Dr. Freeman has; and, if the parallel holds no further here, they will again meet on the ground of their love of old books and young society.

On Sunday morning, after breakfast, Mr. Jefferson asked me into his library, and there I spent the forenoon of that day as I had that of yesterday. This collection of books, now so much talked about, consists of about seven thousand volumes, contained in a suite of fine rooms, and is arranged in the catalogue, and on the shelves, according to the divisions and subdivisions of human learning by Lord Bacon. In so short a time I could not, of course, estimate its value, even if I had been competent to do so.

Perhaps the most curious single specimen—or, at least, the most characteristic of the man and expressive of his hatred of royalty—was a collection which he had bound up in six volumes, and lettered "The Book of Kings," consisting of the "Memoires de la Princesse de Bareith," two volumes; "Les Memoires de la Comtesse de la Motte," two volumes; the "Trial of the Duke of York," one volume; and *"The Book,"* one volume. These documents of regal scandal seemed to be favorites with the philosopher, who pointed them out to me with a satisfaction somewhat inconsistent with the measured gravity he claims in relation to such subjects generally.

On Monday morning I spent a couple of hours with him in his study. He gave me there an account of the manner in which he passed the portion of his time in Europe which he could rescue from public business; told me that while he was in France he had formed a plan of going to Italy, Sicily, and Greece, and that he should have executed it, if he had not left Europe in the full conviction that he should immediately return there, and find a better opportunity. He spoke of my intention to go, and, without my even hinting any purpose to ask him for letters, told me he was now seventy-two years old, and that most of his friends and correspondents in Europe had died, but that he would gladly furnish me with the means of becoming acquainted with some of the remainder, and regretted that their number was so reduced.

The afternoon and evening passed as on the two days previous; for everything is done with such regularity, that when you know how one day is filled, I suppose you know how it is with the others. At eight o'clock the first bell is rung in the great hall, and at nine the second summons you to the breakfast-room, where you find everything ready. After breakfast every one goes, as inclination leads him, to his chamber, the drawing-room, or the library. The children retire to their school-room with their mother, Mr. Jefferson rides to his mills on the Rivanna, and returns about twelve. At half past three the great bell rings, and those who are disposed resort to the drawing-room at the second call of the bell, which is at four o'clock. The dinner was always choice, and served in the French style; but no wine was set on the table till the cloth was removed. The ladies sat until about six, then retired, but returned with the tea-tray a little before seven, and spent the evening with the gentlemen; which was always pleasant, for they are obviously accustomed to join in the conversation, however high the topic may be. At about half past ten, which seemed to be their usual hour of retiring, I went to my chamber, found there a fire, candle, and a servant in waiting to receive my orders for the morning, and in the morning was waked by his return to build the fire.

To-day, Tuesday, we told Mr. Jefferson that we should leave Monticello in the afternoon. He seemed much surprised, and said as much as politeness would permit on the badness of the roads and the prospect of bad weather, to induce us to remain longer. It was evident, I thought, that they had calculated on our staying a week. At dinner, Mr. Jefferson again urged us to stay, not in an oppressive way, but with kind politeness; and when the horses were at the door, asked if he should not send them away; but as he found us resolved on going, he bade us farewell in the heartiest style of Southern hospitality. I came away thinking, with General Hamilton, that he was a perfect gentleman in his own house.

A little incident which occurred while we were at Monticello should not be passed by. The night before we left, young Randolph came up late from Charlottesville, and brought the astounding news that the English had been defeated before New Orleans by General Jackson. Mr. Jefferson had made up his mind that the city would fall. He had gone to bed, like the rest of us; but of course his grandson went to his chamber with the paper containing the news. But the old philosopher refused to open his door, saying he could wait till the morning; and when we met at breakfast I found he had not yet seen it.

There is a breathing of notional philosophy in Mr. Jefferson,—in his dress, his house, his conversation. His setness, for instance, in wearing very sharp toed shoes, corduroy small-clothes, and a red plush waistcoat, which have been laughed at till he might perhaps wisely have dismissed them.

So, though he told me he thought Charron, "De la Sagesse," the best treatise on moral philosophy ever written, and an obscure Review of Montesquieu, by Dupont de Nemours, the best political work that had been printed for fifty years,—though he talked very freely of the natural impossibility that one generation should bind another to pay a public debt, and of the expediency of vesting all the legislative authority of a State in one branch, and the executive authority in another, and leaving them to govern it by joint discretion,—I considered such opinions simply as curious *indicia* of an extraordinary character.

16

The Creoles of Louisiana, 1812

Amos Stoddard was born in Woodbury, Connecticut in 1762. Though occupied for a time in politics and the law in the district of Maine, his true love appears to have been the army. He had served in the Revolution and, during the French crisis of 1798, re-entered military service with the rank of captain. In 1804, directly after the purchase of Louisiana, he was made military and civil governor of the territory. It appears that he served with distinction and popularity and was especially noteworthy in his efforts to reconcile the inhab-

itants with the change in their political status. With an archival sense, he made elaborate compilations of the geography, ethnology, and history of the territory during his term of office. These he gathered together and published in 1812 as Sketches, Historical and Descriptive, of Louisiana. *The work is comprehensive and detailed and speaks with the accuracy and authority of a man with eight years' experience in the area. In the following year he died from wounds received while serving in the War of 1812.*

In contemplating the character of the French people in Louisiana, the old observation, "that ignorance tends to happiness," seems in a degree to be verified among them; for of all people on the globe these French appear to be the happiest. Indolence is prevalent among them; but they are honest in their dealings. They obtain but little, and little satisfies their desires. They usually live within their incomes, and are never so uneasy as when in debt. While the English Americans are hard at labor, and sweat under the burning rays of a meridian sun, they will be seated in their houses, or under some cooling shade, amusing themselves with their pipes and tobacco, and in drinking of coffee. When occasion presses, however, they are not deficient in exertion. Many of them follow boating and the Indian trade; and these require much labor, activity, and circumspection. They are very patient under fatigues, and will subsist for months on such food as the woods afford without a murmur. They enjoy what they have, and are perfectly contented with it.

The Creole French are at least a century behind other civilized nations in the arts and sciences, if not in the amenities of life. Three causes have contributed to keep them stationary. The first is, that most of the original settlers were extremely illiterate, and this in some measure accounts for the same condition of their posterity: Their attention was almost wholly drawn to such laborious pursuits as were calculated to yield them a subsistence, and left them no time for the acquisition of learning. The second is, the inattention of the government, or, in other words, the defect of their social institutions. These were not of a nature to encourage literature, but rather to repress it; and the people had no ambition to excel, especially as the highest literary attainment was never considered as a passport to fame, except perhaps in the religious orders. The third is, that Louisiana was in a manner insulated from the rest of the world; the inhabitants seldom mixed with strangers; and strangers had no inducements to visit them; the trade of the country was either prohibited, or the products of its soil, till a late period, too unimportant to tempt their enterprise.

Notwithstanding these impediments, the people appear to much more advantage than others under like circumstances. Many of the most opulent planters along the Delta and Red River cannot either read or write; and yet they will converse fluently, and with much seeming confidence, on a variety of subjects, where mathematical learning is necessary to a solution. They will debate on complicated machines, the utility or defects of which cannot be determined without a knowledge of mechanics, and propose substitutes and experiments with as much apparent judgment as if they were complete masters of the principles of the art. This want of information cannot be imputed to all; for some of the Creoles possess real intelligence, and are well instructed in several branches of useful learning, though their number is too limited to afford, in this respect, a very favourable reputation to the country.

Perhaps these defects are less apparent from the native vivacity of the Louisianians. This vivacity, indeed, is peculiar to the French, and, in no situation does it wholly forsake them. To this may be ascribed their passion for social intercourse, which is always gratified when opportunities permit. They are particularly attached to the exercise of dancing, and carry it to an incredible excess. Neither the severity of the cold, nor the oppression of the heat, ever restrains them from this amusement, which usually commences early in the evening, and is seldom suspended till late the next morning. They even attend the balls not unfrequently for two or three days in succession, and without the least apparent fatigue. At this exercise the females, in particular, are extremely active, and those of the United States must submit to be called their inferiors.

The dancing assemblies of the *Quarterons,* or free people of color, in New-Orleans, are not the least interesting in point of beauty and dress. They enjoy much more consideration in that country than is usual in any other. They never associate with blacks; and as there is a strong barrier between them and the whites with respect to marriage, they may be said to form a distinct class. The females possess the most beautiful forms and features. If they are accustomed to bestow their favors on the higher orders of society, it is always for stipulated periods, and no depravation of manners is observable among them. Gentlemen of distinction resort to their ball-rooms, and other places of amusement, where decency and decorum maintain their empire.

To the social nature of the French may in part be attributed their fondness for games of hazard, and in part to occasional relaxations from toil and fatigue, when amusements become necessary to their active and volatile dispositions. The repetition of any one soon ceases to afford pleasure; what pleases them one day will disgust the next, and nothing short of a variety will satisfy them. Hence it is, that they escape from the ball-room to cards, from cards to billiards, from billiards to dice, from dice back again to the ball-room, or to some other pastime, and so on alternately. Gambling in New-Orleans is reduced to a profession, where members of the fraternity from the United States rendezvous in great numbers. It is not known in Upper Louisiana as a science, though it is becoming prevalent, especially among the English Americans. The loss of time is never considered by the French as an evil, because if it were not spent in this way, it would be wasted in some other, perhaps equally injurious, and more prejudicial to health. Indolence often induces them to seek repose on the sofa or mattress.

The French are prompted to marry early in life; the climate dictates this practice; and they are usually blessed with a numerous progeny. The women have more influence over their husbands than is common in most other countries. Perhaps this arises in part from the example of the parent state; in part from the respect, which the men entertain for their wives; and perhaps still more from the almost exclusive right, which the women have to the property, in consequence of marriage contracts. Matches are often made by the parents, and the affections and inclinations of the children are not always consulted.

A short acquaintance with the women might lead a prudish observer to believe, that there existed a laxity in their morals. Nothing would be more unjust than such a conclusion. If, in their manners and conversation, they are less guarded than their female neighbors on the east side of the Mississippi, it proceeds from a national habit, and from an unsuspicious temper, and not in the least degree from a corruption of principle or sentiment. To whom shall we appeal as the criterion of purity? Nations essentially differ in their conceptions of virtue and vice. This difference has been created by habit; and the French consider their women, (and they consider justly) as much exempt from impropriety as those of some other countries, who remain almost invisible during their lives.

It has been observed in another place, that the Creoles, or native inhabitants, are partly the descendants of the French Canadians, and partly of those who migrated under some of the first governors of Louisiana. These are intermixed with some natives of France, Spain, Germany, and the United States, and in many instances with the Aborigines.

Most of them are small in statue, and slender in their make, though their bodies and limbs are remarkably well proportioned, supple, and active. Their complexions are somewhat sallow, and exhibit a sickly aspect, though they experience a good degree of health, which results in a great measure from the nature of their food, (most of the vegetable kind) and their manner of dressing it. They usually possess a keen piercing eye, and retain their sight longer than most other people. They are almost strangers to the gout, consumption, the gravel and stone in the bladder, and in general to all chronic complaints. The hair of the old people in the Delta, and neighborhood of it, retains a dark brown color; while that of the old people in Upper Louisiana commonly becomes grey. The young men at this time manifest no great passion for long hair; not many years ago they were seen with queues dangling about their legs. Most of the laboring class disregard dress, and appear no better at home than on a trading voyage among the Indians.

The complexions of the women are, in general, much fairer than those of the men; perhaps because they are less exposed to the vicissitudes of the seasons, particularly the burning rays of the sun. They are usually handsome when young, but when arrived to the age of thirty-five or forty, their bloom mostly forsakes them, and they become wrinkled and withered. This observation is particularly applicable to those of the Low Country, about the Delta and Red River. They are extremely fond of dress; they possess ease, grace, and penetration; they are remarkably loquacious, and their manners are more polished than those of the men; they are hospitable, and manifest much pleasure in offering to their guests and visitors the best things they are able to furnish. They have one fault not easily extenuated; they are habitually cruel to their slaves.

Louisiana contains more than forty thousand slaves. The climate, the productive nature of the lands in that country, and the accumulation of wealth beyond all former example, seem to render it highly probable, that their number will soon exceed that of the whites.

Experience has long since convinced the more intelligent planters, that the profits they derive from the labor of their slaves are in proportion to the good or bad treatment of them. But those planters of an opposite character are much the most numerous, perhaps they form nine tenths of the whole, especially among the French and Spanish settlers in Lower Louisiana. In no part of the world are slaves better treated than in the Mississippi Territory, where the planters generally allow them salted meat, as much corn meal as they can consume, cows to furnish milk for their families, land for gardens, and the privilege of raising fowls. They also allow them one suit of clothes for summer, and another for winter. Their slaves are active and robust, and enabled to perform their alloted portions of work with ease. Such treatment renders them contented and honest, and punishments are rare among them. Each good slave, well clothed and fed, will yield a yearly clear profit of two hundred and fifty or three hundred dollars. No small degree of satisfaction is derived from the performance of good actions; and happy is he, who is not accused by his conscience of aggravated wrongs done to the human species.

When we pass into Louisiana, we behold a different and more disgusting picture. The French and Spanish planters, in particular, treat their slaves with great rigor; and this has been uniformly the case from the first establishment of the colony. They were at first too poor to supply their slaves with clothing and food: Add to this, their families stood in need of the avails of their labors; and every expense incurred on account of their comfort and support was viewed as a serious evil. Hence this original defect in the system has been considered as a precedent by subsequent generations, not because they view the examples of their ancestors with reverence, but because they conceive it redounds to their interest. These planters are extremely ignorant of agricultural pursuits, and of the quantum of labor in the power of a slave to perform in a given time. Few of them allow any clothing to their slaves, or any kind of food, except a small quantity of corn; and even this they are obliged to pound, or grind, while they ought to be at rest. The consequence is, that the slaves are extremely debilitated, and incapable of much labor. One well fed negro is nearly equal to three of them. Their masters and overseers affect to believe, that their want of industry arises from laziness, and a perverse disposition. Hence cruel and even unusual punishments are daily inflicted on these wretched creatures, enfeebled, oppressed with hunger, labor, and the lash. The scenes of misery and distress constantly witnessed along the coast of the Delta, the wounds and lacerations occasioned by demoralized masters and overseers, most of whom exhibit a strange compound of ignorance and depravity, torture the feelings of the passing stranger, and wring blood from his heart.

If the manners of the Creole women be more polished than those of the men, it ought not to be wondered at. The estimation in which they are held, no doubt contributes to it. They mix more in society. The men, except along the Delta, are more or less engaged in trade among the Indians. This is sufficient to give a peculiar cast to their manners; and the pride they take in filling the wardrobes of their family females, contributes in no small degree to the inequality between them. It is not uncommon to see thirty or forty charming females in a ball-room, dressed with taste and even elegance, suited to the most fashionable society, when perhaps the males of their own families appear in their blanket coats and moccasons. It is rare to see in such an assembly more than four or five young men, whose appearance is even tolerable. This strange diversity is prevalent in the detached settlements of the country, and it even appears in some of the villages.

The French Creoles are temperate; they mostly limit their desires to vegetables, soups, and coffee. They are great smokers of tobacco, and no doubt this gives a yellow tinge to the skin. Ardent spirits are seldom used, except by the most laborious classes of society. They even dislike white wines, because they possess too much spirit. No doubt the warmth of the climate is, in some measure, the cause of this aversion. Claret, and other light red wines, are common among them; and those who can afford it are not sparing of this beverage.

Great economy is displayed in their family meals. This is not the effect of a parsimonious disposition, nor always of the want of adequate means; it results from the nature of the climate, and from a conviction of what their constitutions require; they readily sacrifice what may be termed luxury for the preservation of health, and it is seldom they contract diseases from intemperate excesses. Naturally volatile in their dispostions, they sometimes precipitate themselves from one extreme to another. Hence it is, that, in making entertainments for their friends, especially for strangers of distinction, they study to render them sumptuous; their tables are covered with a great variety of dishes; almost every sort of food dressed in all manner of ways, is exhibited in profusion. The master of the house, out of respect to his guests, frequently waits on them himself. On such occasions no trouble or expense is spared in procuring the best wines, and other liquors, the country affords. Their deserts are no less plentiful, and there is no want of delicacy in their quality or variety. Many of these entertainments cost from two hundred and fifty to four hundred dollars, especially in Upper Louisiana, where the luxuries of the table are much more expensive than in the Delta.

This occasional display of luxury may be imputed by some to fastidious pride. The reputation of poverty is almost as dreadful to them as the reality; and even the appearance of wealth affords some satisfaction, if they are not worth a cent in the world. Pride, indeed, is a predominant feature in their character, and sometimes proves injurious to them, because it is the pride of appearing to as much advantage as their more wealthy neighbors, and of feeling the deep mortification of a disadvantageous comparison.

The Louisianians, particularly about the Delta, indulge, to some excess, one of the fashionable vices of older countries. Most of the married men lavish their attentions on dissolute females, whom they usually take under their protection. These, in most instances, are selected from the mixed breeds; except among the Spanish settlers, who prefer a fat black wench to any other female! It is not easy to account for this depravity of taste. The Spaniards carry their impure connexions to a much greater extent than any other description of inhabitants.

The Creoles in general are remarkably neat and cleanly in their houses. Their furniture, usually fabricated by the artizans of the country, is rough and misshapen; yet it is polished to a high degree. Their floors in many instances are waxed, and as smooth and bright as a mahogany dining table. This passion for cleanliness is particularly exhibited by the women, who frequently carry it to excess. All house affairs exclusively belong to them, and the men incur no small danger when they attempt to interfere with their prerogatives. Even in most instances or purchases and sales, the women are consulted; and they not unfrequently assume the management of property.

The mode of building, as practised by the first settlers, is still preserved. The houses are mostly built of wood, except in those villages situated in the neighborhood of stone quarries. The manufacture of brick is of recent date in Louisiana. Several houses in New-Orleans have been constructed of this material, and the inhabitants begin to appreciate its value. The houses in general are of one story high only, and either wholly or partly surrounded by arcades or piazzas, from eight to twelve feet broad. They usually have a spacious hall in the centre, which communicates with the rooms on each side of it. Houses of two stories high are less safe on account of the sudden and violent squalls of wind in that country. This mode of building is convenient in other respects. The arcades or piazzas afford agreeable shades, under which the inhabitants repose themselves during the heat of the day; they likewise serve to shelter them from the dews and rains; and many families eat and sleep under them in summer.

It is said, that the French language in Louisiana has become considerably corrupted, especially among the lower classes. This need not be wondered at, as they are mostly the descendants of those, who settled in North America about two centuries ago; during which period no great intercourse subsisted between them and the mother country, nor were the migrations sufficiently numerous to afford a progressive improvement in the language. Many individuals, however, speak the French language in its purity; they have made it a point to acquire it, and to forget their provincial dialects.

It is hardly necessary to add, that the Creoles are obstinately attached to the Roman catholic religion. If health and prosperity in some measure divert their attention from it; yet in the hour of affliction, particularly when apprehensive of death, they cling to it as the only anchor of their hope. They are strict observers of the festivals prescribed by their religion, and of the days devoted to their favorite saints.

17

Slaves and Rivermen: Western Virginia, 1816

The Letters from the South, *which James K. Paulding (see p. 95) published soon after his excursion to the southern mountains, is less a book of
travels than a springboard for the author's essays on city living, books, Ameri-
canism, and other topics. There are, however, descriptive passages of both
charm and insight.*

*It is evident that Paulding was no Abolitionist, and, indeed, he vigorously
defended the institution in his* Slavery in America. *Like many literary men
confronted with a social problem, Paulding would clearly have liked to think
of slavery in its patriarchal and romantic aspects; and, indeed, in 1816, it was
not too difficult to do so. Yet at times reality so forcefully obtruded itself
upon him, as in the extract here given, that his indignation could not be suppressed. Perhaps Paulding's literary skill appears to better advantage when
his fancy and his ethics were not in conflict, as in the case of the amusing
account of the Shenandoah rivermen.*

AN EARLY VIEW OF THE SLAVE TRADE

The negroes are in general a harmless race and wo to those, who, tempted
by avarice, or impelled by vengeance, shall divide the parent from its offspring, and sell them apart in distant land. A cruel and inhuman act;—for it
is seldom we see the ties of kindred or of conjugal affection stronger than in
the poor negro. He will travel twelve, fifteen, or twenty miles, to see his wife

and children, after his daily labour is over, and return in the morning to his labour again. If he obtains his liberty, he will often devote the first years of his liberty to buying their freedom;—thus setting an example of conjugal and parental affection, which the white man may indeed admire; but, is feared, would seldom imitate.

I am led into these reflections by a rencontre we had yesterday with a caitiff who was on one of those expeditions to buy slaves for the southern market. At one of the taverns along the road, we were set down in the same room with an elderly man, and a youth who conversed together familiarly, and with true republican independence—for they did not mind who heard them. From the tenor of his conversation, I was induced to look particularly at the elder, who was an ill-looking, hard-featured, pock-marked, black-bearded fellow, whom a jury would have hanged upon very doubtful evidence.

He was telling the youth something like the following detested tale:— He was going, it seems, to Richmond, to inquire about a draft for seven thousand dollars, which he had sent by mail, but which, not having been acknowledged by his correspondent, he was afraid had been stolen, and the money received by the thief. "I should not like to lose it," says he, "for I worked hard for it, and sold many a poor d——l of a blacky to Carolina and Georgia to scrape it together." He then went on to tell many a black perfidious tale, which I tried to forget, and threw them from my memory as the stomach does poisons. All along the road, it seems, he made it his business to inquire where lived a man who might perhaps be tempted to become a party in this accursed traffic; and when he had got some half a dozen of these poor creatures, he tied their hands behind their backs, and drove them three or four hundred miles, or more, bare-headed, and half naked, through the burning southern sun. Fearful that even southern humanity would revolt at such an exhibition of human misery, and human barbarity, he gave out that they were runaway slaves he was carrying home to their masters. On one occasion a poor black woman exposed this fallacy, and told the story of her being kidnapped; and when he got her into a wood out of hearing, he beat her, to use his own expression, "till her back was white."

I would not tell such tales, except that chance may bring them to the ears of magistrates who will enforce the laws, if any there be, against this inhuman trade,—or if there be none, that the legislatures may be induced to wipe away this foul stain. There was a singular mixture of guilty hardihood, and affected sancity, about this *animal,*—for he could not be a man. It seems he married all the men and women he bought, himself, because they would sell better for being man and wife! Once,—he told it with high glee,—he sold a negro who was almost blind "to a *parson*," these were his very words, "for eight hundred dollars." Returning that way some time after, the *parson* (can it be possible?) accused him of cheating him, by selling him a fellow who couldn't see half a yard, after sun-down. "I denied it stoutly," continued this fine fellow,—"the parson insisted; and at last I bought the fellow back again for fifty dollars less than I sold him for. When the bargain was concluded,—Pomp, said I,—go and water my horse. Pomp pretended he could not see,—for it was then dusk:—but I took a good cudgel, and laid on till the fellow saw as plain as daylight, and did what he was bid as well as any body could have done it. There, said I, you see the fellow is no more blind than you or I. The parson wanted to get him back: so I sold him again for eight hundred dollars, and made fifty by the speculation."

"But," said the youth, "were you not afraid in travelling through the wild country, and sleeping in lone houses, these slaves would rise and kill you." "To be sure I was," said the other, "but I always fastened my door, put a chair on a table before it, so that it might wake me in falling, and slept with a loaded pistol in each hand. It was a bad life; and I left it off *as soon as I could live without it:* for many is the time I have separated wives from husbands, and husbands from wives, and parents from children; but then I made them amends by marrying them again as soon as I had a chance. That is to say, I made them call each other man and wife, and sleep together,—which is quite enough for negroes. I made one bad purchase, though," continued he,—"I bought a young mulatto girl, a likely creature,—a great bargain. She had been the favourite of her master, who had lately married. The difficulty was, to get her to go; for the poor creature loved her master. However, I swore most bitterly I was only going to take her to her mother at ———, and she went with me; though she seemed to doubt me very much. But when she discovered at last that we were out of the State, I thought she would go mad; and, in fact, the next night, drowned herself in the river close by. I lost a good five hundred dollars by this foolish trick, and began to think seriously of quitting this business; which I did soon after, and set up a shop. But though I lie to every body, somehow or other, I don't get on very well; and sometimes think of returning to my old trade again."

Oliver and I had intended to sleep at this place, but the confession of this abominable caitiff determined us to rid ourselves of his society, for fear the house would fall, or earth open and swallow us up for being in such company. So we left the house, praying that Providence, in pity to a miserable race, would either permit the caitiff to prosper in his present business, or graciously cause him to be speedily hanged. In justice to our own country I ought to mention this caitiff was not a native of the United States: had he been, I would have suppressed this story,—for such a monster is sufficient to disgrace a whole nation.

I ought to have mentioned, that the negroes of Maryland and Virginia, for some reason or other, have an invincible repugnance to being sold to the southward. Whether this repugnance arises from an idea that they will be treated with more severity, or is only the natural dislike every human being, except our fashionable ladies, feels to going to live in a strange land, far from all association with early scenes, and first-born attachments, I cannot tell. I know not that these poor souls are worse treated in Carolina and Georgia, nor have I any reason to believe so; certain it is, however, that they discover an unwillingness amounting almost to horror, at the idea of being sold there; and have a simple song which they some times, as I am told, sing with a mournful melancholy cadence, as they row along the rivers, in remembrance of home. It is merely the language of nature:

> Going away to Georgia, ho, heave, O!
> Massa sell poor negro, ho, heave, O!
> Leave poor wife and children, ho, heave, O! &c. &c.

The negroes have a great number of songs, of their own composition, and founded on various little domestic incidents; particularly the death of their masters and mistresses, who, if they have been kind to them, are remembered in their homely strains, some of which sound very affectingly, but would probably make no great figure on paper. I have heard that in some instances they go to their graves, and invoke their spirits to interpose, if they are treated ill, or threatened to be sold at a distance. There is something of the true pathetic in all this, were these people not negroes. This spoils all; for we have got such an inveterate habit of divesting them of all the best attributes of humanity, in order to justify our oppressions, that the idea of connecting feeling or sentiment with a slave, actually makes us laugh. I have read, that after the death of the famous Alphonso Albuquerque, called the Conqueror of India, it was long the practice of the natives, when they were oppressed, to go to his grave, and call upon his gallant spirit to arise and be again their protector. Such things touch the innermost heart, when told of Indians; but black sentiment, feeling, or gratitude, is not of the real fashionable colour.

Jogging along from the house where we left the caitiff, who will one day, I fear, bring down some great calamity on the country of his birth, it was our fate to meet with another example of the tricks men will play before high Heaven, when not only custom, but the laws, sanction oppression. The sun was shining out very hot,—and in turning an angle of the road, we encountered the following group: first, a little cart, drawn by one horse, in which five or six half naked black children were tumbled, like pigs, together. The cart had no covering—and they seemed to have been actually broiled to sleep. Behind the cart marched three black women, with head, neck, and breasts uncovered, and without shoes or stockings: next came three men, bareheaded, half naked, and chained together with an ox-chain. Last of all came a white man,—a white man!—on horseback, carrying pistols in his belt, and who, as we passed him, had the impudence to look us in the face without blushing. A little further on, we learned, that he had bought these miserable beings in Maryland, and was marching them in this manner to some one of the more southern States. Shame on the State of Maryland! Shame on the State of Virginia!—and every State through which this wretched cavalcade was permitted to pass!

SHENANDOAH BOATMEN

Yesterday we lay by at the little town of W——. It was court time, and two lawyers were to take the field against each other, in a suit between a wagoner and a batteauxman, in a case of assault and battery. You are to understand, the beautiful river Shenandoah passes not far from this town, and is navigable for batteaux; while at no great distance runs the great western road, which is travelled by the west country wagoners—some of whom, you know, are "half horse, half alligator"; others "part earthquake, and a little of the steam-boat." The batteauxmen are for the most part composed of materials equally combustible; and the consequence is, that occasionally, when they meet, they strike fire, and blow up the powder magazine each carries about him in the form of a heart.

The history of the present contest is as follows: One summer evening, when the mild air, the purple light, the green earth, and the blue sky, all seemed to invite peace and repose, the batteauxman fastened his boat to the stump of a tree, lighted his fire to broil his bacon, and began to sing that famous song of "The opossum up the gum-tree." By and by a west country wagoner chanced to come jingling his bells that way, and stopping his wagon, unhooked his horse, carried them round to the little trough at the back of his vehicle, gave them some *shorts,* sat himself down at the top of the bank, below which the batteauxman was sitting in his boat, and began to whistle "The batteauxman robb'd the old woman's hen-roost." The batteauxman cocked up his eye at the wagoner, and the wagoner looking askance down on the batteauxman, took a chew of tobacco with a leer that was particularly irritating. The batteauxman drew out his whiskey-bottle, took a drink, and put the cork in again, at the same time thrusting his tongue in his cheek in a manner not to be borne. The wagoner flapped his hands against his hips, and crowed like a cock; the batteauxman curved his neck, and neighed like a horse. Being, however, men of rather phlegmatic habits, they kept their tempers so far as not to come to blows just then. In a few minutes the wagoner swore "he had the handsomest sweetheart of any man in all Greenbriar." The batteauxman jumped up in a passion, but sat down again, and took a drink. In a few minutes the wagoner swore "he had the finest horse of any man in a hundred miles." The batteauxman bounced up, pulled the waistband of his trowsers, took another drink, and bounced down again. A minute after the wagoner swore "he had a better rifle than any man that ever wore a blue jacket." This was too much—for the batteauxman wore a jacket of that colour, and of course this amounted to a personal insult. Besides, to attack a man's rifle! He could have borne any reflection on his sweetheart, or his horse; but to touch his rifle, was to touch his honour. Off went the blue jacket; the batteauxman scrambled up the bank, and a set to commenced, that ended in the total discomfiture of the wagoner, with the loss of three of his grinders, and the gain of "divers black and bloody bruises," as honest Lithgow says. The batteauxman waited till the moon rose, when he went whistling down the stream to carry the news of his victory to Old Potomac; and the poor wagoner went "to take the law," as a man says, when the law is about to take him.

The honest batteauxman was arrested on his return for assault and battery on the west country wagoner. It being you know the great object of the law to find out which party is in the wrong, the lawyer of each side of course labours to throw the imputation on his adversary's client. It appeared clearly enough that the batteauxman made the first assault, but it also appeared in evidence that crowing like a cock was a direct challenge, according to the understanding of these people; that to undervalue a batteauxman's sweetheart or horse, whether he had any or not, was a mortal insult; and that to insinuate any inferiority in his rifle, was an offence which no one could put up with without dishonour. That such points of honour constituted the chivalry of these people, that no class of mankind is without something of this nature —that however low a man may be, there are insults he cannot submit to, without being disgraced among his equals, who constitute his world—and that to oblige him, in any situation, to put up with disgrace, was to debase his nature, and to destroy every manly principle within him. Trifling as this case may appear, it called forth a display of talent, and a depth of investigation as to how far it was possible, and if possible, how far it was salutary to attempt to repress the operation of those feelings which spur men in all situations to avoid disgrace at the risk of every thing, that gave me a high idea of the two advocates.

18

A New England Poet in Virginia and Kentucky, 1818

*H*enry C. Knight's life was both brief and outwardly uneventful. He was born in Newburyport, Massachusetts, in 1789. Though his education was extensive, it was apparently unrewarding, but he did manage to get a degree from Brown University eventually. He wrote a great deal of poetry, good enough to be published but not good enough to be remembered. When he was twenty-five, he began a long and leisurely trip through the South—a trip which lasted five years. On his return he was ordained in the Episcopal church and served out the few remaining years of his life as a priest in that church. He died in 1835.

The Letters from the South and West *was the result of his observations in the South. It is a brief account of Philadelphia, Washington, Virginia and Kentucky (which states he reached in 1818), New Orleans, and the sea voyage home to Boston. Packed into the pages of this short work is a tremendous amount of information, much of it unusual. Perhaps because he was a poet, Knight possessed the special power of making the scene he described come to life. He wrote well, despite eccentricities of style and punctuation, often with wit, always with discernment. In consequence the* Letters *is his most valuable and enduring work, as it is one of the most interesting travel books by an American.*

LIFE AND MANNERS IN THE OLD DOMINION

Virginia, called after the virgin queen Elizabeth, appears like a new-settled, not an old one. You pass no stone-walls; but hedge, or *in-and-out* zig-zag cedar rails, or wattled fences, if indeed any, on the main roads. At the south, a few houses, though not incorporated, are called a town. If you visit a plantation, you strike off the main road, up or down the banks of the long rivers, that run from the western mountains to the sea-coast; or you mount into the ridge forests. You feel a solitary emotion, as you find a house and out-buildings, on a spot cleared in the middle of the woods, and surrounded by broad wheat and corn fields; not fifteen or twenty acres of arable land, but from one to five hundred; not tilled by five or six hired men, but by from thirty to one or two hundred slaves; and, in harvest time, are in motion, from twenty to fifty reapers, men, women, and children. They do not reap with a sickle, as on the New England small farms, and thresh with a flail; but mow with a scythe fitted into a wooden-cradle with five long curved fingers to ingather the stalks; and tread out the grain in a *wheat-ring,* by ten or twenty horses and mules.

Although there is not, in this vicinity, a stone big enough to kill a quail; yet, it is said that, near the mountains, the soil is so plenteous with them, that one can hear their ploughs for three miles. The Virginians usually plant *twice,* and *pull and reset* their corn, which is left five feet apart, and but *one* stalk, instead of three or four, in a hill, as with us; but that one grows up like a tree. One gentleman, on the James River, who is wealthy beyond all reason, sold, one fall, I am told, fifteen thousand bushels of grain. Colonel Taylor, near Port Royal, a scientific planter, and political author, who cultivates about eight hundred of unctuous acres annually, in *four shifts,* is a firm advocate for the use of gypsum; not so much as a manure, as a medium to draw manure from the atmosphere; so that one, he says, may include, fix, and divide, and bestow to his children, atmosphere to any enclosed extent.

As the Virginians in common are called buckskins, so those, who live in poorer classes on the second-ridges from the James, are called foresters. Over these ridges are commonly soaring large turkey-buzzards, which are never shot, as they gorge upon the carrion.

Every thing here has a certain loose, uncompacted, unappropriated appear-

CABLE FERRY

ance. The ancient Episcopal churches, which once were so predominant, are mostly in a state of dilapidation. The rank reeds rustle round their doors; the fox looks out at their windows. But, as a new bishop has been lately consecrated for Virginia, it is hoped that the churches will soon be re-edified.

Almost every gentleman's seat, even if not presidential, has some romantic appellation, as—Farmer's Hall, Hunter's Hill, Mount-Pleasant; but you need not suppose all these *swells* to be mountains. In walking around a plantation, you deviate into a hundred narrow Indian-like foot, or bridle-paths; and, in going from one plantation to another, you ride through an infinite of swing-gates. Now, for me, rather less land, and better cultivated.

It is delightful, to stroll through the forests, and listen to the susurration of the umbrageous branches, and to pause and admire at trees, infrequent, if found, at the colder East:—the dark glossy evergreen holly, with its scarlet berry; the broad-leafed catalpa; the persimmon, with its tap-root, on which account it is often left for shade in the wheat-fields; the honey-locust; the chinquipin-bushes, which in the fall bear a nut little inferior to the filbert, and which fattens the gluttonous herds of swine, which run free; the gum-tree; the Dutch-elm, with its beautiful thick foliage, and blotchy corky excrescences of bark; the willow-oak; the superb fringe or snowdrop tree; and many others, of which I do not know the names.

In autumn, the tall climbing wild vines, with their yellowy leaves, intermingled with the green of the forest oaks, look a pleasing melancholy. In the sultry months, the under-brushwood is powdered with *chiegoes,* minim insects, too minute to be inspected, but which get into the skin, and sting like nettles; and the tops of the trees are vociferous with sawyers, other larger insects of the locust tribe, called also *katy dids;* because one seems to say "katy did," and the other to reply "katy didn't."

The plantation houses, in general, are of frame, and unexpensive; having the chimney-stacks outside, and therefore no closets inside; and the roof-shingles *shelled* on the edges. The kitchen is usually detached a few rods from the house. Mine Honourable Landlord's mansion, however, is of brick, and one hundred feet in front. In his garden, and orchard, he has more fruits, than most gentlemen in Virginia:—the fig bush, the hard and soft shelled almond; varieties of cherries; peaches, white-blossomed and double-rose-blossomed, rich and luscious that they melt two inches before they reach your lips. He has an apricot, and a nectarine from Pope's garden at Twickenham. Peach orchards, of from fifteen hundred to some thousands, are common here; for distillation into brandy. Pears, but not apples, are scarce. Most planters have a small patch of tobacco, and of cotton, for domestic use; the former plant being extensively cultivated in the southern borders of this state.

The white vegetable wool of the cotton-plant is prefered to the nankin-coloured boll.

The young Virginian ladies take pleasure in nurturing their hortulan shrubbery, and fostering their parlour pot-plants. Here are breathing beds of mignionette, and there the geranium "boasts her crimson honours"; and here vie, in their ranges, the orange-tree, the union or red and white York and Lancaster rose, the moss rose, the yellow rose, the undying globe amaranth, the Otaheite plant with its long-hanging filmy veiny tendrils, the coiling snake plant, the sparkling ice or dewplant, the prickly pear, whose beauty consists in its ugliness, and the evervarying and superb hydrangea. Indeed, the smiling damsels run about among their flowers, until they look as fresh and glowing, as their own rosebushes.

As to the *Manners* of the Virginians, they are a sallow, mercurial, liberal race; abroad, extravagant in dress; at home, slouching in homespun; the children of rich planters not disdaining to wear check not quite tartan. They ride fine horses; a wealthy landlord keeping his saddle, his racing, his carriage, and his plough horses, distinct. They teach the riding horses to pace over their smooth sands, and dislike trotters; ride without cruppers, and, about home, with *one* spur; thinking that if they get one side along, the other will not hang ashank. Instead of a chaise, they use a chair, which is very light, but unsocial, as they are usually single; and which, moreover, being without a top, exposes them to the weather.

Wherever the Virginians go, a slave or two moves behind as their shadow, to hold the horses, pull off their boots and pantaloons at bed time, and, if cold, to blow up the fire in their bed-rooms with their mouths; bellows being unknown in a slave state. All are fox-hunters, and duck shooters; some keeping parks of deer, and others a ducker for the season. As game is plenteous near their enclosures, on a cloudy drizzly day, or a clear frosty night, when the hounds can scent the trail along the dew, out start young lads and bring home the partridge, the groundhog, the rabbit, and the opossum with her offspring not bigger than a bean clinging to her teats in her false pouch.

Accustomed from boyhood to athletic sports, the Virginians are muscular and elastic in limb; and leaving draughts, whist, backgammon, and chess, for the evening; they are out at sling-fist, and sling-foot; or outjumping, or outrunning each other. I saw a young man betted upon, for five hundred dollars, at a foot race. Indeed, every thing is by wager. Dr. and Maj. wagered, whether a serpent ejected his poison from the sac through a groove in the inner side of the tooth, or through a hollow up the middle of the tooth? Maj. lost a year's medical practice upon his family, and Dr. won his gray poney. What would a northern man think, to see a father, and a sensible, and a respected one too, go out with a company, and play at marbles? At some cross-roads, or smooth-shaven greens, you may see a wooden-wall, high and broad as the side of a church, erected for men to play ball against.

Most young Virginians are too convivial; and not a few, however splendid in talents and fortune, are open "votaries of Bacchus," and devotees "of the Paphian Dame." But among the lower classes, worse than this is sometimes met, the pandemonium of a whiskey-shop; where houseless, pennyless, famished idlers endeavour to "keep their spirits up, by pouring spirits down."

The Virginians are fierce marksmen, and duelling is not discountenanced. They sometimes meet, and shoot at a target for a fish-fry. Fish-fries are held about once in a fortnight, during the fish season; when twenty or thirty men collect, to regale on whiskey, and fresh fish, and soft crabs, cooked under a spreading tree, near a running stream, by the slaves. At these fries, the talk is of slaves, crops, shooting-matches, and quaffing revels; their ideas ever in a muddy channel.

A more genteel festival is the barbecue, expensive and elegant; where a numerous party of ladies and gentlemen assemble by invitation, or ticket, and feast, and dance, in beautiful decorum, under an artificial arbour. This, as the Virginians, living so isolated, are fond of company, produces a course of visiting for weeks afterwards. A Virginian visit is not an afternoon merely; but they go to week it, and to month it, and to summer it. Nothing is contracted about the Virginians. Although all classes are proverbially hospitable, yet there is a wide disparity between the different *castes* in this state. The haughty and purse-proud landlords form an aristocracy over the dependent democracy of the poorer planters. Their gymnastic education insures all to be bold riders, and brave fighters; but leaves a more than moiety surprisingly wanting in literature. Latin is not uncommon but rare is any Greek. At William and Mary College, where the course is but *three,* instead of *four* years as with us, there is now no funded professorship of languages. They care but little for belles-lettres.

As to religion, the Virginians are less zealous than were our Plymouth sires. Being brought up without many churches, too few regard the sabbath, except as a holiday; or wherein to begin or end a journey. In some places, toward Norfolk, shops are kept open, only the buyer may walk round to the side door, to evade the law. Yet the Virginians are sticklers for orthodoxy. For example, Richmond is faith without works; Boston works without faith. But do not conclude, that there are no christians in Virginia. There are many; many, who will cheerfully ride twenty miles to hear one sermon.

As they reside so far apart, each plantation has its God's acre, or *corner of graves;* and the funeral service is not infrequently performed a month after the deceased is buried; as they must send, perhaps, a score or two of miles for a clergyman.

It is very common for rich planters to remain bachelors. In families, the mistress usually carries about a ponderous bunch of keys; as articles are kept under lock from the slaves, and doled out each day for use. Where there are children, each single babe, if there be a dozen, has its particular nurse, or black *mamma;* to spy it, and *tote* it up and down all day upon her shoulder, until it is three or four years old. The matrons, in the upper classes, are industrious, affable, and accomplished, in a high degree. The young ladies, with their pensive, but imaginative countenances, frequently dip into the heart. What is amiable, I have seen a little miss sit down at the side-table, on an evening, to instruct an aged house-slave to spell in the Bible. When out on the green terraces, or in the orchards, the young girls run wild as the boys; wearing, to preserve their delicacy, broad sun-bonnets, deep enough for small cradles; so that they appear all head and feet. They will run up a tree like a squirrel.

The chief sickness, in this *ancientest dominion,* is in the autumn; when you may chance to shake, on one day, so that you cannot hold yourself in your chair; and, on the next, to burn so as to scorch your clothes. In this vicinity, they do not often suffer from hydrophobia; although surrounded by families of hounds, pointers, and spaniels.

As to the *Diet* of the Virginians, I may tell you what I observe. Once for all, they are plentiful livers. The first thing in the morning, with many, is the silver goblet of mint-julap. At breakfast, besides their wheaten rolls, they usually have, in their seasons, apple-bread, or hominy, with a relish of honey or herring. They have none of the rye-and-indian loaves, the rural bread of New England.—At dinner, which is about three o'clock, whatever other varieties they may have, a tureen of soup, and a chine, jole, or ham of bacon, imbedded with greens about it, are standing dishes. A meat-house is one of the first houses built; hung on all sides with chines, middlings, joles, and hams; perhaps finer flavoured for having run wild, and fed chiefly upon mash. One of the common petty larcencies of the slaves, is breaking into the smoke-house. It is remarked that, north of the Potomac, one may find good beef, and bad bacon; and south of the Potomac, good bacon and bad beef. They do not here eat the terrapin, which is esteemed a luxury at the north; but they highly relish the sturgeon, which is seldom eaten at the east. They never fail of having hominy, which is broken corn and beans mixed; coarse or fine ground; fried, baked, or boiled. It is a good substitute for potatoes, which do not here keep sound throughout the winter, although fine in the summer, which will sometimes, it is said, grow so large, that you may sit on one end, and roast and eat the other. They seldom have any puddings, or pastries; but have, for variety, six or seven kinds of meats, flesh, fowl, and fish; frequently, in its season, the exquisite canvass-back duck, with rich catsups, and anchovies. They have no cider or common beverage for table-drink; but, instead, for the ladies, water unqualified, weak toddy, and for the gentlemen, either whiskey, or apple or peach brandy, of their own distilling. Instead of a glass before the plate of each person, as with us, the decanters rest upon the sideboard until you call upon the waiter. Most planters have an ice-house, and contrive to keep the ice cool all summer.

As the kitchens are some rods removed from the dining-hall, at dinner-hours you may count long trains of slaves pacing to and fro, with the different viands, for a long time; for, although they have so much help, they are ever in getting a thing done; and thus the dinner is comfortably cool before you sit down to it. And one need not to be over-fastidious, since, however neat the mistress, good luck is it if the kitchen is not lined with little half-naked smutchy implings, rolling and clawing about, and listening with impatient delight to the slow revolutions of the spits, and the soft warblings of the caldrons. It is difficult to get over first prejudices against black servants.

As the Virginians expend all their strength upon dinner, their supper is a mere ceremony. They have not, as we have, a table, and toast, and pies, and cake; but, at about dusk, is sent around to each one, as he sits in the hall, or under the piazza, a cup of coffee, or tea, or both. Then follows round a plate of biscuits on a tray, hot, and about as large as a small letter-waifer; and perhaps a Virginian may sip a whole cup, and nibble a half or even a whole biscuit; but as frequently neither. Some epicures, after this apology, have a flesh or crawfish supper, at ten o'clock, to sleep on, and to accommodate them with the fashionable dyspepsy.

You will expect me to say something of the *Slaves*. The plantations are blotched over, every twenty or forty rods, with slave-cabins. These cabins, as they are called, are built of small straight timbers, crossed four-square, and interlocked at the corners, very like children's cob-houses; and daubed at the interstices with clay, having a chimney of rough stones at one end outside, and a hard dry ground floor. They are cheap and mean, but healthy and comfortable. The industrious slaves have little garden-plats, and keep poultry. The field slaves are allowed a cap, shirt, and drawers, and a blanket in winter. The field-slaves are the plebians; the house-slaves the patricians. It is amusing that the blacks monopolize the most classical and romantic names; Caesar, Plato, Pompey, Cato; Flora, Florilla, Rose and Lily; our cook is Minerva, and our waiting-boy McIvor, out of Waverly.

On a plantation, is usually one of each trade; a coachman, a gardener, and a vulcan; and if one breaks off a leg, they make a tailor, or a shoemaker, out of him. The house-servants and nurses, although they do not work so hard as a labouring-slave, and live better, yet are they more stinted in leisure. The house-slaves frequently sleep down before the embers, in a row, on rough rugs. With the field-slaves, Sunday is usually a holiday; wherein they deck themselves out for a frolic, or for their unintelligible methodist meetings; where those, who are tender in spirit, are said to be "seeking." Where they have kind masters, the slaves look cheerful, and happy; and do not labor harder than a free white labourer. The little ones, which in summer wear nothing more than a remnant of a shirt, and not infrequently go literally nude, and look like little imps, will yet be seen singing, and kicking, and wallowing about in the yellow sand right merrily.

In slave states, there is little economy of labour; and, though overrun with help, it seems as if nothing could ever be done in season. Although extravagant, and even princely, in many expenditures, the planters seldom have a well, or pump, near the house; but the slaves must go twenty or thirty rods, twenty or thirty times every day, to a spring-house, and *tote* up a tub, or a huge stone-jar, upon their heads, on which they sustain all weights. Instead of having a cheap apple-mill for cider, they scoop out a long trough, and into this empty the apples; and then may you see long rows of slaves, of both sexes, arranged up and down the sides, with ponderous pounders, and their shining black arms lifted up and down in order, as they quash the pomace; and, as they drink what juice they please, they get merry, and sing lustily to the strokes of their tall weighty wooden pestles.

Sometimes you will see three or four slaves on each side of a long horizontal tree-body, cutting in a row; one axe playing up, as the other axe is playing down, in alteration; so that, when the logs are of equal diameter, they all get done at one time.

When a slave dies, the master gives the rest a day, of their own choosing, to celebrate the funeral. This, perhaps a month after the corpse is interred, is a jovial day with them; they sing and dance and drink the dead to his new home, which some believe to be in old Guinea. Indeed, a wedding, and a funeral, are equally agreeable to those not personally interested in them, as then comes a holiday. It appears to be an instinct of these creatures to dance, to equivocate, and to pilfer; but, for the two latter propensities, ignorance and necessity plead loudly. The slaves have black tempers when affronted, and no white man is near by; they will jabber, and rave, and fight, like madmen.

The treatment of the slaves is quite different under different masters, and overseers. It is certified, that a black overseer is always more domineering, and more of an eye-servant, in the bad sense of the word, than a white one.

This is true also in the treatment of their own children, and dogs; which they frequently delight to abuse. What slaves I have seen, have fared coarsely, upon their hoe-cakes and ash-pone; but have been treated humanely, and not hard tasked.

There are many planters, who wish there never had been a slave brought into the country; and who would make great sacrifices to emancipate them, if it could be safely done. But this must be done gradually, and provision be made for them when free; or they would soon wish to be re-inthralled. The planters stand in dread of the free blacks in the state, who act as a kind of

NATURAL BRIDGE, VA.

medium of intrigue between the slaves and the whites; and on this account they approve of a Colonization Society, in order to induce the free negroes to quit the country.[1]

I know not whether the slaves, in general, are not as happy as their masters. They have no thought of to-morrow for a whole life, and have provision for sickness, and for old age; whereas a poor white, or black free labourer, if sick for a week, or when become infirm from age, perhaps breaks the hopes and dependence of a whole family, or casts them upon the county. In fine, although I certainly hold a high estimation of the Virginian character, in many respects; and of their thousand-and-one acre plantations; yet, I never should covet to live so secluded in the woods; and to have my eye offended, and my heart pained, by the degradation of so many of the human species.

1. [A reference to the American Colonization Society, founded in 1817, which, with influential support, proposed to solve the Negro problem by transporting all the blacks to Africa.—ED.]

The Virginian *phraseology* sounds a little peculiar to a northern ear at times. There is the executive *belittle* for demean, which, however, being an expressive word, the ex-president hath rather *belarged* his fame by adding it to our vocabulary. As the New Englanders guess, so do the Virginians reckon. What in New England is called the husk of corn, in Virginia is called the *shuck;* and what we call cob, they call husk. The Virginians use clever for intelligent; whereas we use it for a kind of negative character of weak intellect, but good disposition; the correct meaning is rather with them, than with us, as shrewd, cunning, dextrous. What they call chamber, is the room where the madam sleeps, and is usually *below* stairs; and what we call afternoon, they call evening, making no quarter divisions of the day. *Tote,* a slave word, is much used; implying both sustension and locomotion. They say—to grow a crop, for, to raise a crop; he was raised, for, he was educated; mad for angry, as do the Irish; and madam and mistress, instead of our abbreviations. Children learn from the slaves some odd phrases; as, every which way; will you *all* do this? and the epithet *mighty* is quite popular with old and young, as, for instance, mighty weak. Nor is their pronunciation without some slight peculiarities, as, stars for stairs, arr for air, bar for bear; and Talliaferro, a surname, of which they had a governor, is pronounced Tollifer.

OLD KENTUCKY HOME

On the map, this country appears like a new world, divided from the Atlantic states by the everlasting Alleghanies, which seem to uplift an impassable separation wall between the east, and the west. Of this state, and some of the other western states, the growth is almost a miracle. About thirty years ago, there were only one hundred and seventy returned militia, on the east side of Kentucky river. I was informed, by a lawyer of Lexington, that, thirty years ago also, three thousand acres of prime land, but ten miles from the town, were sold by a young woman, for as little money as would buy her a *new silk gown* to attend a ball in. Patrick Henry, of Virginia, moreover, sold, to his brother-in-law, about fifty years since, more than three thousand acres, and another parcel of two thousand acres of land, in this Scott county, for *two brood mares.*

The larger towns in this state, as Lexington and Frankfort, and especially Cincinnati, in a neighbouring state, across the Ohio river, are very city-like, and thriving; and in them, as also among many of the planters, is much wealth, and gentility. One indication of a new country is, that the shops are variety-shops; each one keeping piece-goods, groceries, cutlery, porcelain, and stationery, in different corners; there not yet being that partition of trade, which we meet in older states. In Lexington is a college of a classic-sounding name, Transylvania, i.e. Backwoods College. In Frankfort, the state-house vaulting is covered with little ruddy chubby cherubs.

This country conceals strata of limestone, which spread about six feet below the surface, and render the fountains somewhat cathartic for a time to most strangers. In this vicinage, the champaign lands are undulating, which causes a wholesome ventilation of atmosphere. The western roads, from their rich loamy soil, after a rain, become very miry; but soon dry under a hot sun, or brisk air. The hills are covered with large loose stones, almost impassable for wheels. Along these rough roads, the mail-carrier rides upon one horse, with long reins and whip, guiding and driving another horse before him, which bears the mail-bag.

The plantation-mansions are in general mean; so that many a rich planter, were it not for his far-spreading fields, would by a northern man, be accounted poor. The houses are usually of hewn timber, with stone chimnies outjutting from the end walls, and the out-doors opening directly into the parlours, so that in winter they are quite comfortless. Some few of the plantation-seats, however, are of brick, and are accommodated with ample out-buildings. There is commonly in the front yard a horse-rack, with bridle pins over head for a dozen steeds; and upon one of which, from my casement, I now see a peacock perched on his long black legs, and screeching for joy.

This is not yet a country of books. Most professional gentlemen here, for want of early opportunity, have little taste for literature; but the lawyers are well grounded in land-claims, the most general and lucrative part of their practice. In lieu of three or five years, as they have or have not received degrees, county pettifoggers here sometimes come forth to plead, and to counsel, after perhaps six months of desultory reading. As to Latin, ten years ago, very few were the youths, who advanced farther than the *licet recedere;* and, as to Greek, rare was the native minister, attorney, or physician, that ever dreamed in any language but English. Such are now entitled buck-eyes; yet often well succeed, by an undiverted application of their mental faculties, and an unabashed assurance.

In the lower counties, you may meet with young men, urbane, fashionable, and enterprising, who cannot indite a familiar epistle passably; and others, who cannot read nor write; as one of wealthy exterior said to me, when I offered him a state-trial, that I was perusing:—"He was not *scribe* enough to *read."* This is not mentioned from marvel, but from regret; since the deficiency originated in the paucity of means in the early modes of a new country, and is a constant disquietude to them. In the towns, and among rich planters, no people are more liberal in support of public, and private tutors.

If the young men cannot easily translate the Iliad of War, they can readily construe the Oeilaid of Love. The Kentuckians frequently marry very young; men at eighteen or twenty; girls at fourteen or sixteen; and, on the day after the wedding, at the bridegroom's father's hall, is usually a sumptuous festival, called an *inn-fare*.

The men of this state have iron-bound constitutions; they are a people of enterprise, and of bravery; none were braver in the last war. Military titles are here inflicted upon one; few escaping the honour of either captain, major, colonel, or general. A gun is a child's play-thing. Let a little Western lad espy but the velvet ear of a gray-squirrel, which he has *tree'd,* on the top bough of a hackberry, and he *downs him,* as he calls it. These early habits of the youths lead to a venturousness of disposition, which is not found in more refined, and effeminate states, where sedentary philosophy and literature have prevailed.

Among the lower classes of society, the Canaan richness of the land is productive, among better fruits, of much indolence. Too many, instead of resting one day in seven, work only on one day in six; and therefore ever remain poor. In some of the inferior hovels, are seen little once-white boys sitting at table in their long shirts; and running half the summer with nothing else on; which freedom renders them hardy. Some mothers here *hip* their infants. Men of this rank, if they cannot thrive in one occupation, often commute it for another; never distrusting their capabilities. Among this class, the riotous roisters, or, as they are here called, *rowdies,* will fight, not only from patriotism, but from mere love of fighting; it being one of their habitual amusements. These merry Shamgars are said to have fifteen ribs upon each side. A pistol, and a dirk, are as familiar, as a watch, and a penknife. When maddened, an affront is followed by a battery upon the bones; for, as they cannot comprehend reason, their arguments are generally palpable. I have heard of more pugnacious affrays during the past year, than in all my life before. The impious and senseless duel-murder is frequent in this state.

Whiskey slays many a strong man here; and too many of the groceries are grogeries. I lately saw an advertisement for a pedagogue; and, in a *nota bene:* —"One that is not addicted to ardent spirits would be prefered." At elections, where they vote *viva voce,* not by ballot, you may see a barrel afloat, offered by the successful candidates, and the vulgar portion of the voters crowding, and dipping up the spirit, if not in their hats and shoes, in their palms. At such times, they feel their freedom, and vociferate their propensities. At the polls, not an age since, as the candidates sat in the clerk's office, to thank each voter for his suffrage, according to custom, one voter cried out, as he obliquely eyed them:—"I vote for that little black man, over that huge yellow man."

Most wealthy planters in this state keep their coach and pair; their chaises are here called gigs. But, on account of the roughness of the roads in a lately settled country, the men, in general, travel on horseback, with their valise behind them, and no cruppers. To prevent the mire from dishonouring their legs, the horsemen wear short galligaskins, or long cherevalls; though they mar these words into uncouth sounds. The youths, from early practice, ride gracefully; not like clodhoppers, the rider in a gallop, the horse in a long trot. Like their progenitors, the Virginians, they are partial to pacers. The little maidens here, of eight or ten years old, will pace, or canter off, on their side-saddles, like young huntress Dianas.

You meet in this country with more renowned names, than a late wilderness might promise. Scarce a lad, or damsel, but is called after some redoubtable scholar, philosopher, statesman, or warrior; some nymph of mythology, or maid of romance: Cyrus, Junius, Newton, Manlius Valerius, Euclid, Darwin, Napoleon; characters, which frequently were all "unknown to mam', or daddy O."

The Kentuckians in general have numerous families, the fruitfulness of the climate extending even to the wives; and, it is noticed, that brides, who were as Rachels in the Atlantic states, having migrated to the west, become as Leahs; and that they esteem it no unusual compliment to receive even the double blessing of Rebeccahs. From the poorer states, when there is a famine in the land, they are fain to send to this Egypt to buy corn. In this state, all are plentiful, and bountiful livers. Sugar is eaten by spoonfuls, the maple-sugar not cloying like the cane-sugar. Melons here ofttimes expand their cheeks to unedible compass. At table, is a huge pitcher of mantling milk, towering in the middle of a circle of glasses. Here is sometimes used frumenty, a pottage of wheat and milk seethed. Bonny-clabber, in its season, is with *some* a favourite cooling-dish. If their coarse ash-pones irritate the palate as they descend, their soft waffles, with their hollow cheeks floating in honey, soothe all again. In fine, the rich Kentuckians live like lords.

Camp-meetings are common in Kentucky, and are doleful curiosities. The ministers are a species of without-method Methodists; happy compounds of illiterateness and fanaticism. If the weather be rainy, and it be convenient, they enter a meeting-house; many of which are built with a door back of the pulpit, so that the preacher may turn, and exhort those, who chose to lie grouped out on the grass; and which houses have long parallel seats, instead of pews, which are deemed too aristocratical. But, in fine weather, the preachers, and their followers, encamp in the woods, or fields, for some days, or even weeks; migrating from one county to another. They preach in part-coloured suits, gray or drab, with yellow or white buttons. With most of these apostles, the text is but a pitching of the tones to the nasal key; for, although they name a text when they commence, that is commonly the last you hear of it. Their long harangues are ludicrously solemn, and sometimes accidently sensible. When the whole vast circumvened crowd lift up their voices, they outsing all music. At a baptism, they appear to imagine an immersion into a creek an ablution of sin. The shores are lined with the picturesque multitudes, and you would smile in sadness, at the blushing unhallowed mode of submerging the women. For, as they do not close gather the borders of their white flannel robes, nor sink them by leaden knobs, when a female wades into the stream, her robe opens, and spreads, like an umbrella. The gospel is indeed, in a too literal sense, revealed unto babes and sucklings, if such have it.

In slave states, the white conversation is apt to be darkened in its complexion; indeed, three quarters of sociable discourse is often engrossed by the topic of slaves. If a young widow be inquired of, it is asked, is she a good manager? and instead of the phrase, how rich? how many slaves has she? Although, south and west, men boast of being most democratic, yet what is more contradictory to their principles, than their tyranny over three fifths of their population?

I saw one slave corded up to a tree, with his hands above his head, for wagging an evil tongue at a white man, and stripped, and knouted with a raw-hide thong, until his back was carbonadoed into ridges, and crimson. If two slaves are found quarrelling, it is customary to tie their left wrists together, and order them to lash each other, until one asks of the other pardon. A mistress is often obliged to wield the cowskin over her refractory young female house servants; and the practice is, when they scream aloud, to chastise them until they smother their sobs. Yet, in truth, as might be expected, almost every slave is an eye-servant, more easily governed by fear, than by affection; and, as the mansion, and yard, and plantation, are overrun with them, there could be, perhaps, no safety without severity.

The Phraseology in this state is sometimes novel. When you arrive at a house, the first inquiry is, where is your plunder? as if you were a bandit; and out is sent a slave to bring in your plunder; i.e. your trunk, or valise. Instead of saying of a promised mother, with Shakespearean delicacy, that she is "nigh fainting under the pleasing punishment, that women bear"; the hint is quite Shaker-like, that she is "about to tumble to pieces." I have often heard the word *human* used here as a noun. The word *great* is sometimes used to signify *little;* as, that a lady has a great foot, meaning, without irony, a little foot. Many from habit, like the Virginians, tuck a *t* at the end of such words as onct, twict, skifft. They here call a river, a run; a lot, a section of land; they say to stall, i.e. overload, a horse; and cupping for milking. Some words are used, even by genteel people, from their imperfect educations, in a new sense; and others, by the lower classes in society, pronounced very uncouthly, as:—to eat a liquid, to quile for to quiet, to suspicion one, to legerize an account, to prize for to raise by a lever, to fayz for to fix, offer for the candidacy, best book I have ever read after, well liked of, heap of times, did done do it, done done did it, painter for panther, varmont for vermin, contràry, hȳmn, breethren, an oxen, I seen, I brung, exhibition, schrowd, yearth, yearn for earn, bresh, hommer, sketes, drap, fotch, mought, and so forth.

19

Sundry Observations on Southern Life, 1818–29

*M*rs. *Royall was an indefatigable traveler. Between 1818 and 1822 she visited Alabama, mostly in the area along the Tennessee River. Later she journeyed northward (see p. 48) and, again in 1828 and 1829, made an extensive trip through the Atlantic and Gulf South, from Virginia southward through the Carolinas and Georgia, then westward along the Gulf to Mobile.*

Mrs. Royall was certainly not without her prejudices. On the other hand, when stripped of their invective and personalities, her observations cannot be ignored, for she described features of southern life too frequently omitted by other travelers. Almost alone in the travel literature of the South, she refused to be absorbed by the institution of slavery, recognizing that other phenomena existed in the southern community. She caught in her lively way the frontier aspects of Alabama; she searched into the educational and

humanitarian conditions of Charleston; she saw people, too, in their every-
day life. Considering how bitterly she could attack what she did not like,
it is remarkable how detached and universal were her interests, with what
adroitness she escaped being engulfed by the single theme of the plantation,
and with what lively insight she could re-create the life of the people.

MORALS AND POLITICS ON THE ALABAMA FRONTIER

After packing up last evening for Melton's Bluff, I sat musing in my parlour at the inn, when all at once my ear was saluted with the sound of mirth
and jollity below. Eager to learn what was going on, I descended to the public
parlour, and there found the sweet girl, the grave matron, the sparkling belle,
the conceited fop, the modest young gentleman, the veteran soldier, and a
sociable old planter. They were all talking and laughing about planting
cotton, courting, philosophy, biography, &c. Every one expressed themselves
with freedom and good humour; but I perceived great deference was paid to
the old planter, a Virginian by birth, immensely rich, and a *widower*.

I had scarcely seated myself when my landlady, a sprightly black-eyed
woman, and no fool either, joked the old planter about the girls.

"Poh, poh," said the planter, "I don't care a cent for the girls: why, they
won't let such an old fellow come within a squirrel's jump of 'em."

"But you must persevere—don't give up the ship—I'll engage you will
succeed—many a girl would jump at you."

"Faith, that's the greatest fault I find with them; but instead of jumping
at me, they jump away; and if I offer to lay my hand on one, she runs and
squalls, as though I were a robber, and were tempting her life."

"But," says the sprightly landlady, "there you are wrong: no one offers
to touch a lady in these days. I am surprised at you. When you court a girl,
you must set off at a distance and talk to her; and write verses in her praise,
and send them to her; the old time's fashion, when you and my mother were
young people, will not do now-a-days."

"The devil it won't; then they may all die old maids for me. I tell you
what, I think the *gals* was as virtuous in my young days, and may be, a little
more so, than they are now—and many an arm have I laid round 'em, see."

"Oh, fie! don't talk so—you will make the ladies faint. Those were old
times, the fashions have changed."

"Faith, I believe so; but it is from good to bad. I am opposed to all these
new kick-ups. Whenever I see a gal so very coy and prudish, and won't let
a man come near her, it gives me a bad opinion of her; and I'll tell you why—
when I was a young man, I happened to be at a ball—your mother was there

too. So, there was one gal there; a m-i-g-h-t-y precise creature, and would not let me touch the tip of her finger. 'No, Sir, I don't d-a-n-c-e t-o-n-i-g-h-t'; and primped up and tossed her head, and cried out to a friend, sitting by her, 'how odious it was, for men to be taking hold of ladies' hands—she was surprised at my presumption'; and not long after this, this same nice lady met with a misfortune, ladies, which I leave you to guess. Ever since that I marks 'em—I has my own opinions of 'em."

"La, what nonsense," said the belle; "such talk *ar* quite ridiculous."

The next morning, while we were sitting at breakfast, a stranger stepped in, who proved to be one of the neighbors. He was rather coarsely dressed, but had a pleasing aspect.

"Well, old fellow," said the Colonel, "how goes it"; shaking hands cordially. "How do you do? Come, Sir, sit down, and take some breakfast with us—(Maria, bring a plate, and knife and fork)—Come, Sir, take a dram first—(Hand a glass Maria)."

The stranger took a dram, and then seated himself at the table; and the Colonel and him carried on a kind of dialogue, for some time.

"How is your family, Sir?"

"Why I'm 'bliged to you, Colonel, the'r all about, but Mary: She's got her ager yet. How's it wi' yourself?"

"We are all well thank you, Sir. Let me help you to another piece of steak. Have some gravy, Sir. Well, lets hear the news: who do the people talk of voting for—(take some butter, Sir)—in your part? What do they talk about?"

"Why, some on 'em is mighty feared, see, of losing their land; and some on 'em agin is 'mind to stand 'em a pull. I tell you what, Colonel, it's hard upon a poor man, after all, after clearin on himself a smart patch of ground, and puttin it under a good fence, see, and buildin on him a snug cabin, and then for a rich man like you, Colonel, because he rebounds in most money, to come to buy it from over his head, see, I'll tell 'e what, it's little sort o' hard. But I reviewed it so from the first. I saw how it was a goin and sold out. If they fool me they have but one more to fool."

"Well, but tell me, old fellow—(Sam put more wood on the fire)—who do the people talk of voting for on Flint?—(Pour out some more coffee, Maria)"

"Why, to tell the truth, Colonel, they'r purty much divided. Some on 'em talks a runnin Doctor Crab, and some on 'em agin talk o' votin for Lawyer L."

"(Maria set that decanter on the table)—Take some whiskey, Sir. But tell me, who do you intend to vote for?"

"Well, I was jist goin to say, I don't hold with sendin none of these here doctors, and lawyers, and 'losophers.—I look upon it, see, that these here men of larnin jist lay their heads together, and cologe,[1] and jist make laws to 'press the poor. I'm for 'sportin a plain farmer, like myself, Colonel, that will act upon nimical principles—an't I right?"

"But tell us, old fellow, have you any corn to sell up your way?"

"Why, it's purty tol'able sca'ce. I raised a fine chance this year, and my wife had the finest passel of *truck*—I da'e say, she had greens enough to a 'splied the whole neighborhood; but Jim Wilson's critters broke in and most 'stroyed the whole affair: so it is, I shall have to buy. The neighbors told me, if it had abin them, as it was me, they would a shot the critters. But that would abin too sneakin.—But an't you comin to the barbacue, next Friday? Doctor Crab is goin to have a great barbacue, and goin to make a stump speech; and there's to be the greatest doins that ever was heard on. He's sent up two barrels of whiskey, and—"

"Where is it to be?"

"Why it's to be at Elum's Mill; and old Molly's going to do her best. I dare say sh'll make her own out on 'em. She's one of your most inactive women folks in all my knowin, and she has plenty to go upon. Come up, Thursday, to my house, and bring your gun, and we'll take the hounds and have a hunt. Thank God, I have plenty to go upon, anough to eat and drink, and plenty to feed your critter. We'll knock up a fat chicken or two, and my wife is first rate at a cup of coffee. Stay all night, and we'll take a hunt in the mornin."

"Well, Sir, I believe I will."

"That's clever: I shall look for you."

"So, some of your neighbors are a mind to contest the public sales?"

"They say so. Tom Towns says he has a friend that will help him out. But you know how it was the first land sales; every poor fellow as *fout* for his country, was forgotten, see, and kicked off, and thought nothin of—Don't tell me about *premptions;* oh! I seed enough! Colonel Donalson said it was a diabolical business."

Though through this conversation I was unable to discover the Colonel's candidate, I was pleased with the blunt honesty of the countryman, for it is in the rude state of the species, we are to seek for the true characteristics of man. When he becomes polished, his resources enable him to conceal his real character. Thus the Colonel and his guest talked and laughed—drank whiskey, electioneered, and finally settled the affairs of the nation between themselves.

The Colonel has been appointed to marry people, and at a late hour today,

1. [Collude?—ED.]

he had to marry a couple who had been waiting for him from an early hour in the day. Imagine our surprise, at seeing an old man of about sixty, and the bride little under. The Colonel, being a man of humour, blends sundry ceremonies with the marriage contract, suited to his fancy and the persons he marries.

In the first place he told the couple to stand forth, asked them several ludicrous questions—made them repeat the Lord's prayer—and when the ceremony was ended, (being put up to it by the young men who boarded with him) directed them to a room of his own house, to spend the night. We then separated, and retired to rest, and this morning we were thrown into convulsions with laughter, at the merry dance the lovers were led after they left us.

Several young doctors and lawyers have their residence here. Being young, wild, and frolicksome, they are always devising some means of amusement, and the old couple were selected as a subject of sport, upon whom it appeared they played sundry mischievous pranks, in the course of the night. They removed every thing out of their room which might serve as weapons of defense, and carefully disposed some plank in a corner of the room, and was at no small pains to dress up one of the party like a ghost, and ensconsed him behind the plank.

The houses are nothing but rude cabins built with logs, with cracks between the logs, so that any one without can see what passes within. These mischievous wags, had fixed the bed upon a lilt, which by pulling a rope fastened to it, would fall down. This rope they drew through, in the outside, between the logs. They had also provided themselves with a number of canes, of different sizes—the cane being hollow, served as bugles, and make a hollow, doleful sound, when blown through with the mouth. Some of the canes were large, and others small, so as to have *treble, tenour, bass.* Thus, the bride and bridegroom were no sooner bedded, and a bright fire in the hearth, than the ghost, upwards of six feet in height, stalked forth with a white sheet round it, and advanced towards the lovers, with a slow grave step. Those without began to blow their bugles, at the same time. The bride shrieked out, and covered her head—not so the bridegroom—being an old soldier, it would have taken more ghosts than one to have frightened him. Finding the ghost continued to advance, he sprang out of bed, and looked about for some weapon of defence; finding nothing but a box of nails, which from its weight he was unable to wield, he flew round the room for something else. Meanwhile the ghost slipped out of doors.—The hero finding he had fled, exclaimed, "Ah, damn you, if you had only waited a moment longer, I'd a tore your long trappings for you."

"Oh, my dear," said the bride, "what was that? Listen—only hear—Oh, mercy, we'll be carried away—we'll be murdered—help me up—I always heard old Melton haunted the Bluff."

"Haunt the devil; it's them fellows, I tell you, makin their fun—lie still. Oh, blow away and be damned," said the old man. "But you don't come in here again," and pushed the door to; but finding neither bolt nor latch, he placed one of the planks against it, and betook himself to bed again.

The imps watching him through the cracks all the while, he no sooner drew the clothes over him than down came the bed and all, with a sudden crash! Report says, instead of praying for his enemies, he uttered many hard names; and running out of doors, swore vengeance against every *shoe-boot* gentleman on the Bluff. He flew round the cabin with the agility of a youth of fifteen; and the gentlemen took to flight.

"Where are you," cried the enraged lover; "I dare you to show your faces; I'll whip the best of you; I'll take you one by one, and whip the whole of you. Pretty gentlemen with your high crowned hats, and shoe-boots, a screaking."

It was to no purpose he drove his enemies from one position to another; he would no sooner return to bed, than his tormentors renewed the music of canes—sometimes putting them through the cracks of the house, near to the ear of the bride: the old man losing all patience, left the place with his bride before day, and it is supposed without sleep!

The other day a most laughable scene occurred here. The first we heard of it was the voice of a female entering the town, on foot, in a violent rage, cursing and swearing (for it appears ladies do swear). She smote her fists together violently, and (passing over about ninety-nine oaths, at least) declared vengeance against every young man in Florence. Those who were in the secret, began to laugh; others laughed for company; but the most of the people were astonished.

"Twenty-four miles here I've walked, and torn myself to pieces with thorns, and bruises; look at my arms damn you; look at my clothes; yes, laugh, laugh, see my shoes and stockings, wading all the creeks, you sons of bitches. Oh, yes, you're the ones." Her face was red as scarlet, from the heat and rage together.

Briefly—a number of boats are generally lying at the landing, and it appears that the young men of Florence are no better than the young men of other towns, or what I would say, rather, that all young men are alike. Parties of both sexes, for want of house room, doubtless, often spent the night in these boats.

Let this be as it may, a very decent and respectable young man was seen leading a lady in the dusk of the evening into one of these boats; and sometime in the night, somebody untied the cable of the boat, and down the river she sailed of her own accord. There are shoals in Tennessee River, about 20 or 24 miles below Florence, and the first intelligence the inmates of the boat had of being under way, was the noise of the Shoals, which awakened them from a sound sleep! The woman waked first, and being alarmed at the noise, roused the young man. Upon looking out, and rubbing his eyes, the truth burst upon him; but there was no remedy, and their fears were no little, lest the boat might hang or rest upon a rock. Fortunately the boat lodged against an island, fair and softly—and there the gentleman and his companion had to remain, till fortune might send a boat for their relief, either up or down the river, which, by chance, happened sometime the ensuing day. But it appears the gentleman proved rather ungallant, in the end, as he left the lady to shift for herself, the moment he set foot on shore; and turning back to back, he went down the river, and she came up to Florence. It is supposed he had two reasons for this: First—he did not wish to be seen walking side by side with the lady into Florence, which would have subjected him to the ridicule of his friends. Secondly—within six or seven miles below "Lover's Landing," there was a small town, where he wished to refresh himself, and procure a horse, to ride back, being clerk of the court, his absence could not well be dispensed with.

AN ALABAMA REVIVAL

I have met with several excellent orators since I have been in this country; the best I ever heard, men of handsome delivery. These are methodists. I was truly astonished, as I never saw one of that sect, before, hardly worth hearing. The baptists, and the Cumberland presbyterians, are continually preaching and *covaulting* also. When that busybody, Mr. *They say,* reported Mr. Porter was to preach here to day, that is, out at the stand in the woods, I observed, "I will go and hear Mr. Porter."

"Oh," said a bystander, "it is another preacher than Mr. Porter that preaches to-day—there is not such another preacher in the known world—he's a monstrous fine preacher."

As I had heard some fine preaching, for the oratory I went to hear this none-such. But never was I so disappointed. I placed myself in front of the preacher, (a great rough looking man,) and the congregation sat some on fallen timber, some on benches carried there for the purpose—some sat flat on the ground, and many stood up—about 500 in all. His text was, "He that hath ears to hear, let him hear." The people must have been deaf indeed that could not have heard him. He neither made division nor subdivision. He is one of the Cumberland presbyterians. They are Calvinists, it is said, but do not deem education a necessary qualification to preach the Gospel. But to the sermon: he began low but soon bawled to deafening. He spit in his hands, rubbed them against each other, and then would smite them together, till he made the woods ring. The people now began to covault, and dance, and shout, till they fairly drowned the speaker. Many of the people, however, burst out into a laugh. Seeing this, the preacher cried out, pointing to them with his finger, "Now look at them sinners there—You'll see how they will come tumbling down presently—I'll bring them down." He now redoubled his strength; spit in his hands and smote them together, till he made the forest resound, and took a fresh start; and sure enough the sinners came tumbling down. The scene that succeeded baffles description. Principally confined to women and children, the young women had carefully taken out their combs, from their hair, and laid them and their bonnets in a place of safety, as though they were going to set in for a fight; and it was much like a battle. After tumbling on the ground, and kicking sometime, the old women were employed in keeping their clothes civil, and the young men (never saw an old man go near them) would help them up, and taking them by each hand, by *their* assistance, and their own agility, they would spring nearly a yard from the ground at every jump, one jump after another, crying out, glory, glory, as loud as their strength would admit; others would be singing a lively tune to which they kept time—hundreds might be seen and heard going on in this manner at once. Others, again, exhausted by this jumping, would fall down, and here they lay cross and pile, heads and points, yelling and screaming like wild beasts of the forest, rolling on the ground, like hogs in a mire,—very much like they do at camp meetings in our country, but more shameless; their clothes were the color of the dirt; and like those who attend the camp meetings, they were all of the lower class of the people. I saw no genteel person among them. Are not people of education answerable for this degradation of society? It appears to me, since I have had opportunities of mixing with the world, that there are a certain class of citizens, whose interest it is to keep their fellow men in ignorance. I am very sure, half a dozen words of common sense, well applied, would convince those infatuated young women that they were acting like fools. In fact a fool is more rational. Not one of those but would think it a crying sin to dance.

The noise of the preacher was effectually drowned at length, and a universal uproar succeeded louder than ever.—Whilst this was going on, I observed an old woman near me, snivelling and turning up the whites of her eyes, (she was a widow—all the widows, old and young, covaulted,) and often applying her handkerchief to her eyes, and throwing herself into contortions, but it would not do, she could not raise the steam.

I pointed to one young woman, with a red scarf, who had tired down several young men, and was still covaulting, and seeing she jumped higher than the rest, I asked "who she might be?" One of the gentlemen, a Mr. Gallagher, who was standing near, gave such an account of her (men know these things) as would shock a modest ear. "D——n her, she gets converted every meeting she goes to." How much better had she been at a ball, (if they must dance,) where they would be obliged to behave decent, and where vile characters dare not appear.

Shortly after they began to rear and covault, a daughter of my host began too. He walked up to her, and left her off some distance, and sat her down at the root of a tree. When he returned, I inquired "if she was sick?"

"No," he answered, "but she was beginning to go on as the rest, and I told her if she wished to worship God, to do it there, and not to expose herself before faces."

The preacher having spent all his ammunition, made a pause, and then called upon all the sinners to approach and be prayed for. Numbers went forward, all women and children, (children of ten years old get religion!) and the priest began to pray; when a decent looking man approached the stand, and took a female by the arm, and led her away. As he walked along, the preacher pointed to him, and said, "God, strike that sinner down!" The man turned around, and in an angry tone said, "God has more sense than to mind such a damned fool as you are!" and resumed his course.

Being tired of such an abominable scene, I proposed returning home, and, taking a near cut through a slip of woodland, we surprised the red scarf lady in a manner that gave us no favorable opinion of her piety.

There is a great deal of preaching here; and a great many ill natured remarks pass between the presbyterians and methodists; but whether it be to determine which shall save the most souls, or receive most money, I am too ignorant to discover. From what I have heard, it appears the methodists have braved every danger, and preached to the people gratis, in the settling of the country; and now that there is no danger, and the people have become wealthy, those sly fellows, the presbyterians, are creeping in to reap the harvest. But the methodists have a great advantage, in point of talent, many of them being the best orators in the country. But they all draw too many women after them, in my humble opinion.

REMOVAL OF THE INDIANS FROM ALABAMA

It is unnecessary to state what you have learned from the newspapers, that this land was abandoned last fall by the Indians. The fires were still smoking, when the white people took possession. Although I had travelled through a beautiful country, the two preceding days, and my mind had been raised to the highest pitch of expectation by repeated descriptions of this land; yet, it far exceeded all I anticipated. On quitting the impervious river-bottom, I emerged into an open country, high and dry. The exuberance of cane and timber subsides. This enables the eye to see to a great distance. No hill nor dale, but a surface gently undulating. The eye can range without controul in all directions.

About ten o'clock we came in sight of the first Indian farm—but Indian farm no longer! The smoke was issuing slowly through the chimney. Why, these Indians have been like us!—could not be savage—cornfields—apple trees, and peach-trees. Fences like ours, but not so high—trusted to their neighbor's honesty—perhaps these being more civilized had more reason to fear their neighbor. Provoked with my guide because he could not tell me the original cause of these enclosures among the Indians—from four to five rails high—this would not do among us—'twould breed a civil war.—There were the lusty corn-stalks—looked grayish—some were standing erect, some were broken off at the middle and hung together still, some were prostrate. The house looked tight and comfortable; the fruit-trees are large, and show age— there the Indian sat under their shade, or stood up and plucked the apples— wonder he did not plant more—suppose he did not know how to make cider. Blockhead!—better than whiskey.

My guide says peaches are delightful in this country.

Poor Gourd! That was the Indian's name; had he still been there, I would have called to see him: but I felt no desire to see his successor. Guide says Gourd was very kind; he knew him for fifteen years. He helped to subdue the Creeks, and made an excellent soldier. There was a portico over the door —there Gourd used to sit in the warm summer days. We rode close to the fence, built by his hands, or perhaps his wife's; no matter which it was, it was no less dear!—It was his home! The sun, at this moment, overcast with clouds, threw a solemn gloom upon the Indian farm. Nothing moved but the smoke from the chimney—all was silent and hushed as death!—Poor Gourd had to leave his home, his cornfield, and his apple trees.

There could not exist a greater evidence of unbounded avarice and ambition which distinguished the Christian world, than the one that lay before me. There was a time when the owners of this beauteous country flattered themselves that *distance* alone would screen them from the intrusion of the whites. Vain hope!

Melton's Bluff is a town, and takes its name from a person by the name of John Melton, a white man, deceased two years since, at an advanced age. Various stories are related of this man; but all agree in this; that he was an Irishman by birth; became displeased with the white people; attached himself to the Cherokee Indians; married a squaw, and settled at this place many years ago; that, with the assistance of the Indians, he used to rob the boats which passed down the river, and murder the crews. By these means he became immensely rich; owned a great number of slaves; most of whom he robbed from these boats. Thus it is said he continued his piracies until the treaty between the United States and the Cherokees.

He had several children by his Indian wife, one of whom married Rhea, the pilot. After peace was signed with the Indians, Melton lived quietly at home, and cultivated his farm; but towards the latter part of his life he became alarmed from the threats of the Creeks, and removed over the river, where he also had a large farm, and built a fine house, (which I have seen,) and died rich in a good old age. Most of his children married white people.

Rhea married one of Melton's daughters—a most amiable woman, and very lame. When the Cherokee Indians abandoned this territory last fall, some of them went up the river to the Cherokee nation, there to remain, till boats were provided for their removal to the west, by the government; others went directly down the river to Arkansas—of whom Rhea's wife was one. The order for their departure was sudden and unexpected.[2] Rhea, at that time was absent from home, but returned on the same day, and learning what had happened, was almost frantic—jumped into a canoe, and soon overtook the boats. He flew to his wife, and clasped her in his arms. Neither spoke a word, but both wept bitterly. In a few moments he resumed his canoe and returned to the Bluff, and she went on. They had no children.

Whether Rhea was prohibited by the treaty from accompanying his wife, or whether he was under a prior engagement, none here are able to inform me—but certain it is, he is now married to a white woman.

Hearing eleven boats had arrived about two miles from hence, and had haulted up the river, we set off, as I said before, in a little canoe, to see the Indians, which are on their way to their destination beyond the Mississippi. Government, agreeably to their contract, having completed the boats, the news of the arrival of the Indians had been received with much interest; but being unable to proceed by water, we quit the canoe, and proceeded by land in our wet shoes and hose.

2. Such was the eagerness of the white people to possess these lands, that the fires were not extinguished when they took possession.

We arrived at the Indian camps about eleven o'clock. There were several encampments at the distance of three hundred yards from each other, containing three hundred Indians. The camps were nothing but some forks of wood driven into the ground, and a stick laid across them, on which hung a pot in which they were boiling meat; I took it to be venison. Around these fires were seated, some on the ground, some on logs, and some on chairs, females of all ages; and all employed, except the old women. There were some very old gray-haired women, and several children at each camp. The children were very pretty; but the grown females were not. I saw but few men. I asked the interpreter where they were: he said they had gone to hunt; some of them had returned, and were skinning and others preparing their game for their journey. But none of them were near the women's department; they kept at a very respectful distance.

Some of the women were engaged in sewing, some in cooking, and some in nursing their babies, which were the prettiest little creatures I ever beheld. Their manner of nursing is singular. They do not hold their infants in their arms, or on their laps, as our women do; but on their backs, confined in such a manner that they are in no danger of falling, or moving in any direction. This is done by means of a blanket, or part of one, drawn tight round the infant, leaving its head and arms out. This blanket is fastened round the waist of the mother, and the top I do not know exactly how; but the utmost confidence seems to be reposed in its tenacity, as the mother never touches the child with her hands, or is at any more trouble with it whatever. The little things clasp their arms round the necks of their mothers, which they never move: no crying, no fretting, nor any apprehension of danger disturbed the serenity of these little philosophers, on our approaching them. The mothers suckle them, where they are, by raising the breast up to the child's mouth. The Indian women appear to sustain no inconvenience from the incumbrance of their children. They went through the different vocations of pounding their corn into meal, carrying wood and water, with the same apparent ease as those that had no children.

Although there were such a number of Indians, so near together as to be seen from one camp to the other, yet there was the greatest order imaginable: not the least noise was to be heard. Even their dogs were not permitted to bark at us. The poor dogs! I felt for them: they were nothing but skin and bones! The same word that we use to encourage our dogs to seize on any thing, or to bark, the Indians use to control theirs, which is *hiss!* One of our party told me that it was *hiska!* which means "be still."

These Cherokees are far advanced in civilized arts and manners. This great work was accomplished by the indefatigable labors of the Reverend

Gideon Blackburn! And yet, what an aversion they manifest toward our language! I was told that nearly all those that I saw, both understood and could talk good English; but not one word could I get out of them, of any sort. Their inter-communications were carried on by signs. I saw many of the half-breed, as they are called, here; the offspring of a white and an Indian—but they were as unsociable as the others. I was thinking that this would be a good plan to promote their civilization but the result proves that any plan would not succeed. It is very probable, that the most effectual means have been resorted to by our government to overcome their prejudices. I mean our rifles.

A VISIT WITH DOLLY MADISON

Early one morning while I was in Richmond, I called for a hack to wait on Mrs. Madison, as she lived some distance from my residence. The ruffian who keeps hacks at the Union, said he must have $1 for hitching, and $2 an hour—I took it afoot! Mr. and Mr. Madison boarded at Hon. A. Stevenson's, a mile and a quarter; but I walked nearly three miles before I found it. The ignorance of the people is such, that they can only tell where the Church, the Prison, and the Court-room is; after walking my very soul out, I found the house, and was quite mortified that Mrs. Madison was not at home.

"Where is Mr. Stevenson?"

"Mr. Stevenson is very ill, and his family cannot leave him!"

"Where is Mrs. Madison's servant?" The servant was out.

I spoke then with spirit and desired them to say, "Mrs. R. was in the house."

Mrs. Madison heard it, and sent word she would be down in a minute. I listened for her step, and never was I more astonished. I expected to have seen a little dried up woman; instead of this, a tall, young, active, elegant woman stood before me.

"This Mrs. Madison—impossible"; yet she was the self-same lady of whom I had heard more anecdotes than any family in Europe or America. No wonder she was the idol of Washington—at once in possession of every thing that could enoble woman. But chiefly she captivates by her artless though warm affability—affectation and her, are further asunder than the poles; and her full fine eye and countenance, display a majestic brilliancy found in no other face. She is a stout, tall, straight woman, muscular but not fat, and as active on her feet as a girl. Her face is large, full and oval, rather dark than fair, her eye is dark, large and expressive; her face is not handsome nor does it appear ever to have been so. It is diffused with a slight tinge of red, and rather wide in the middle—but her power to please sheds such a charm over all she says and does, that it is impossible not to admire her. She was dressed in a plain black silk dress, and wore a silk checked turban on her head, and black glossy curls. But to witness how active she would run out—bring a glass of water, wipe the mud off my shoes and tie them—seeing I was fatigued she pressed me with much earnestness to await dinner. I was greatly surprised in her size and height, but much more in her youthful appearance. She appears young enough for Mr. Madison's daughter; there is more indulgence in her eye than any mortal's.

A DIM VIEW OF THE ARMED FORCES

We took in a few *midshipmen* of the *Porpoise,* which had just arrived at Norfolk, and for the first time I had a sight of a genuine sailor. Jack was amongst those who remained on shore, and had come down to the wharf to take leave of a black comrade, (another fine fellow) whom their highness' were taking to *wait* on them. He was fully six feet high, very young and stout limbed; dressed in a blue sailor's Jacket and Pants, and about 3 sheets in the wind. He staggered up to the Boat which lay close to shore, and grasping the hand of his black friend some time, he reeled off, and after dipping the air, and fetching a circle round of 20 feet or so, he approached the Boat again, when I expected nothing else but to see him fall into the water. Jack, however, swinging round with his heart in his eyes, extending his hand toward his comrade, exclaimed "good by, old boy." This he repeated till the steamboat moved off, staggering and waving his hat as far as we could see him; and a stouter or more noble looking Blue-jacket never trod a deck.

Since my residence in Washington, my ears have been deafened, and my feelings tortured, by the endless applications of silly fathers and mothers to have their sons admitted as midshipmen.

"Oh, if I could only, Sir, *only* get my son William in the Navy, it would make a man of him.—It would be the making of us all. Oh dear, Sir, my son William is such a smart boy, now do this one time oblige me, oh do beg for me."

The Secretary replies, "I cannot, Madam, I cannot, Sir, the navy is full, I can take no more."

"Can't you slip him in?"

"Impossible, madam, I have slipped in too many already."

"Well, if you sometimes do it, do it now. My Billy has a pain in his breast, he cannot work; work disagrees with him."

"I cannot."

This refusal does not discourage the applicant, and every citizen in the

District, of any distinction, is teazed out of all patience on the subject, until the Darling is placed on the navy-list.

Had these silly Parents been present to-day, it would have cured them of the navy fever forever. There were three of those *dear ones* of the Porpoise on Board with us; and the first introduction I had to them was, a "volley of oaths"—turning round to see whence the oaths proceeded, I discovered a youth, sitting on the Guard of the boat, with one of those Hurricane deck caps; every one knows them—as flat and as large as a candle-stand. He seemed to be from 16 to 17 years of age—pulled his cap over his eyes—threw his head back to bring his eye in contact with the mighty vulgar objects that might happen to meet with them. He sat sideways on the guard, slinging one of his *folio* feet backwards and forwards, while his Admiralship seemed to be profoundly engaged in thoughts, when some insolent fellow disturbed his musing. Leaving him, I found the two other Mr. *Portholes* on their way to join the first. Another lady and myself, giving their Bumshels the way, turned to one side, pumping some water ourselves from the water-Barrel, and took a drink out of a tin cup. This proved to the men of *war,* that we knew nothing of life, and to show us *they* did, one of them cocked his hurricane cap, and putting his hands a-kimbo, bawled out to a very genteel elderly Blackman, (Jack's friend) "Tom, I want some water." Tom knowing his cue, procured a glass and waiter, pumped some water from the Barrel, and uncovered, presented it to his commandant with admirable grace, winking at us at the same time. They then turned off, casting a glance of contempt at us, with an air and commenced a conversation with each other, and in every word repeating, "by G——d." They were confirmed Topers in appearance, their faces being scruffy and bloated, their eyes red, with the State prison painted in their countenance. Finding the general respect of the company directed toward myself, whilst no one would introduce *them,* their insolence knew no bounds; and finding their *struts,* their *swells* and their oaths were regarded with the contempt due to such conduct, they intruded upon me and my friends, as we sat chatting in the gentlemen's cabin.

"Mrs. R., your most obe't., have you any books to sell?"

I ordered them to be-gone. "I had no books for ruffians."

"By G——d, there it is again." They ran off on deck, but whenever I appeared, they were sure to throw themselves in the way, and discharge a volley, not of Bombs, but oaths; I never saw a match for their profligacy, excepting the infamous females in the work-house, in New York.

Such were the Midshipmen of the Porpoise, and doubtless, the whole of these midshipmen are equally guilty, particularly to judge of the conduct of the Navy-Board in admitting such into the Department.

The mother of these boys, like others, had their Darlings clapped into the navy, to make gentlemen of them and keep them from work; we have many such gentlemen in the State prisons, and these Mr. Midshipmen are candidates for like honors.

The prospect of our Army and navy is gloomy.—The people of the U.S. seem bent upon becoming slaves to some power or other. Any man who is contented to work hard, to support a profligate set of men under any pretense, deserves to spend his days in a dungeon, and live on bread and water: they certainly are not aware of their privileges, or they would elect no man to Congress, who would not promise to purge the army and navy, and remonstrate against Midshipmen in toto.

THE LADIES OF RALEIGH TAKE SNUFF

My pen is now to give pain, not only to the parties concerned, but to all that part of mankind not lost to feeling: I allude to a strange infatuation of the females in Raleigh, from the oldest to the youngest, in an unbounded use of snuff!!!—real tobacco snuff! They do not snuff it up the nose, but take it into the mouth—they call it dipping. It was first resorted to, to clean the teeth, and has grown into a confirmed habit! It is simply dipping a small wooden brush, a little stick (bruised or chewed at one end) into a common box of snuff and rubbing the teeth, and they are so besotted, that they sit for hours rubbing their teeth, merely as it is said, for the pleasure of intoxication—like a toper over his bottle, which is affirmed to be the effect. But why snuff would occasion intoxication when grown into a habit, more than *chewing* tobacco, I cannot discover: some say it is more apt to reach the system by the saliva. Let this be as it may, it has a powerful effect on the system, and must finally destroy the health. The ladies of Raleigh are deadly, pale, and emaciated, old and young; even little girls look like ghosts. A knott of young ladies will assemble in a room as though it were a tea party and lock themselves in, and dip for hours, chatting and amusing themselves all the while with anecdotes and stories—cooks, chamber-maids and washer-women, all dip. I have seen little girls walking in the streets, with their lips besmeared with snuff and saliva, which rendered them objects of disgust, and it evidently distends the mouth.

Besides the expense and loss of health, and color, it evidently must engross all their time. These little and big girls never go without their box, and the stick in it, either in their reticule or their bosom; and the cook hardly waits to get her dinner dished, till she is eagerly engaged in *dipping*. It is strange they do not take some measures to stop the evil amongst the children, that the mania might end with the mother. This lamentable practice is said to be spreading into the neighborhood of Raleigh; and, some do say, it is in use in some of the adjoining towns. They generally strive to keep it a secret but it is, alas, but too well known. Several respectable gentlemen, married and single, with deep felt regret, mentioned the ruinous habit to me; and requested me to expose a habit so offensive, and one which threatened to destroy the intercourse of the sexes. The young men of Raleigh, seemed to deplore the unfortunate habit.

This is one of the many proofs we have, that women and not men rule the nation. I hope my fair Sisters will never require another public lecture, and that the prospect of dying old maids may induce them to quit *dipping*.

CHARLESTON AND SAVANNAH

Charleston Harbor is as handsome a sight as I ever saw, not excepting that of New York; and the appearance of the city, as you approach it, is the most happy and triumphant specimen of beauty on the Atlantic shore. Charleston, like New York, lies between two rivers, Ashley and Cooper; but New York runs into the harbor in a sharp point, and you see but little of the city excepting the steeples. Charleston meets you in an even and deep front—Cooper river running parallel with the shore some distance, meets the Ashley at a right angle; but the business part of the city ranges along the shore of Cooper river, where a long line of warehouses rear themselves up in full view at once. Charleston, too, is more elevated, and is not hid by the dense clouds of smoke which constantly hover over New York—the houses are lofty and bright; these with Sullivan's island on our right, also covered with buildings, made a splendid appearance.

Next morning, between daylight and sunrise, I hastened to see the *Market* where I very justly expected to see the whole world of fruit and vegetables. The market of Charleston, at least to me, is much more interesting than any (even that of Philadelphia,) in our northern states, as it not only puts the seasons forward about one-fourth of the year, but also presents us with the productions of the West Indies. The market-house, like that of Philadelphia, occupies nearly a whole street, leaving room for the cross streets, but the market-house of Charleston is not only wider but higher and neater; the floors, stalls, and shelves are as neat as a lady's parlor, and is much more pleasant to walk through, as there are but few people in this, compared to the Philadelphia market, the reason for which is, that white people do not, for the most part, attend the former. Vegetables are brought in by negroes, also fruit; but the most of the fruit in the Charleston market, is brought from the West Indies, and supplied from the vessels.—There is more West India fruit in Charleston market, perhaps, in one day, than can be found in the northern markets in six months, and some that is never seen there, much of which I was unable to learn the names, the sellers being averse to converse with you, unless they think you are going to purchase. Besides every species of orange is to be seen, in astonishing quantities, even to the wild orange, which grows in the neighborhood; this is about the size of an egg, supposing it to be round, they are of a deep yellow, and sour as a lemon. Lemons in cart

CHARLESTON IN 1837

loads, and the *banana;* this is in taste, substance and color, like our *pawpaus,* but not in shape: it is long, perhaps four inches, and crooked like a long-necked squash; it has a sweetish, insipid taste, and grows in clusters upon a small twig, to the amount of a peck, and are brought into market hanging upon the stalk. Besides these, there were a great variety of fruits, and all the nuts of the globe, the names of which I could not learn.

This was in the month of March, and I saw all kinds of vegetables, excepting green beans; peas, cabbages, onions, turnips, and every other species of garden vegetable, were in great profusion, and very neat: the meat was thin and poor, it would be condemned in our market. Butter is neither plenty nor good; fowls are only tolerable; fish is pretty good, I think bass mostly, they are fresh and neat. But I did not dream that such a variety of sweet potatoes, peas (dried) and beans existed on the globe, as I saw in Charleston market.

The stalls are different from ours, which are between, or outside of the pillars—these are inside under the cover, and are boxed up with a species of railing and raised from the floor, and have a gate opening from the outside: these stalls are filled with vegetables, and negro women to sell them. The negro goes in and shuts herself up, and is seated, and hands the articles over. These stalls are on both sides, and the whole is very neat.

But the *Buzzards,* they are all through the market as gentle as dogs. They were the only polite gentlemen I saw, and made me very many handsome bows; and one who strikes one of these pays a fine of $5. It is laughable to see how assiduous they inspect the meat and fish market, and how quietly and soberly they walk about the houses; and the chimnies are covered with them. They seem fond of smoke: they breed over Ashley river, near the town. They are a great advantage to the citizens in removing all kinds of filth and carrion: the moment a cow, horse, or any animal dies, hundreds of these Buzzards light on it, and in a few minutes it disappears (even before it is known by the owner that the animal is dead) except the bones, which are stript clean, not a vestige of flesh or sinew is left. They are not so large as the Buzzard in our country and are properly called carrion Crows. But to return to the Market—I saw no white ladies in market, and few white gentlemen— these mostly rode in their gigs, with a market basket hung under the chair or gig, and a negro boy rides behind.

Veal sells from 10 to 14 cents per pound, beef from 6 to 8, sausages 12, pork 8 to 9, butter 18¾ to 20, mutton 12 cents.

As I drove on through the streets the town burst upon me in a new dress. Near the harbor, the shops and streets are thronged with negroes and hucksters; but the heart of the town displays fine wide streets, cool alleys running quite through to every back yard; elegant shops, and dry good stores, and well dressed people, with great activity of business—every part of the town filled with hacks, private carriages, stages, waggons, and drays. There are, however, no licensed hacks in Charleston. To all this we may add *fops* and fruitsellers, crying (or screaching rather) at every turn; the buildings are low, mostly of wood: but the most striking objects to me were the horses, by far the handsomest in the Union. There is no society in the place—business is done by low, unprincipled Yankees, low Irish, and Scotch. I visited most of the business men, and found very few gentlemen among them. In justice to Charleston, however, the importation of dry-goods, in particular, for richness, beauty and quality, are greatly superior to any in the United States. We have nothing like them in the northern cities—compared to the goods of Charleston, those of New-York and Philadelphia, appear to be the refuse; every species of millinery and wearing stuff is superior to any thing of the same sort I have met with, in any part of the Union.

The streets are paved and well lighted, and planted with the china tree, which was just putting forth leaves, and formed a delightful shade. It would grow very high, but the citizens keep them trimmed. They likewise have a night watch, who cry the hour, and a man goes daily through the streets, with a cart and barrel of water, so contrived as to wet the streets while he drives through them.

The cellar-doors are left open during the day, and there is a wide alley between almost every house, and an extensive backyard, kept surprisingly neat, and cooly shaded, attached to each dwelling. The town, however, I mean the buildings, are not handsome in the general, being mostly of wood, and low, many of them have piazzas. The water is not good, though better than that of New-York.

I have heard many great tales of the streets in Charleston deluging the people and houses with sand; this can only be said of the streets on the Bays. There are some handsome bridges and machinery near the city, and when the rail-road, which is now under way, is finished, Charleston will doubtless revive. It is contemplated to extend the rail-road to Hamburg and Augusta. It will certainly be a great advantage to the market; but I fear there is neither enterprise nor talent enough in Charleston to prosecute the plan.

The Court House made a handsome appearance, though I did not see the inside. But the *Prison,* I despair of credit, when I state there were but *six* prisoners in it, and not a woman—out of these six, but one criminal, and that was a doubtful case! This is for the population of the city and the State, too, without parallel in the *world!* All the rooms were empty but one. The jailor has very little trouble in Charleston. I was so struck with astonishment that I could not for some time believe the jailor. But the fact was too plain for doubt. I have seen 27 committed in one day in New York, and Philadelphia, the police officers set every day in the week, and from 10 to 1500 prisoners in each place. I enquired why they had so few criminals—they said "they hung them all." But this was doubtless a jest, as I hear of more hanging in the north than in the south. Let the cause be what it may, the fact certainly exists.

I saw very few, in fact none but negroes in the *Work House,* to which is attached a *Stepping Mill.* This stepping mill is much lighter than that at Philadelphia: it is designed as a punishment for house-servants, and has been substituted in place of the cowskin; when a slave displeases his master, he or she is sent to the Work House or Stepping Mill, as they work and grind alternately. There were 70 in the Workhouse, and these were changing daily, some going home, and others coming in.

As to the cruelty so much talked of, of masters to slaves—I saw no instance of it: so far from it, they are 10 times better fed, and better clothed than the poor white people of Philadelphia and New York, and particularly Washington City. I think those would make a happy exchange to swap situations with the negroes of the South. In fact, these negroes, though they are called slaves, are the most independent people I saw in Charleston, and more than one half of them deserved flogging, as they are the most impudent people by far, in the city, and no gentlemen or ladies dress finer. Whoever has seen an Irish hackman, in New York, may form some idea of those negroes. I beg their pardon,—colored gentlemen. I have never heard a slave receive an angry word from Washington City to this place, and as to living, very few live half so well. I fancy the poor people of Washington City would be very glad to jump at the leavings of these slaves. I am no advocate of Slavery, but I despise the infamous hypocrites who can fabricate such falsehoods, and slander the innocent. But the appearance of the slaves gives the lie to the report. Let every one who has seen black people in New York or Philadelphia, and those any where in the South and say what a difference in appearance—the first lazy, ragged, slothful, drunken and stupid, and the latter neat, active, wholesome and lively.

The Tread Mill is a very slight punishment, in fact it is play, it is in the disgrace of the thing the punishment lies. I found a great difference between the Tread Mill of Philadelphia and this; there were *nine* white men on the former, and but three on this, it being easier to turn. Two of these were bucksome young lassies, very modest, plump, and seemed to blush at my arrival, one of them particularly, as her handkerchief dropped from her handsome round bosom. The third was a man, also young. The girls were neatly dressed, and were doubtless house servants. They grind corn into coarse meal, called *grits* and half *grits,* a kind of small hominy. I left them laughing at the idea of being an object of curiosity to strangers.

SCHOOLS

"Amongst other things Mrs. R. you must visit Mr. Courtney's School" or Academy (I do not recollect) said a friend. Accordingly I called at the Seminary. As I approached the building which sits on a large square in the heart of the town, I discovered a number of youths at play on the square—but as the School hour drew near I walked on and entered the building: I found a few more youths at the door, and upon inquiry for the tutor or principal, they did not understand what I meant, and replied only by stupid grins: I walked in at the first door that offered, and finding a young man only in a large School room, I inquired for the teacher: he replied he was not in, and saying this, he walked out without further notice, and I took a seat to await the coming of the master. Meantime, the pupils surrounded the building, and assembled at the windows peeping in, yelling and using every indecent epithet: I locked the door to keep them out, expecting the teacher would silence them when he came in. They soon however, collected at the inner door. They now began to thunder at the door, and continued to yell like wild beasts, and finally would have broken the door if I had not unlocked it; and such another rabble I never beheld. They were all well dressed to be sure, but such language and behaviour, would disgrace pickpockets. At this moment the teacher came to my relief. He was much hurt at the conduct of the pupils, and after forcing them to their rooms, very politely attended me part of the way home.

What are called Medical Colleges, are nothing more than so many dens of speculators, to swindle the public first out of their money, and then turn armies of literal murderers loose upon them. From 140 to 150 of these legal murderers were licensed at Charleston, while I was there.

Ignorant as the people are in the city, they despise these medical murderers; and the evil is viewed with pain and horror. These students are a vulgar herd—from the interior, from the mountains, from little villages, and are mostly people of no fortune, no learning, no principle, and wishing to live without work, attend lectures at Charleston. But why need I say Charleston, it is the case throughout the Union. But to resume, these ignorant cubs are the terror of the citizens during winter, chasing negro women, insulting white women, frightening children, pilfering and rummaging shops, taking the streets and sidewalks, blackguarding and insulting every one they meet, and as ignorant, and more so than one half the negroes.

"I am a Physician madam," said one of these hopefuls to me one day, when I asked some one "if that was not a *medical*." A medical student is the lowest character in Charleston, and always coupled with disgrace: to say they are impudence itself, is giving but a faint idea of a medical student. Now the faculty cannot help the ignorance of these fellows, but they could help giving them a license.

These fellows previous to their licensing receive certain subjects from the Faculty, upon which they are requested to diffuse, for instance, one is requested to explain the cause, symptoms and cure of one disease; and another must explain another. This they are requested to hand in or deliver, I did not learn which, to the Faculty previous to receiving their license. They immediately refer to some medical book and transcribe it. Many of them however, are not able to do this, and procure some one to do it for him.

It was amusing to see them running into the book-stores and druggists, purchasing a few dollars worth of books and medicines, to commence killing forthwith. "I hope I see you," is all they can say; you hear this whenever they meet, and this "I hope I see you," passes for ton; meet them an hundred times a day, you hear nothing but "I hope I see you," and the response, "I hope I do." These are pretty fellows to tamper with human lives.

Savannah being built upon a bluff, makes a handsome appearance as we approach it; the steeples first,—the houses soon after become visible. The river spreads out to a great width, and the harbor exhibited a number of steam-boats, and some shipping, and almost rivals the beauty of Charleston harbor.

The streets of Savannah are one sea of sand; the novelty of this, and the pride of China (*alias* China-tree) in full bloom, filling the air with the sweetest fragrance, the profusion of its foliage, and the soft tinge of its exuberant flowers, the hum of insects, the fruit shops, the genial shade, and the pleasant sunshine,—I have no name for the scene!

Savannah is the garden spot of the south, whether as to opulence, trade, refinement, hospitality, or site. The buildings of Savannah are rather indifferent, like those of Charleston, and much inferior to those of Augusta. They seem to take most pride in decorating their streets with those beautiful trees, and their despatch of business. Of all people, they take the most pleasure in an unwearied attention to business. The business season commences late in the fall, and ends in June, and such is their industry, that they scarcely leave time for refreshment or repose. After the business season is over, they then enjoy themselves with their friends—travel to the north, or amuse themselves as they please, till the business season comes round again. This is the routine of all the southern towns. Though Savannah is an even sandy plain, this plain is considerably elevated above the river, and rises still higher in the rear.

From the top of the Exchange, we have one of the handsomest prospects in the southern country, and by a long way the most extensive. For the distance of eight miles, you see one continued plain of rice and cotton fields. Splendid mansions, groves of live oak, magnolia gardens, the river with its islands, steamboats, and shipping, the whole city with its squares, and regular streets, lined with the pride of Savannah, (I would say instead) of China, with the endless cotton warehouses, the marble monument, erected to the memory of Green and Pulaski, present to the eye, a most ravishing picture of beauty, or rather novelty to a traveller. The harbor excepted, it greatly exceeds any view of Charleston. Its chief beauty consists in the symmetry, extent, and uniform evenness of the great rice and cotton plantations, and the alternate rows of those exquisitely variegated trees and houses.

The wharves and streets near the river, were alive with people and drays. Having often mentioned the china-tree, I never saw it in bloom till now, and one of them, growing opposite my window, so near that I could put out my hand and pluck the flowers. The China-tree is in symmetry and attitude, something like the apple tree, if we allow it about twice its height, and it would grow much taller, but they are topped from time to time, and neatly pruned. The color and form of the flower, is much like the liloc. It is, however, more deeply tinged with red—on the outside of its tiny petals, which are exactly like those of the liloc, and like it, grows in large bunches, the stem not so long, nor is the body of the flower so pointed—very narrow hair stripes of a blood red, appear on the outward part of the petal, and it is somewhat deeper shaded than the liloc. These hang in bunches on the boughs of the tree, as thick as the leaves, which are in heavy clusters of a beautiful bright green, in shape like the elder,—thus mingled and shaded, the tree is extremely beautiful and very ornamentive.

Market is held on Sunday morning in Savannah, all the negroes (who reap the benefit) for many miles round come in, and the market is numerously attended. It is hardly necessary to say this is a special privilege of leniency, and accommodation to the slaves, who cannot attend with their own perquisites and manufactures in the week; and it is also a day of visits and finery. This privilege is not the only one they are allowed: the poorer sort traverse the streets during Sunday, with brooms, and various other manufactures of their own.

Among the novelties of Savannah, I was amused with the gait of the people, as they walked the streets. They are so much accustomed to wade through the sand, that they have contracted a habit, something like a wading step, as one would walk through a bed of tough brick-mortar. Their gait is slow and regular, their step long, their head thrown back—the better to breathe, I suspect—and they rise and fall every step. This is more strongly marked in the men. My visit to Savannah happened to be at one of the busiest seasons in the year: in those times, the people scarcely take time to eat, or sleep. All the produce of the State and a large portion of South Carolina, comes here to be shipped, and the time being limited, they work themselves nearly to death.

All the streets cross at right angles, laying the city off into squares. The streets are wide, and paved on the sides; but such is the depth of the sand in the middle of the street, that carriages sink into it, and people can scarcely drag themselves through it; and yet this difficulty is entirely eclipsed by the beauty of the trees, which line the streets, and the profusion of delicious fruit.

To sum up the whole in a few words, so far as I have travelled, Savannah is the first city of the south, by a long way. The citizens are wealthy, sober, intelligent, hospitable, industrious, and high-minded, to a degree which few towns in the United States, can ever reach. I cannot say the society is better than in Camden, S.C. and Wilmington, N.C. but it greatly excels in wealth and numbers. I met with more of what we call gentlemen in Savannah, than in any town in the United States.

20

A Yankee Falls in Love with the South, 1835

*J*oseph H. Ingraham is remembered today, when he is remembered at all, *as the prolific writer of superdramatic and sensational novels, of which La-fitte: The Pirate of the Gulf and the later, religious Prince of the House of David are representative. Contemporary opinion recognized that his writings were enormously popular and totally without literary merit. Longfellow notes in his diary for April 6, 1846: "Ingraham the novelist called. A young, dark man, with soft voice. He says he has written eighty novels, and of these twenty during the last year; till it has grown to be merely mechanical with him. These novels are published in the newspapers. They pay him something more than three thousand dollars a year."*

Ingraham was born in Portland, Maine, in 1809 and attended Bowdoin College. His career was somewhat varied. In his youth he was a sailor. Later he became a schoolteacher—which accounts for the title "Professor" found on the title-pages of his works—married the daughter of a wealthy Mississippi planter, and ended his career as an Episcopalian clergyman. He died at Holly Springs, Mississippi, in 1866.

When still a young man in his twenties, he visited New Orleans and the Natchez area of Mississippi. The result was his first and, without much doubt, his best book, the anonymous The South-West. By a Yankee. *Stylistically, the book is wordy, "over literary," and displays many of the romantic notions which appear so prominently in his later fiction. At the same time, with a novelist's insight, he catches vividly the color and vitality of the half-foreign, half-strange life of New Orleans and the Mississippi plantations. He was certainly not the type of New Englander who went to disapprove of what he saw in the South. He tended to palliate slavery and to dwell on the picturesque features of plantation life. Yet, if he undoubtedly surveyed the South with rose-colored glasses, he was most assuredly not blind to the evils of southern life; and many of his comments show both shrewdness and insight.*

SHIPS ON THE LEVEE AT NEW ORLEANS

Double lines of market and fish-boats, secured to the Levée, form a small connecting link with the long chain of shipping and steamboats that extend for a league in front of New Orleans. At the lower part of the town lie generally those ships, which having their cargoes on board, have dropped down the river to await their turn to be towed to sea. Fronting this station there are no stores, but several elegant private dwellings, constructed after the combined French and Spanish style of achitecture, almost embowered in dark, green foliage, and surrounded by parterres. The next station above, and immediately adjoining this, is usually occupied by vessels, which, just arrived, have not yet obtained a berth where they can discharge their cargoes; though not unfrequently ships here discharge and receive their freight, stretching some distance up the Levée to the link of market-boats just mentioned.

From the market to the vicinity of Bienville-street, lies an extensive tier of shipping, often "six deep," discharging and receiving cargo, or waiting for freight. The next link of the huge chain is usually occupied by Spanish and French coasting vessels,—traders to Mexico, Texas, Florida, &c. These are usually polaccas, schooners, and other small craft—and particularly black, rakish craft, some of them are in appearance.

Next to this station (as you will perceive, the whole Levée is divided into *stations* appropriated to peculiar classes of shipping,) commences the range of steamboats, or steamers, as they are usually termed here, rivaling in magnitude the extensive line of ships below. The appearance of so large a collection of steamboats is truly novel, and must always strike a stranger with peculiar interest.

The next station, though it presents a more humble appearance than the others, is not the least interesting. Here are congregated the primitive navies of Indiana, Ohio, and the adjoining states, manned (I have not understood whether they are *officered* or not) by "real Kentucks"—"Buckeyes"—"Hooshers"—and "Snorters." There were about two hundred of these craft without masts, consisting of "flat-boats," and "keel-boats," which are one remove from the flat-boat, having some pretensions to a keel; they somewhat resemble freighting canal-boats. Besides these are "arks," most appropriately named, their *contents* having probably some influence with their god-fathers in selecting an appellation, and other non-descript-craft. These are filled with produce of all kinds, brought from the "Upper country," (as the north western states are here termed) by the farmers themselves who have raised it;—also, horses, cattle, hogs, poultry, mules, and every other thing raiseable and saleable are piled into these huge flats, which an old farmer and a half a dozen Goliaths of sons can begin and complete in less than a week, from felling of the first tree to the driving of the last pin.

These boats, on arriving here, are taken to pieces and sold as lumber, while their former owners with well-lined purses return home as deck passengers on board steamboats. An immense quantity of whiskey from Pittsburgh and Cincinnati, besides, is brought down in these boats, and not unfrequently, they are crowded with slaves for the southern market. The late excellent laws relative to the introduction of slaves, however, have checked, in a great measure, this traffic here, and the Mississippi market at Natchez has consequently become inundated, by having poured into it, in addition to its usual stock, the Louisianian supply.

The line of flats may be considered the last link of the great chain of shipping in front of New-Orleans, unless we consider as attached to it a kind of dock adjoining, where ships and steamers often lie, either worn out or undergoing repairs. From this place to the first station I have mentioned, runs along the Levée, fronting the shipping, an uninteresting block of stores, (except where they are intersected by streets,) some of which are lofty and elegant, while others are clumsy piles of French and Spanish construction, browned and blackened by age.

THE STREETS OF NEW ORLEANS BY NIGHT

We commenced our long, delightful walk just as the loud report of the evening gun broke over the city, rattling and reverberating through the long massively built streets, like the echoing of distant thunder along mountain ravines. On a firm, smooth, gravelled walk elevated four feet, by a gradual ascent from the street—one side open to the river, and the other lined with the "Pride of China," or India tree, we pursued our way to Chartres-street, the "Broadway" of New-Orleans. The moon shone with uncommon brilliancy, and thousands, even in this lower faubourg, were abroad, enjoying the beauty and richness of the scene. Now, a trio of lively young Frenchmen would pass us, laughing and conversing gayly upon some merry subject, followed by a slow moving and stately figure, whose haughty tread, and dark *roque-laure* gathered with classic elegance around his form in graceful folds, yet so arranged as to conceal every feature beneath his slouched *sombrero,* except a burning, black, penetrating eye,—denoted the exiled Spaniard.

We passed on—and soon the lively sounds of the French language, uttered by soft voices, were heard nearer and nearer, and the next moment, two or three duenna-like old ladies, remarkable for their "embonpoint" dimensions, preceded a bevy of fair girls, without that most hideous of all excrescences, with which women see fit to disfigure their heads, denominated a "bonnet"— their brown, raven or auburn hair floating in ringlets behind them.

As we passed on, the number of promenaders increased, but scarcely a lady was now to be seen. Every other gentleman we met was enveloped in a cloud, not of bacchanalian, but tobacconalian incense, which gave a peculiar atmosphere to the Levée.

Every, or nearly every gentleman carried a sword cane, apparently, and occasionally the bright hilt of a Spanish knife, or dirk, would gleam for an instant in the moon-beams from the open bosom of its possessor, as, with the lowering brow, and active tread or wary suspicion, he moved rapidly by us, his roundabout thrown over the left shoulder and secured by the sleeves in a knot under the arm, which was thrust into his breast, while the other arm was at liberty to attend to his segar, or engage in any mischief to which its owner might be inclined. This class of men are very numerous here. They are easily distinguished by their shabby appearance, language, and foreign way of wearing their apparel. In groups—promenading, lounging, and sleeping upon the seats along the Levée—we passed several hundred of this *canaille* of Orleans, before we arrived at the "Parade," the public square in front of the cathedral. They are mostly Spaniards and Portuguese, though there are among them representatives from all the unlucky families which, at the building of Babel, were dispersed over the earth. As to their mode and means of existence, I have not as yet informed myself; but I venture to presume that they resort to no means beneath the dignity of "caballeros"!

After passing the market on our right, a massive colonnade, about two hundred and fifty feet in length, we left the Levée, and its endless tier of shipping which had bordered one side of our walk all the way, and passing under the China-trees, that still preserved their unbroken line along the river, we crossed Levée-street, a broad, spacious esplanade, running along the front of the main block of the city, separating it from the Levée, and forming a magnificent thoroughfare along the whole extensive river-line.

We entered Rue St. Pierre, which issues from it south of the grand square. This square is an open green, surrounded by a lofty iron railing, within which troops of boys were playing. The front of this extensive square was open to the river, bordered with its dark line of ships; on each side were blocks of rusty looking brick buildings of Spanish and French construction, with projecting balconies, heavy cornices, and lofty jalousies or barricaded windows. The lower stories of these buildings were occupied by retailers of fancy wares, vintners, segar manufacturers, dried fruit sellers, and all the other members of the innumerable occupations, to which the volatile, ever ready Frenchman can always turn himself and a *sous* into the bargain. As we passed along, these shops were all lighted up, and the happy faces, merry songs, and gay dances therein, occasionally contrasted with the shrill tone of feminine anger in a foreign tongue, and the loud, fierce, rapid voices of men mingling in dispute, added to the novelty and amusement of our walk. I enumerated ten, out of seventeen successive shops or *cabarets,* upon the shelves of which I could discover nothing but myriads of claret and Madeira bottles, tier upon tier to the ceiling; and from this fact I came to the conclusion, that some of the worthy citizens of New-Orleans must be most unconscionable "wine-bibbers," if not "publicans and sinners," as subsequent observation has led me to surmise.

On the remaining side of this square stood the cathedral, its dark moorish-looking towers flinging their vast shadows far over the water. The whole front of the large edifice was thrown into deep shade, so that when we approached, it presented one black mingled mass, frowning in stern and majestic silence upon the surrounding scene.

Leaving this venerable building at the right, we turned into Chartres-street, the second parallel with the Levée, and the most fashionable, as well as greatest business street in the city. As we proceeded, *cafés,* confectioners, fancy stores, millineries, parfumeurs, &c. &c., were passed in rapid succession; each one of them presenting something new, and always something to strike the attention of strangers, like ourselves, for the first time in the only "foreign" city in the United States.

At the corner of one of the streets intersecting Chartres-street—Rue St. Louis I believe—we passed a large building, the lofty basement story of which was lighted with a glare brighter than that of noon. In the back ground, over the heads of two or three hundred loud-talking, noisy gentlemen, who were promenading and vehemently gesticulating, in all directions, through the spacious room—I discovered a bar, with its peculiar dazzling array of glasses and decanters containing "spirits"—not of "the vasty deep" certainly, but of whose potent spells many were apparently trying the power, by frequent libations. This building—of which and its uses more anon—I was informed, was the "French" or "New Exchange." After passing Rue Toulouse, the streets began to assume a new character; the buildings were loftier and more modern—the signs over the doors bore English names, and the characteristic arrangements of a northern dry goods store were perceived, as we peered in at the now closing doors of many stores by which we passed. We had now attained the upper part of Chartres-street, which is occupied almost exclusively by retail and wholesale dry goods dealers, jewellers, book-sellers, &c., from the northern states, and I could almost realize that I was taking an evening promenade in Cornhill, so great was the resemblance.

As we successively crossed Rues Conti, Bienville and Douane, and looked down these long straight avenues, the endless row of lamps, suspended in the middle of these streets, as well as in all others in New-Orleans, by chains or ropes, extended from house to house across, had a fine and brilliant effect, which we delayed for a moment on the flagstone to admire, endeavouring to reach with our eyes the almost invisible extremity of this line of flame. Just before we reached the head of Chartres-street, near Bienville, our way was impeded by a party of gentlemen in violent altercation in English and French, who completely blocked up the "trottoir." "Sir," said one of the party—a handsome, resolute-looking young man—in a calm deliberate voice, which was heard above every other, and listened to as well—"Sir, you have grossly insulted me, and I shall expect from you, immediately—before we separate— an acknowledgment, adequate to the injury." "Monsieur," replied a young Frenchman whom he had addressed, in French, "Monsieur, I never did insult you—a gentleman never insults! you have misunderstood me, and refuse to listen to a candid explanation." "The explanation you have given, sir," reiterated the first speaker, "is not sufficient—it is a subterfuge"; here many voices mingled in loud confusion, and a renewed and more violent altercation ensued which prevented our hearing distinctly; and as we had already crossed to the opposite side of the street, having ladies under escort, we rapidly passed on our way, but had not gained half a square before the clamour increased to an uproar—steel struck steel—one, then another pistol was discharged in rapid succession—"guards," "gens d'armes, gens d'armes," "guards! guards!" resounded along the streets, and we arrived at our hotel, just in time to escape being run down, or run through at their option probably, by half a dozen *gens d'armes* in plain blue uniforms, who were rushing with drawn swords in their hands to the scene of contest, perfectly well assured in our own minds, that we had most certainly arrived at NEW-ORLEANS!

Though affairs of the kind just described are no uncommon thing here, and are seldom noticed in the papers of the day—yet the following allusion to the event of last evening may not be uninteresting to you, and I will therefore copy it, and terminate my letter with the extract.

"An affray occurred last night in the vicinity of Bienville-street, in which one young gentleman was severely wounded by the discharge of a pistol, and another slightly injured by a dirk. An *'affaire d'honneur'* originated from this, and the parties met this morning. Dr. —— of New-York, one of the principals, was mortally wounded by his antagonist M. Le —— of this city."

NEW ORLEANS COFFEE HOUSES AND GAMBLING HELLS

A French coffee-house is a place well worth visiting by a stranger, more especially a Yankee stranger. I will therefore detain you a little longer and introduce you for a moment into this café and to its inmates. As the coffee houses here do not differ materially from each other except in size and richness of decoration, though some of them certainly are more fashionable resorts than others, the description of one of them will enable you perhaps to form some idea of other similar establishments in this city. Though their usual denomination is "coffee-house," they have no earthly, whatever may be their spiritual, right to such a distinction; it is merely a *"nomme de profession,"* assumed, I know not for what object. We entered from the street, after passing round a large Venetian screen within the door, into a spacious room, lighted by numerous lamps, at the extremity of which stood an extensive bar, arranged, in addition to the usual array of glass ware, with innumerable French decorations. There were several attendants, some of whom spoke English, as one of the requirements of their station. This is the case of all *employés* throughout New-Orleans; nearly every store and place of public resort being provided with individuals in attendance who speak both languages. Around the room were suspended splendid engravings and fine paintings, most of them of the most licentious description, and though many of their subjects were classical, of a voluptuous and luxurious character. This is French taste however. There are suspended in the Exchange in Chartres-street—one of the most magnificent public rooms in the city—paintings which, did they occupy an equally conspicuous situation in Merchant's Hall, in Boston, would be instantly defaced by the populace.

Around the room, beneath the paintings, were arranged many small tables, at most of which three or four individuals were seated, some alternately sipping negus and puffing their segars, which are as indispensable necessaries to a Creole at all times, as his right hand, eyebrows, and left shoulder in conversation. Others were reading newspapers, and occasionally assisting their comprehension of abstruse paragraphs, by hot "coffee," alias warm punch and slings, with which, on little japanned salvers, the active attendants were flying in all directions through the spacious room, at the beck and call of customers. The large circular bar was surrounded by a score of noisy applicants for the liquid treasures which held out to them such strong temptations. Trios, couples and units of gentlemen were promenading the well sanded floor, talking in loud tones, and gesticulating with the peculiar vehemence and rapidity of Frenchmen. Others, and by far the majority, were gathered by twos and by fours around the little tables, deeply engaged in playing that most intricate, scientific, and mathematical of games termed "Domino." This is the most common game resorted to by the Creoles. In every café and cabaret, from early in the morning, when the luxurious mint-julep has thawed out their intellects and expanded their organ of combativeness, till late at night, devotees to this childish amusement will be found clustered around the tables, with a tonic, often renewed and properly sangareed, at their elbows. Enveloped in dense clouds of tobacco-smoke issuing from their eternal segars—those inspirers of pleasant thoughts,—to whose density, with commendable perseverance and apparent good will, all in the café contribute,—they manoeuvre their little, dotted, black and white parallelograms with wonderful pertinacity and skill.

There are certainly one hundred coffee-houses in this city—how many more, I know not,—and they have, throughout the day, a constant ingress and egress of thirsty, time-killing, news-seeking visitors. As custom authorized this frequenting of these popular places of resort, the citizens of New-Orleans do not, like those of Boston, attach any disapprobation to the houses or their visitors. And as there is, in New-Orleans, from the renewal of one half of its inhabitants every few years, and the constant influx of strangers, strictly speaking no exclusive *clique* or aristocracy, to give a tone to society and establish a standard of propriety and respectability, as among the worthy Bostonians, one cannot say to another, "It is not genteel to resort here—it will injure your reputation to be seen entering this or that café." The inhabitants have no fixed criterion of what is and what is not "respectable," in the northern acceptation of the term. They are neither guided nor restrained from following their own inclinations, by any laws of long established society, regulating their movements, and saying "thus far shalt thou go, and no farther." Consequently, every man minds his own affairs, pursues his own business or amusement, and lets his neighbours and fellow-citizens do the same; without the fear of the moral lash (not law) before his eyes, or expulsion from "caste" for doing that "in which the soul delighteth."

Thus you see that society here is a perfect democracy, presenting variety and novelty enough to a stranger, who chooses to mingle in it freely, and feels a disposition impartially to study character.

Proceeding along the corridor, we left the billiard-room on our left, in which no sound was heard (though every richly-carved, green-covered table was surrounded by players, while numerous spectators reclined on sofas or settees around the room) save the sharp *teck! teck!* of the balls as they came in contact with each other, and the rattling occasioned by the "markers" as they noted the progress of the game on the large parti-coloured "rosaries" extended over the centre of the tables. Lingering here but a moment, we turned an angle of the gallery, and at the farther extremity came to a glass door curtained on the inner side, so as effectually to prevent all observation of the interior. Entering this,—for New Orleans,—so carefully guarded room, we beheld a scene, which, to an uninitiated, ultra city-bred northerner, would be both novel and interesting.

The first noise which struck our ears on entering, was the clear ringing and clinking of silver, mingled with the technical cries of the gamblers, of "all set"—"seven red"—"few cards"—"ten black," &c.—the eager exclamations of joy or disappointment by the players, and the incessant clattering of the little ivory ball racing its endless round in the roulette-table. On one side of the room was a faro-table, and on the opposite side a roulette. We approached the former, which was thronged on three sides with players, while on the other, toward the wall, was seated the dealer of the game—the "gentleman professeur." He was a portly, respectable looking, jolly-faced Frenchman, with so little of the "black-leg" character stamped upon his physiognomy, that one would be far from suspecting him to be a gambler by profession. This is a profession difficult to be conceived as the permanent and only pursuit of an individual. Your conception of it has probably been taken, as in my own case, from the fashionable novels of the day; and perhaps you have regarded the character as merely the creation of an author's brain, and "the profession" *as* a profession, existing nowhere in the various scenes and circumstances of life.

There are in this city a very great number of these *infernos*, (*anglicè* "hells") all of which—with the exception of a few private ones, resorted to by those gentlemen who may have some regard for appearances—are open from twelve at noon till two in the morning, and thronged by all classes, from the lowest blackguard upward. They are situated in the most public streets,

THE LEVEE AT NEW ORLEANS

and in the most conspicuous locations. Each house has a bank, as the amount of funds owned by it is termed. Some of the houses have on hand twenty thousand dollars in specie; and when likely to be hard run by heavy losses, can draw for three or four times that amount upon the directors of the "bank company." The establishing of one of these banks is effected much as that of any other. Shares are sold, and many respectable moneyed men, I am informed, become stockholders; though not ambitious, I believe, to have their names made public. It is some of the best stock in the city, often returning an enormous dividend. They are regularly licensed, and pay into the state or city treasury, I forget which, annually more than sixty thousand dollars. From six to twelve well-dressed, genteel looking individuals, are always to be found in attendance, to whom salaries are regularly paid by the directors; and to this salary, and this occupation, they look for as permanent a support through life as do members of any other profession. It is this class of men who are emphatically denominated "gamblers and black legs." The majority of them are Frenchmen, though they usually speak both French and English. Individuals, allured by the hope of winning, are constantly passing in and out of these houses, in "broad noon," with the same indifference to what is termed "public opinion," as they would feel were they going into or out of a store.

Those places which are situated in the vicinity of Canal-street and along the Levée, are generally of a lower order, and thronged with the *canaille* of the city, sailors, Kentucky boatmen, crews of steam-boats, and poor Gallic gentlemen, in threadbare long-skirted coats and huge whiskers. The room we were now visiting was of a somewhat higher order, though not exclusively devoted to the more genteel adventurers, as, in the very nature of the thing, such an exclusion would be impossible. But if unruly persons intrude, and are disposed to be obstreperous, the conductors of the rooms, of course, have the power of expelling them at pleasure.

Being merely spectators of the game, we managed to obtain an advantageous position for viewing it, from a vacant settee placed by the side of the portly dealer, who occupied, as his exclusive right, one side of the large table. Before him were placed in two rows thirteen cards; the odd thirteenth capping the double file, like a militia captain at the head of his company, when marching "two by two"; the files of cards, however, unlike these martial files of men, are *straight*. You will readily see by the number, that these cards represent every variety in a pack. The dealer, in addition, has a complete pack, fitting closely in a silver box, from which, by the action of a sliding lid, he adroitly and accurately turns off the cards in dealing. The players, or "betters," as they are termed, place their money in various positions as it respects the thirteen cards upon the table, putting it either on a single card or between two, as their skill, judgment, or fancy may dictate.

As I took my station near the faro-board, the dealer was just shuffling the cards for a new game. There were eleven persons clustered around the table, and as the game was about to commence, arm after arm was reached forth to the prostrate cards, depositing one, five, ten, twenty, or fifty dollars, according to the faith or depth of purse of their owners. On, around, and between the cards, dollars were strewed singly or in piles, while the eyes of every better were fixed immoveably, and, as the game went on, with a painful intensity, upon his own deposit, perhaps his last stake. When the stakes were all laid, the dealer announced it by drawling out in bad English, "all saat." Then, damping his forefinger and thumb, by a summary process—not quite so elegant as common—he began drawing off the cards in succession. The card taken off does not count in the game; the betters all looking to the one turned up in the box to read the fate of their stakes. As the cards are turned, the winners are paid, the money won by the bank swept off with a long wand into the reservoir by the side of the banker, and down go new stakes, doubled or lessened according to the success of the winners—again is drawled out the mechanical "all set," and the same routine is repeated until long past midnight, while the dealers are relieved every two or three hours by their fellow-partners in the house.

At the right hand of the dealer, upon the table, is placed what is denominated "the bank," though it is merely its representative. This is a shallow, yet heavy metal box, about twenty inches long, half as many wide, and two deep, with a strong network of wire, so constructed as to cover the box like a lid, and be secured by a lock. Casting my eye into this receptacle through its latticed top, I noticed several layers of U.S. bank notes, from five to five hundred dollars, which were kept down by pieces of gold laid upon each pile. About one-fifth of the case was parted off from the rest, in which were a very large number of gold ounces and rouleaus of guineas. The whole amount contained in it, so far as I could judge, was about six thousand dollars, while there was more than three thousand dollars in silver, piled openly and most temptingly upon the table around the case, in dollars, halves, and quarters, ready for immediate use. From policy, five franc pieces are substituted for dollars in playing; but the winner of any number of them can, when he ceases playing, immediately exchange them at the bank for an equal number of dollars. It often happens that players, either from ignorance or carelessness, leave the rooms with the five franc pieces; but should they, five minutes afterward, discover their neglect and return to exchange them, the dealer exclaims with an air of surprise—"Saar! it will be one mistake, saar.

I nevair look you in de fas before, saar!" Thousands of dollars are got off annually in this manner, and a very pretty interest the banks derive from their ingenious method of *franking*.

Having seen some thousands of dollars change hands in the course of an hour, and, with feelings somewhat allied to pity, marked the expression of despair, darkening the features of the unfortunate loser, as he rushed from the room with clenched hands and bent brow, muttering indistinctly within his teeth fierce curses upon his luck; and observed, with no sympathizing sensations of pleasure, the satisfaction with which the winners hugged within their arms their piles of silver, we turned from the faro, and crossed the room to the roulette table. These two tables are as inseparable as the shark and the pilot fish, being always found together in every gambling room, ready to make prey of all who come within their influence. At faro there is no betting less than a dollar; here, stakes as low as a quarter are permitted. The players were more numerous at this table than at the former, and generally less genteel in their appearance. The roulette table is a large, long, green-covered board or platform, in the centre of which, placed horizontally upon a pivot, is a richly plated round mahogany table, or wheel, often inlaid with ivory and pearl, and elaborately carved, about two feet in diameter, with the bottom closed like an inverted box cover. Around this wheel, on the inner border, on alternate little black and red squares, are marked numbers as high as thirty-six, with two squares additional, in one a single cipher, in the other two ciphers; while on the green cloth-covered board, the same numbers are marked in squares. The dealer, who occupies one side of the table, with his metal, latticed case of bank notes and gold at his right hand, and piles of silver before him, sets the wheel revolving rapidly, and adroitly spins into it from the end of his thumb, as a boy would snap a marble, an ivory ball, one quarter the size of a billiard ball. The betters, at the same instant, place their money upon such one of the figures drawn upon the cloth as they fancy the most likely to favour them, and intently watch the ball as it races round within the revolving wheel. When the wheel stops, the ball necessarily rests upon some one of the figures in the wheel, and the fortunate player, whose stake is upon the corresponding number on the cloth, is immediately paid his winning, while the stakes of the losers are coolly transferred by the dealer to the constantly accumulating heap before him; again the wheel is set revolving, the little ball rattles around it, and purses are again made lighter and the bank increased.

As we were about to depart, I noticed in an interior room a table spread for nearly a dozen persons, and loaded with all the substantials for a hearty supper. The dealers, or conductors of the bank, are almost all bachelors, I believe, or ought to be, and keep "hall" accordingly, in the same building where lies their theatre of action, in the most independent and uproarious style. After the rooms are closed, which is at about two in the morning, they retire to their supper table, inviting all the betters, both winners and losers, who are present when the playing breaks up, to partake with them. The invitations are generally accepted; and those poor devils who in the course of the evening have been so unfortunate as to have "pockets to let," have at least the satisfaction of enjoying a good repast, *gratis,* before they go home and hang themselves.

SUNDAY IN NEW ORLEANS

The spacious bar-room of our magnificent hotel, as I descended to it on Sabbath morning, resounded to the footsteps of a hundred gentlemen, some promenading and in earnest conversation—some hastening to, or lounging about the bar, on which was displayed a row of rapidly disappearing glasses, containing the tempting, green-leaved, mint-julep—while others, some *tête à tête,* some smoking, were sipping in quiet their morning potation. A few, with legs *à la Trollope,* upon the tables, were reading stray papers, at the farther extremity of the hall.

My northern friend met me at the door of the hotel, around which, upon the side-walk, was gathered a knot of fashionably dressed, cane-wearing young men, talking, all together, of a duel. The morning was cloudless, the air mild. The sun shone down warm and as we passed from Camp-street across Canal, into Chartres-street, all the gay inhabitants, one would verily believe, had turned out as to a gala. The long, narrow streets were thronged with moving multitudes, and flashing with scarfs, ribbons, and feathers. Children, with large expressive eyes, their heads surmounted with tasselled caps and fancy hats, arrayed in their "brightest and best," bounded along behind their more soberly arrayed, but not less gay parents, followed by gaudily dressed slaves, who chattered incessantly with half-suppressed laughter to their acquaintances on the opposite trottoir. Clerks, just such looking young men as you will meet on Sabbath mornings in Broadway, or Cornhill—released from their six day's confinement—lounged by us arm in arm, as fine as the tailor and hair-dresser could make them. Crowds, or gangs of American and English sailors, mingling most companionably, on a cruise through the city, rolled jollily along—the same careless independent fellows that they are all the world over. I have observed that in foreign ports, the seamen of these once hostile nations link together like brothers. This is as it should be. The good feeling existing generally among all classes of Americans toward the mother country, must be gratifying both to reflecting Americans and to Englishmen.

These sons of Neptune were all dressed nearly alike in blue jackets, and full white trowsers, with black silk handkerchiefs knotted carelessly around their necks, and confined by some nautical breast-pin, in the shape of a foul anchor, a ship under her three top-sails, or plain gold hearts, pierced by arrows. Sailors are very sentimental fellows on shore! In direct contrast to these frank-looking, open-browed tars, who yawed along the side-walk, as a landsman would walk on a ship's deck at sea, we passed, near the head of Bienville-street, a straggling crew of some Spanish trader, clothed in tarry pantaloons and woollen shirts, and girt about with red and blue sashes, bucanier fashion, with filthy black whiskers, and stealthy glowing eyes, who glided warily along with lowering brows. The unsailor-like French sailor—the half horse and half alligator Kentucky boatman—the gentlemanly, carelessly-dressed cotton planter—the pale valetudinarian, from the north, whose deep sunken eye told of suicidal vigils over the midnight lamp—a noble looking foreigner, and a wretched beggar—a troop of Swiss emigrants, from the grandsire to the infant, and a gang of Erin's toil-worn exiles—all mingled *en masse*—swept along in this living current; while, gazing down upon the moving multitude from lofty balconies, were clusters of bright eyes, and sunny faces flashed from every window.

As we approached the cathedral, a dark-hued and finely moulded quadroon, with only a flowing veil upon her head, glided majestically past us. The elegant olive-browned Louisianese—the rosy-cheeked maiden from *La belle riviere*—the Parisian gentil-homme—a dignified, light-mustachoed palsgrave, and a portly sea-captain—the haughty Englishman and prouder southerner—a blanketed Choctaw, and a negro in uniform—slaves and freed-men of every shade, elbowed each other very familiarly as they traversed in various directions the crowded side-walks.

Crossing rue St. Louis, we came in collision with a party of gens d'armes with drawn swords in their hands, which they used as walking canes, leading an unlucky culprit to the callaboose—that "black-hole" of the city. Soldiers in splendid uniforms, with clashing and jingling accoutrements, were continually hurrying past us to parade.

At the corner of Toulouse-street we met a straggling procession of bare-headed, sturdy-looking priests, in soiled black surplices and fashionable boots, preceded by half a dozen white-robed boys, bare-legged and dirty. By this dignified procession, among which the crowd promiscuously mingled as they passed along, and whose august approach is usually notified by the jingling of the "sacring bell," was borne the sacred "host." They hastily passed us, shoved and jostled by the crowd, who scarcely gave way to them as they hastened on their ghostly message. These things are done differently in Buenos Ayres or Rio Janeiro, where such a procession is escorted by an armed guard, and a bayonet thrust, or a night in a Spanish prison, is the penalty for neglecting to genuflect, or uncover the heretical head.

As we issued from Chartres-street—where all "nations and kingdoms and tongues" seemed to have united to form its pageant of life—upon the esplanade in front of the cathedral, we were surprised by the sound of martial music pealing clearly above the confusion of tongues, the tramp of feet, and the rattling of carriages. On and around the noble green, soldiers in various uniforms, some of them of a gorgeous and splendid description, were assembling for parade. Members of the creole regiment—the finest body of military men I ever beheld, with the exception of a Brazilian regiment of blacks—were rapidly marshalling in the square. And mounted huzzars, with lofty caps and in glittering mail, were thundering in from the various streets, their spurs, chains and sabres, ringing and jingling warlike music, as they dashed up to the rendezvous.

At the head of this noble square, so variegated and tumultuous with its dazzling mimicry of war, rose in solemn and imposing grandeur the venerable cathedral, lifting its heavy towers high above the emmet-crowd beneath. Its doors, in front of which was extended a line of carriages, were thronged with a motley crowd, whose attention was equally divided between the religious ceremonies within the temple and the military display without. We forced our way through the mass, which was composed of strangers like ourselves—casual spectators—servants—hack-drivers—fruit sellers, and some few, who, like the publican, worshipped "afar off."

"Do you attend the *Theatre d'Orleans* to-night?" inquired a young Bostonian, forgetful of his orthodox habits—twirling while he spoke a ticket in his fingers—"you know the maxim—when in Rome"—

"I have not been here quite long enough yet to apply the rule," said I; "is not the theatre open on other evenings of the week?"

"Very seldom," he replied, "unless in the gayest part of the season—though I believe there is to be a performance some night this week; I will ascertain when and accompany you."

You are aware that the rituals, or established forms of the Roman church, do not prohibit amusements on this sacred day. The Sabbath, consequently, in a city, the majority of whose inhabitants are Catholics, is not observed as in the estimation of New-Englanders, or Protestants it should be. The lively Orleanese defend the custom of crowding their theatres, attending military parades, assembling in ballrooms, and mingling in the dangerous masquerade on this day, by wielding the scriptural weapon—"the Sabbath was made for man—not man for the Sabbath"; and then making their own inductions, they argue that the Sabbath is, literally, as the term imports, a day of rest, and not a day of religious labour.

That evening as I entered my room, I discovered, lying upon my table, a ticket for the American or Camp-street theatre, folded in a narrow slip of a play-bill, which informed me that the laughable entertainment of the "Three Hunchbacks," with the interesting play of "Cinderella," was to constitute the performance of the night: In a few moments afterward my Boston friend, who had left the ticket in my room, came in with another for the French theatre. I decided upon attending both, dividing the evening between them.

After tea we sallied out, in company with half of those who were at the supper-table, on our way to the theatre. The street and adjacent buildings shone brilliantly, with the glare of many lamps suspended from the theatre and coffee houses in the vicinity. A noisy crowd was gathered around the ticket-office—the side-walks were filled with boys and negroes—and the curbstone was lined with coloured females, each surrounded by bonbons, fruit, nuts, cakes, pies, gingerbread, and all the other et cetera of a "cake-woman's commodity." Entering the theatre, which is a plain handsome edifice, with a stuccoed front, and ascending a broad flight of steps, we passed across the first lobby, down a narrow aisle, opened through the centre of the boxes into the pit or *parquette,* as it is here termed, which is considered the eligible and fashionable part of the house. This is rather reversing the order of things as found with us at the north. The pews, or slips—for the internal arrangement, were precisely like those of a church—were cushioned with crimson materials, and filled with bonnetless ladies, with their heads dressed *à la Madonna*. We seated ourselves near the orchestra. The large green curtain still concealed the mimic world behind it; and I embraced the few moments of delay previous to its rising, to gaze upon this Thespian temple of the south, and a New Orleans audience.

The "parquette" was brilliant with bright eyes and pretty faces; and upon the bending galaxy of ladies which glittered in the front of the boxes around it, I seemed to gaze through the medium of a rainbow. There were, it must be confessed, some plain enough faces among them; but, at the first glance of the eye, one might verily have believed himself encircled by a gallery of houris. The general character of their faces was decidedly American; exactly such as one gazes upon at the Tremont or Park theatre; and I will henceforward eschew physiognomy, if "I guess" would not have dropped more naturally from the lips of one half who were before me, while conversing, than "I reckon."

There were but few French faces among the females; but, with two or three exceptions, these were extremely pretty. Most of the delicately-reared Creoles, or Louisiana ladies, are eminently beautiful. Their style of beauty is *unique,* and not easily classed. It is neither French nor English, but a combination of both, mellowed and enriched under a southern sky.

The interior of the house was richly decorated; and the panneling in the interior of the boxes was composed of massive mirror-plates, multiplying the audience with a fine effect. The stage was lofty, extensive, and so constructed, either intentionally or accidentally, as to reflect the voice with unusual precision and distinctness. The scenery was in general well executed: one of the forest scenes struck me as remarkably true to nature. While surveying the gaudy interior, variegated with gilding, colouring, and mirrors, the usual cry of "Down, down?—Hats off," warned us to be seated.

The performance was good for the pieces represented. The company, with the indefatigable Caldwell at its head, is strong and of a respectable character. When the second act was concluded we left the house; and passing through a parti-coloured mob, gathered around the entrance, and elbowing a gens d'armes or two, stationed in the lobby—we gained the street, amidst a shouting of "Your check, sir! your check!—Give me your check—Please give me your check!—check!—check!—check!" from a host of boys, who knocked one another about unmercifully in their exertions to secure prizes, which, to escape a mobbing, we threw into the midst of them; and jumping into a carriage in waiting, drove off to the French theatre, leaving them embroiled in a *pêle mêle,* in which the sciences of phlebotomy and phrenology were being "tested" by very practical applications.

After a drive of half a league or more through long and narrow streets, dimly lighted by swinging lamps, we were set down at the door of the Theatre d'Orleans, around which a crowd was assembled of as different a character, from that we had just escaped, as would have met our eyes had we been deposited before the *Theatre Royale* in Paris. The street was illuminated from the brilliantly lighted cafés and cabarets, clustered around this "nucleus" of gayety and amusement. As we crossed the broad *pavé* into the vestibule of the theatre, the rapidly enunciated, nasal sounds of the French language assailed our ears from every side. Ascending the stairs and entering the boxes, I was struck with the liveliness and brilliancy of the scene, which the interior exhibited to the eye. "Magnificent!" was upon my lips— but a moment's observation convinced me that its brilliancy was an illusion, created by numerous lights, and an artful arrangement and lavish display of gilding and colouring. The whole of the interior, including the stage decorations and scenic effect, was much inferior to that of the house we had just quitted.

The boxes—if caverns resembling the interior of a ship's longboat, with one end elevated three feet, and equally convenient, can be so called—were cheerless and uncomfortable. There were but few females in the house, and none of these were in the pit, as at the other theatre. Among them I saw but two or three pretty faces; and evidently none were of the first class of French society in this city. The house was thinly attended, presenting, wherever I turned my eyes, a "beggarly account of empty boxes."

After remaining half an hour, wearied with its tiresome *ritornello* of a popular French air—listening with the devotion of a "Polytechnique" to the blood-stirring Marseillaise hymn—amused at the closing scene of a laughable comédie, and edified by the first of a pantomime, and observing, that with but one lovely exception, the Mesdames *du scene* were very plain, and the Messieurs very handsome, we left the theatre and returned to the hotel, whose deserted bar-room, containing here and there a straggler, presented a striking contrast to the noise and bustle of the multitude by which it was thronged at noonday. In general, strangers consider the *tout ensemble* of this theatre on Sabbath evenings, and on others when the élite of the New-Orleans society is collected there, decidedly superior to that of any other in the United States.

A LOUISIANA SUGAR PLANTATION

A gentleman to whom I brought a letter of introduction called yesterday and invited me to ride with him to his plantation, a few miles from New Orleans. He drove his own phaeton, which was drawn by two beautiful long-tailed bays. After a drive of a mile and a half, we cleared the limits of the straggling, and apparently interminable faubourgs, and, emerging through a long narrow street upon the river road, bounded swiftly over its level surface, which was as smooth as a bowling-green—saving a mud-hole now and then, where a crevasse had let in upon it a portion of the Mississippi. An hour's drive, after clearing the suburbs, past a succession of isolated villas, encircled by slender columns and airy galleries, and surrounded by richly foliaged gardens, whose fences were bursting with the luxuriance which they could scarcely confine, brought us in front of a charming residence situated at the head of a broad, gravelled avenue, bordered by lemon and orange trees, forming in the heat of summer, by arching naturally overhead, a cool and shady promenade. We drew up at the massive gate-way and alighted. As we entered the avenue, three or four children were playing at its farther extremity, with noise enough for Christmas holidays; two of them were trundling hoops in a race, and a third sat astride of a non-locomotive wooden horse, waving a tiny sword, and charging at half a dozen young slaves, who were testifying their bellicose feelings by dancing and shouting around him with the noisiest merriment.

After playful and affectionate congratulations between the noble little fellows and their parent, we walked toward the house, preceded by our trundlers, with the young soldier hand-in-hand between us, followed close behind by the little Africans, whose round shining eyes glistened wistfully —speaking as plainly as eyes could speak the strong desire, with which their half-naked limbs evidently sympathized by their restless motions, to bound ahead, contrary to decorum, "wid de young massas!"

Around the semi-circular flight of steps, ascending to the piazza of the dwelling,—the columns of which were festooned with the golden jasmine and luxuriant multiflora,—stood, in large green vases, a variety of flowers, among which I observed the tiny flowerets of the diamond myrtle, sparkling like crystals of snow, scattered upon rich green leaves—the dark foliaged Arabian jasmine silvered with its opulently-leaved flowers redolent of the sweetest perfume,—and the rose-geranium, breathing gales of fragrance upon the air. From this point the main avenue branches to the right and left, into narrower, yet not less beautiful walks, which, lined with ever-green and flowering shrubs, completely encircled the cottage.

The proprietor of the delightful spot which lay spread out around me—a lake of foliage—fringed by majestic forest trees, and diversified with labyrinthyne walks,—had, the preceding summer, consigned to the tomb the mother of his "beautiful ones." They were under the care of a dignified lady, his sister, and the widow of a gentleman formerly distinguished as a lawyer in New-England. But like many other northern ladies, whose names confer honour upon our literature, and whose talents elevate and enrich our female seminaries of education, she had independence enough to rise superior to her widowed indigence; and had prepared to open a boarding school at the north, when the death of his wife led her wealthier brother to invite her to supply a mother's place to his children, to whom she was now both mother and governess.

The history of this lady is that of hundreds of her country-women. There are, I am informed, many instances in the south-west, of New-England's daughters having sought, with the genuine spirit of independence, thus to repair their broken fortunes. In this country the occupation of instructing, whether invested in the president of a college or in the teacher of a country school, is degraded to a secondary rank. In New-England, on the contrary, the lady of a living collegiate president is of the élite, decidedly, if not at the head, of what is there termed "good society." Here, the same lady, whether a visitor for the winter, or a settled resident, must yield in rank—as the laws of southern society have laid it down—to the lady of the planter. The southerners, however, when they can secure one of our well-educated northern ladies in their families, know well how to appreciate their good fortune. Inmates of the family, they are treated with politeness and kindness; but in the soirée, dinner party, or levée, the governess is thrown more into the back-ground than she would be in a gentleman's family, even in aristocratic England; and her title to an equality with the gay, and fashionable, and wealthy circle by whom she is surrounded, and her challenge to the right of *caste,* is less readily admitted. This illiberal jealousy is the natural consequence of the crude state of American society, where the line of demarcation between its rapidly forming classes is yet uncertainly defined, and each individual who is anxious to be of the better file has to walk circumspectly lest he should be found mingling with the canaille.

After a kind of bachelor's dinner, in a hall open on two sides for ventilation, sumptuous enough for Epicurus, and served by two or three young slaves, who were drilled to a glance of the eye, crowned by a luxurious dessert of fruits and sweet-meats, and graced with wine, not of the vintage common in New England, but of the pure *outre-mer,* we proceeded to the sugar-house or *sucrérie,* through a lawn which nearly surrounded the ornamental grounds about the house, studded here and there with lofty trees, which the good taste of the original proprietor of the domain had left standing in their forest majesty. From this rich green sward, on which two or three fine saddle-horses were grazing, we passed through a turn-stile into a less lovely, but more domestic enclosure, alive with young negroes, sheep, turkies, hogs, and every variety of domestic animal that could be attached to a plantation. From this diversified collection, which afforded a tolerable idea of the interior of Noah's ark, we entered the long street of a village of white cottages, arranged on either side of it with great regularity. They were all exactly alike, and separated by equal spaces; and to every one was attached an enclosed piece of ground, apparently for a vegetable garden; around the doors decrepit and superannuated negroes were basking in the evening sun—mothers were nursing their naked babies, and one or two old and blind negresses were spinning in their doors. In the centre of the street, which was a hundred yards in width, rose to the height of fifty feet a framed belfry, from whose summit was suspended a bell, to regulate the hours of labour. At the foot of this tower, scattered over the grass, lay a half score of black children, *in puris naturalibus,* frolicking or sleeping in the warm sun, under the surveillance of an old African matron, who sat knitting upon a camp-stool in the midst of them.

We soon arrived at the boiling-house, which was an extensive brick building with tower-like chimneys, numerous flues, and a high, steep roof, reminding me of a New England distillery. As we entered after scaling a barrier of sugar-casks with which the building was surrounded, the slaves, who were dressed in coarse trowsers, some with and others without shirts, were engaged in the several departments of their sweet employment; whose fatigues some African Orpheus was lightening with a loud chorus, which was instantly hushed, or rather modified, on our entrance, to a half-assured whistling. A white man, with a very unpleasing physiognomy, carelessly leaned against one of the brick pillars, who raised his hat very respectfully as we passed, but did not change his position. This was the overseer. He held in his hand a short-handled whip, loaded in the butt, which had a lash four or five times the length of the staff. Without noticing us, except when addressed by his employer, he remained watching the motions of the toiling slaves, quickening the steps of a loiterer by a word, or threatening with his whip, those who, tempted by curiosity, turned to gaze after us, as we walked through the building.

The season of sugar-making is termed by the planters of the south, the "rolling season"; and a merry and pleasant time it is too. It commences about the middle or last of October, and continues from three weeks to as many months, according to the season and other circumstances; but more especially the force upon the plantation, and the amount of sugar to be made. As the season approaches, every thing assumes a new and more cheerful aspect. The negroes are more animated, as their winter clothing is distributed, their little crops are harvested, and their wood and other comforts secured for that season; which, to them, if not the freest, is certainly the gayest and happiest portion of the year. As soon as the corn crop and fodder are harvested, every thing is put in motion for the grinding. The horses and oxen are increased in number and better groomed; the carts and other necessary utensils are overhauled and repaired, and some hundred or thousand cords of wood are cut and ready piled for the manufacture of the sugar. The *sucrérie,* or boiling house, is swept and garnished—the mill and engine are polished—the kettles scoured—the coolers caulked, and the *purgerie,* or draining-house, cleaned and put in order, where the casks are arranged to receive the sugar.

The first labour in anticipation of grinding, is that of providing plants for the coming year; and this is done by cutting the cane, and putting it in *matelas,* or matressing it, as it is commonly called. The cane is cut and thrown into parcels in different parts of the field, in quantities sufficient to plant several acres, and so arranged that the tops of one layer may completely cover and protect the stalks of another. After the quantity required is thus secured, the whole plantation force, nearly, is employed in cutting cane, and conveying it to the mill. The cane is divested of its tops, which are thrown aside, unless they are needed for plants, which is often the case, when they are thrown together in rows, and carefully protected from the inclemencies of the weather. The stalks are then cut as near as may be to the ground, and thrown into separate parcels or rows, to be taken to the mill in carts, and expressed as soon as possible. The cane is sometimes bound together in bundles, in the field, which facilitates its transportation, and saves both time and trouble. As soon as it is harvested, it is placed upon a cane-carrier, so called, which conveys it to the mill, where it is twice expressed between iron rollers, and made perfectly dry. The juice passes into vats, or receivers, and the *baggasse* or cane-trash, (called in the West Indies *migass,*) is received into carts and conveyed to a distance from the sugar-house to be burnt as soon as may be. Immediately after the juice is expressed, it is distributed to the boilers, generally four in succession, ranged in solid masonry along the sides of the boiling-room, where it is properly tempered, and its purification and evaporation are progressively advanced. The French have commonly five boilers, distinguished by the fanciful names of *grande—propre—flambeau— sirop,* and *battérie.*

In the first an alkali is generally put to temper the juice; lime is commonly used, and the quantity is determined by the good judgment and experience of the sugar-maker. In the last kettle—the *teach* as it is termed—the sugar is concentrated to the granulating point, and then conveyed into coolers, which hold from two to three hogsheads. After remaining here for twenty-four hours or more, it is removed to the *purgerie,* or draining-house, and placed in hogsheads, which is technically called *potting.* Here it undergoes the process of draining for a few days or weeks, and is then ready for the market. The molasses is received beneath in cisterns, and when they become filled, it is taken out and conveyed into barrels or hogsheads and shipped. When all the molasses is removed from the cistern, an inferior kind of sugar is re-manufactured, which is called *cistern-sugar,* and sold at a lower price. When the grinding has once commenced, there is no cessation of labour till it is completed. From beginning to end, a busy and cheerful scene continues. The negroes work from eighteen to twenty hours though to lighten the burden as much as possible, the gang is divided into two watches, one taking the first, and the other the last part of the night; and notwithstanding this continued labour, the negroes improve in condition, and appear fat and flourishing. They drink freely of cane-juice, and the sickly among them revive and become robust and healthy.

After the grinding is finished, the negroes have several holidays, when they are quite at liberty to dance and frolic as much as they please; and the cane-song—which is improvised by one of the gang, the rest all joining in a prolonged and unintelligible chorus—now breaks night and day upon the ear, in notes "most musical, most melancholy." This over, planting recommences, and the same routine of labour is continued, with an intermission—except during the boiling season, as above stated—upon most, if not all plantations, of twelve hours in twenty-four, and of one day in seven throughout the year.

Leaving the sugar-house, I returned with my polite entertainer to the house. Lingering for a moment on the gallery in the rear of the dwelling-house, I dwelt with pleasure upon the scene which the domain presented.

The lawn, terminated by a snow-white paling, and ornamented here and there by a venerable survivor of the aboriginal forest, was rolled out before me like a carpet, and dotted with sleek cows, and fine horses, peacefully grazing, or indolently reclining upon the thick grass, chewing the cud of contentment. Beyond the lawn, and extending farther into the plantation, lay a pasture containing a great number of horses and cattle, playing together, reposing, feeding, or standing in social clusters around a shaded pool. Beyond, the interminable cane-field, or plantation proper, spread away without fence or swell, till lost in the distant forests which bounded the horizon. On my left, a few hundred yards from the house, and adjoining the pasture, stood the stables and other plantation appurtenances, constituting a village in themselves—for planters always have a separate building for everything. To the right stood the humble yet picturesque village or "Quarter" of the slaves, embowered in trees, beyond which, farther toward the interior of the plantation, arose the lofty walls and turreted chimneys of the sugar-house, which, combined with the bell-tower, presented the appearance of a country village with its church-tower and the walls of some public edifice, lifting themselves above the trees. Some of the sugar-houses are very lofty and extensive, with noble wings and handsome fronts, resembling—aside from their lack of windows—college edifices. It requires almost a fortune to construct one.

The whole scene before me was extremely animated. Human figures were moving in all directions over the place. Some labouring in the distant field, others driving the slow-moving oxen, with a long, drawling cry—half naked negro boys shouting and yelling, were galloping horses as wild as themselves —negresses of all sizes, from one able to carry a tub to the minikin who could "tote" but a pint-dipper, laughing and chattering as they went, were conveying water from a spring to the wash-house, in vessels adroitly balanced upon their heads. Slaves sinking under pieces of machinery, and other burdens, were passing and repassing from the boiling-house and negro quarter. Some were calling to others afar off, and the merry shouts of the black children at their sports in their village, reminding me of a school just let out, mingled with the lowing of cows, the cackling of geese, the bleating of lambs, the loud and unmusical clamour of the guinea-hen, agreeably varied by the barking of dogs, and the roaring of some young African rebel under maternal castigation.

Passing from this plantation scene through the airy hall of the dwelling, which opened from piazza to piazza through the house, to the front gallery, whose light columns were wreathed with the delicately leaved Cape-jasmine, rambling woodbine and honeysuckle, a lovlier and more agreeable scene met my eye. I stood almost embowered in the foliage of exotics and native plants, which stood upon the gallery in handsome vases of marble and China-ware. The main avenue opened a vista to the river through a paradise of althea, orange, lemon, and olive trees, and groves and lawns extended on both sides of this lovely spot, terminating at the villas of the adjoining plantations.

The Mississippi—always majestic and lake-like in its breadth—rolled past her turbid flood, dotted here and there by a market-lugger, with its black crew and clumsy sails. By the Levée, on the opposite shore, lay a brig, taking in a cargo of sugar from the plantation, whose noble colonnaded mansion rose like a palace above its low, grove-lined margin, and an English argosy of great size, with black spars and hull, was moving under full sail down the middle of the river.

As I was under the necessity of returning to the city the same evening, I took leave of the youthful family of my polite host, and rolling like the wind over the level road along the banks of the river, arrived in the city a few minutes after seven.

A MISSISSIPPI STEAMBOAT: NEW ORLEANS TO NATCHEZ

Once more I am floating upon the "Father of rivers." New-Orleans, with its crowd of "mingled nations," is seen indistinctly in the distance. We are now doubling a noble bend in the river, which will soon hide the city from our sight; but scenes of rural enchantment are opening before us as we advance, which will amply and delightfully repay us for its absence.

Below us a few miles, indistinctly seen through the haze, a dense forest of masts, and here and there a tower, designate the emporium of commerce—

the key of the mighty west. The banks are lined and ornamented with elegant mansions, displaying, in their richly adorned grounds, the wealth and taste of their possessors; while the river, now moving onward like a golden flood, reflecting the mellow rays of the setting sun, is full of life. Vessels of every size are gliding in all directions over its waveless bosom, while graceful skiffs dart merrily about like white-winged birds. Huge steamers are dashing and thundering by, leaving long trains of wreathing smoke in their rear. Carriages filled with ladies and attended by gallant horsemen, enliven the smooth road along the Levée; while the green banks of the Levée itself are

RIVERBOAT AT A "WOODING STATION"

covered with gay promenaders. A glimpse through the trees now and then, as we move rapidly past the numerous villas, detects the piazzas, filled with the young, beautiful, and aged of the family, enjoying the rich beauty of the evening, and of the objects upon which my own eyes rest with admiration.

The passengers have descended to the cabin; some to turn in, a few to read, but more to play at the ever-ready card table. The pilot (as the helmsman is here termed) stands in his lonely wheelhouse, comfortably enveloped in his blanket-coat—the hurricane deck is deserted, and the hands are gathered in the bows, listening to the narration of some ludicrous adventure of recent transaction in the city of hair-breadth escapes. Now and then a laugh from the merry auditors, or a loud roar from some ebony-cheeked fireman, as he pitches his wood into the gaping furnace, breaks upon the stillness of night, startling the echoes along the shores. How readily do we accustom ourselves to circumstances! The deep trombone of the steam-pipe—the regular splash of the paddles—and the incessant rippling of the water eddying away astern, as our noble vessel flings it from her sides, no longer affect the senses, unless it may be to lull them into a repose well meet for contemplation.

The plantations along the river extend from the Levée to the swamps in the rear; the distance across the belt of land being, from the irregular encroachment of the marshes, from one to two or three miles. These plantations have been, for a very long period, under cultivation for the production of sugar crops. As the early possessor of large tracts of land had sons to settle, they portioned off parallelograms to each; which, to combine the advantages of exportation and wood, extended from the river to the flooded forest in the rear. These, in time, portioned off to their children, while every occupant of a tract erected his dwelling at the head of his domain, one or two hundred yards from the river. Other plantations retain their original dimensions, crowned, on the borders of the river, with noble mansions, embowered in the ever-green foliage of the dark-leaved orange and lemon trees. The shores, consequently, present, from the lofty deck of a steamer,—from which can be had an extensive prospect of the level country—a very singular appearance.

As we approach Baton Rouge, the character of the scene changes. Hills once more relieve the eye, so long wearied with gazing upon a flat yet beautiful country.

We are now nearly opposite the town, which is pleasantly situated upon the declivity of the hill, retreating over its brow and spreading out on a plain in the rear, where the private dwellings are placed, shaded and half embowered in the rich foliage of that loveliest of all shade-trees, "the pride of China." The stores and other places of business are upon the front street, which runs parallel to the river. The site of the town is about forty feet above the highest flood, and rises by an easy and gentle swell from the water. The barracks, a short distance from the village, are handsome and commodious, constructed around a pentagonal area—four noble buildings forming four sides, while the fifth is open, fronting the river. The buildings are brick, with lofty colonnades and double galleries running along the whole front. The columns are yellow-stuccoed, striking the eye with a more pleasing effect, than the glare of red brick. The view of these noble structures from the river, as we passed, was very fine.

The rich and luxuriant character of the scenery, which charms and attracts the eye of the traveller as he ascends the Mississippi from New-Orleans to Baton Rouge, is now changed. A broad, turbid flood, rolling through a land of vast forests, alone meets the eye, giving sublime yet wild and gloomy features to the scene. On looking from the cabin window, I see only a long, unbroken line of cotton trees, with their pale green foliage, as dull and void of interest as a fog-bank. The opposite shore presents the same appearance; and so it is, with the occasional relief of a plantation and a "landing place," comprising a few buildings, the whole distance to Natchez. A wretched cabin, now and then, varies the wild appearance of the banks—the home of some solitary wood-cutter.

Having secured a berth in one corner of the spacious cabin, where I could draw the rich crimsoned curtains around me, and with book or pen pass the time somewhat removed from the bustle, and undisturbed by the constant passing of the restless passengers, I began this morning to look about me upon my fellow-travellers, seeking familiar faces, or scanning strange ones.

Our passengers are a strange medley, not only representing every state and territory washed by this great river, but nearly every Atlantic and trans-Atlantic state and nation. In the cabin are the merchants and planters of the "up country"; and on deck, emigrants and return-boatmen. There are about forty passengers of both sexes. Two of the most genteel-looking among them, so far as dress goes, I am told, are professed "black-legs"; or, as they more courteously style themselves, "sporting gentlemen."—There is an organized body of these *ci-devant* gentry upon the river, who have local agents in every town, and travelling agents on board the principal steamboats. In the guise of gentlemen, they "take in" the unwary passenger and unskilful player, from whom they often obtain large sums of money. As the same sportsmen do not go twice in the same boat, the captains do not become so familiar with their persons as to refuse them passage, were they so inclined. It is very seldom, however, when they are known, that they are denied a passage, as gambling is not only permitted but encouraged on most of the boats, by carrying a supply of cards in the bar. Even the sanctity of the Sabbath is no check to this amusement: all day yesterday the tables were surrounded with players, at two of which they were dealing "faro"; at the third playing "brag." Indeed the day was utterly disregarded by nearly every individual on board. Travelling is a sad demoralizer.

There are several French gentlemen on board; one important looking personage, who bears the title of general, and seems to feel the dignity it confers; three or four Mississippi cotton planters, in large, low-crowned, broad-brimmed, white fur hats, wearing their clothes in a careless, half sailor-like, half gentleman-like air, dashed with a small touch of the farmer, which style of dressing is peculiar to the Mississippi country gentleman. They are talking about negroes, railroads, and towing shipping. There is also a travelling Yankee lawyer, in a plain, stiff, black coat, closely buttoned up to his chin, strait trowsers, narrow hat, and gloves—the very antipodes, in appearance, to the *non chalant,* easy, care-for-nothing air of his southern neighbours.

A Methodist minister, in a bottle-green frock coat, fancy vest, black stock, white pantaloons and white hat, is sitting apart by the stove, deeply engaged upon the pages of a little volume, like a hymn-book. Any other dress than uniform black for a minister, would, at the north, be deemed highly improper, custom having thus so decided; but here they wear just what Providence sends them or their own taste dictates.

There are two or three fat men, in gray and blue—a brace of bluff, manly-looking Germans—a lynx-eyed, sharp-nosed New-York speculator—four old French Jews, with those noble foreheads, arched brows, and strange-expressioned eyes, that look as though always weeping—the well-known and never to be mistaken characteristic of this remarkable people. The remainder of our passengers present no peculiarities worth remarking. So I throw them all in, tall and short, little and big, and all sorts and sizes, to complete the motley *"ensemble"* of my fellow-travellers.

Among the ladies are a beautiful, dark-eyed, dark-haired Virginian, and an intelligent, young married lady from Vermont, accompanied by her only child, a handsome, spirited boy, between four and five years of age. His mother possessed a highly cultivated mind, and her full share of Yankee inquisitiveness. She was always resolved that nothing worthy of observation should escape her. She was a pure New-England interrogative. With a southerner I might have journied from Montreal to Mexico, without being questioned as often as I have been in this short passage. When a northerner is not inquisitive, the fact may generally be ascribed to intellectual dullness; in a southerner to constitutional indolence.

The loud and startling report of a cannon in the bows of the boat, making her stagger and tremble through every beam, is the signal that Natchez is in sight. At the foot of the bluffs are long straggling lines of wooden buildings, principally stores and store-houses; the levée is fringed with flat boats and steamers, and above all, tower majestically the masts of two or three ships. The whole prospect from the deck presents an interesting scene of commercial life and bustle.

NATCHEZ-UNDER-THE-HILL

Forcing my way through the dingy crowd—for four out of five of them were black, and, "by the same token," as ragged as Falstaff's regiment, of shirtless memory—I followed my athletic pioneer; who, with my heavy baggage poised accurately upon his head, moved as rapidly and carelessly along the thronged Levée as though he carried no weight but his own thick cranium. On looking round me for a moment, on landing, I was far from agreeably impressed with the general appearance of the buildings. This part of the town is not properly Natchez—and strangers passing up and down the river, who have had the opportunity of seeing only this place, have, without dreaming of the beautiful city over their heads, gone on their way, with impressions very inaccurate and unfavourable. These impressions, derived only, but justly, from this repulsive spot, have had a tendency to depreciate the city, and fasten upon it a bad name, which it is very far from meriting. Like the celebrated "Five Points," in New-York, "Natchez under the Hill," as it has been aptly named, has extended its fame throughout the United States, in wretched rhyme and viler story. For many years it has been the nucleus of vice upon the Mississippi. But, for two or three years past, the establishment of respectable mercantile houses, and an excellent hotel, combined with an efficient police, and a spirit of moral reform among the citizens, has, in a great measure, redeemed the place—changed its repulsive character and cancelled its disgraceful name. Though now on the high way of reform, there is still enough of the cloven-hoof visible, to enable the stranger to recognise that its former reputation was well earned.

The principal street, which terminates at the ascent of the hill, runs parallel with the river, and is lined on either side with a row of old wooden houses; which are alternately gambling-houses, brothels, and bar-rooms: a fair assemblage! As we passed through the street—which we gained with difficulty from the boat, picking our way to it as we could, through a filthy alley—the low, broken, half-sunken side-walks, were blocked up with fashionably-dressed young men, smoking or lounging, tawdrily arrayed, highly rouged females, sailors, Kentucky boatmen, negroes, negresses, mulattoes, pigs, dogs, and dirty children. The sounds of profanity and Bacchanalian revels, well harmonizing with the scene, assailed our ears as we passed hastily along, through an atmosphere of tobacco smoke and other equally fragrant odours. After a short walk we emerged into a purer air, and in front of a very neat and well-conducted hotel. From near this place, extending along the Levée to the north, commences the mercantile part of the "landing," lined with stores and extensive warehouses, in which is transacted a very heavy business. The whole of this lower town is built upon a reclaimed flat, from one to two hundred yards broad, and half a mile in length; bounded upon one side by the river, and on the other by the cliff or bluff, upon which Natchez stands, and which rises abruptly from the *Batture,* to the height of one hundred and sixty feet. This bluff extends along the river, more or less varied and broken, for several miles; though at no point so abrupt and bold as here, where it bears the peculiar characteristics of the wild scenery of "Dover cliffs." The face of the cliff at Natchez is not a uniform precipice, but, apparently by the provident foresight of nature, broken by an oblique shelf or platform, gradually inclining from the summit to the base. With but a little excavation, a fine road has been constructed along this way, with an inclination sufficiently gentle to enable the heaviest teams to ascend with comparative ease. One side of the road is of course bounded by a perpendicular cliff; the other by empty air and a dizzy precipice: so that the unwary foot-traveller, involved amid the ascent and descent of drays, carriages, horsemen, and porters, enjoys a tolerably fair alternative of being squeezed uncomfortably close against the bluff, or pitched, with a summerset, into some of the yawning chimneys on the flats beneath. For the whole length of this ascent, which is nearly a quarter of a mile, there is no kind of guard for the protection of the passengers. Yet, I have been told, no lives have ever been lost here. One poor fellow, a short time since, having taken a drop too much, and reeling too near the verge, lost his equilibrium, and over he went. But it is hard to kill a drunkard, except with the "pure spirit" itself; and the actor in this "drop scene" being "a gem of sweet Erin," stuck to the sod, and slid comfortably, though rapidly, to the bottom. The next moment he was seen gathering himself up out of a sand-heap, with "By St. Pathrick! but that was a jewel of a lape!—and it's my bright new baiver castor that's smashed by it to smitherins."

Yesterday was the Sabbath and I had early rambled to the cliff. The majestic Mississippi was spread out before me like a vast sheet of liquid steel —its unruffled bosom, dotted and relieved here and there by a light skiff or a huge steamer, booming and puffing far away in the distance.

From a row of dilapidated yet inhabited dwellings beneath me, at the base of the cliff, sounds of rude merriment, mingled with the tones of loud dispute and blasphemy, rose with appalling distinctness upon the still air, breaking the Sabbath silence of the hour, in harsh discord with its sacredness. The streets of the lower town were alive with boatmen, draymen, buyers and sellers, horsemen and hacks, and scores of negroes, some wrestling, some fighting, others running foot-races, playing quoits or marbles, selling the products of their little gardens, or, with greater probability, their predatory excursions; while from all combined, a confused murmur, not unlike the harmony which floated around Babel, rolled upward to the skies—an incense far from acceptable to Him, who has promulgated amid the thunders of Sinai, "Remember the Sabbath day to keep it holy."

In "Natchez under the hill," the Sabbath, as a day of rest and public worship, is not observed according to the strictest letter of the old "blue laws." On that day the stores are kept open and generally filled with boatmen and negroes. With the latter this day is a short jubilee, and, with the peculiar skill of their race, they make the most of it—condensing the occupation and the jollity of seven days into one. It is customary for planters in the neighbourhood to give their slaves a small piece of land to cultivate for their own use, by which, those who are industrious, generally make enough to keep themselves and their wives in extra finery and spending money throughout the year. They have the Sabbath given them as a holiday, when they are permitted to leave their plantations and come into town to dispose of their produce, and lay in their own little luxuries and private stores. The various avenues to the city are consequently on that day filled with crowds of chatting, laughing negroes, arrayed in their Sunday's best, and adroitly balancing heavily loaded baskets on their heads, which, from long practice in this mode of conveyance, often become indurated, like a petrification, and as flat as the palm of the hand, distending at the sides, and elongating in proportion to the depression, causing a peculiar conformation of the skull, which would set phrenology at defiance. Others mounted on mules or miserable-looking plough-horses, in whose presence Rosinante himself would have looked sleek and respectable—burthened with their marketable commodities, jog on side by side, with their dames or sweethearts riding "double-jaded"—as the Yankees term the mode—behind them; while here and there market carts returning from the city, (as this is also market morning) or from the intersecting roads, pour in upon the highway to increase the life, variety, and motley character of its crowd. But this unpleasing picture of a Sabbath morning, has brighter tints to redeem the graven character of its moral shades. Of all that picturesque multitude of holiday slaves, two-thirds, the majority of whom are women, are on their way to church, into whose galleries they congregate at the hour of divine service in great numbers, and worship with an apparent devoutness and attention, which beings who boast intellects of a higher order might not disdain to imitate. The female slaves very generally attend church in this country; but, whether to display their tawdry finery, of which they are fond to a proverb, or for a better purpose, I will not undertake to determine. The males prefer collecting in little knots in the streets, where, imitating the manners, bearing, and language of their masters, they converse with grave faces and in pompous language, selecting hard, high-sounding words, which are almost universally misapplied, and distorted, from their original sound as well as sense to a most ridiculous degree—astounding their gaping auditors "ob de field nigger class," who cannot boast such enviable accomplishments— parading through the streets from mere listlessness, or gathering around and filling the whiskey shops, spending their little all for the means of intoxication. Though negroes are proverbially lovers of whiskey, but few are to be found among them who get drunk, unless on Christmas holidays, when the sober ones are most easily numbered; this is owing to the discipline of plantations, the little means they have wherewith to purchase, and last, though not least, the fear of punishment—that *"argumentum ad corporem,"* which leaves a stinging conviction behind it, of the painful effects of "old rye" in the abstract upon the body.

That a market should be held upon the Sabbath in this city, is a "bend sinister" upon its escutcheon. But this custom is defended, even by those who admit its evil tendency, upon the plea "that meats in this climate will not keep over night."—These stores are all kept open upon the Sabbath, on which day there is often more business done than on any other. The blacks, who have no other opportunity of making their little purchases, crowd around the counters—the boatmen trade off their cargoes, and the purchasers store them—steamers are constantly arriving and departing, lading and unlading—and the steam ferry-boat makes its oft-repeated trip from shore to shore—all giving a life, bustle, and variety to the scene, of a very un-sabbath-like character. The merchants plead the necessity of supplying steamers. This is readily admitted; but it has given rise to a train of unforeseen evils, which have little relation to this basis of the custom. The numerous drinking shops in the other parts of the Landing are, on that day, as much at least, if not more than on other days, filled with a motley assemblage of black, white, and yellow, drinking and carousing.

Nearly two hundred feet below me, as I stood upon the bluff, and within the huge shadow of the cliff, stretched a long, low building, over which proudly waved the star-spangled banner, and to whose inhabitants the sun, already high in the heavens, had not yet risen. From this building issued the sound of bestial revelry, drowning the hum of business and the shouts of boyish merriment. The coarse gray clothing (a shame to our army) of most of those lounging about the door, designated it, in conjunction with the flag over their heads, as a rendezvous—even had not the martial eloquence of a little, half-tipsy, dapper man in a gray doublet, whose voice now and then reached my ear in the intervals of the uproarous proceedings—expatiating to a gaping crowd of grinning Africans—night-capped or bare-headed white females, in slattern apparel and uncombed locks—two or three straight, blanketed, silent Indians—noisy boys and ragged boatmen—upon the glories of a soldier's life, sufficiently indicated its character. The southern division of the landing consists of one short street, parallel with the river, over which it hangs on one side, while the houses on the other are overhung by a spur of the cliff, which, like an avalanche, threatens every moment to slide and overwhelm it. The street is lined with dancing-houses, tippling-shops, houses of ill-fame, and gambling-rooms. Here may always be heard the sound of the violin, the clink of silver upon the roulette and faro-tables, and the language of profanity and lewdness: and the revellers, so far from being interrupted by the intervention of the Sabbath, actually distinguish it by a closer and more persevering devotion to their unhallowed pursuits and amusements.

THE PLANTERS OF MISSISSIPPI

The towns and villages of Mississippi, as in European states, are located perfectly independent of each other, isolated among its forests, and often many leagues apart, leaving in the intervals large tracts of country covered with plantations, and claiming no minuter subdivision than that of "county." Natchez, for instance, is a corporation one mile square, but from the boundaries of the city to Woodville, the next incorporated town south, there is an interval of thirty-eight miles. It is necessary for the planters who reside between towns so far asunder, to have some more particular address, than the indefinite one arising from their vicinity to one or other of these towns. Hence has originated the pleasing custom of naming estates, as in England; and the names so given are always regarded by the planters themselves, and by the community, as an inseparable part of their address. These names are generally selected with taste, such as "Monmouth," "Laurel-hill," "Grange," "Magnolia grove," "The Forest," "Cottage," "Briars," "Father land," and "Anchorage"— the last given by a retired navy officer to his plantation. The name is sometimes adopted with reference to some characteristic of the domain, as "The Oaks," "China grove," "New Forest," &c., but more frequently it is a mere matter of fancy.

Towns in this state have usually originated from the location of a county seat, after the formation of a new county. Here the court-house is placed, and forms the centre of an area which is soon filled with edifices and inhabitants. If the county lies on a river, another town may arise, for a shipping port, but here the accumulation of towns usually ceases. A county seat, and a cotton mart, are all that an agricultural country requires. The towns in this state are thus dispersed two or three to each county, nor so long as this is a planting country, will there be any great increase in their number.

Each town is the centre of a circle which extends many miles around it into the country, and daily attracts all within its influence. The ladies come in their carriages "to shop," the gentlemen, on horseback, to do business with their commission merchants, visit the banks, hear the news, dine together at the hotels, and ride back in the evening. The southern town is properly the "Exchange" for the neighbouring planters, and the "Broadway" for their wives and daughters. And as no plantation is without a private carriage, the number of these gay vehicles, filling the streets of the larger towns on pleasant mornings in the winter, is surprising. I have counted between thirty and forty private carriages in the streets of Natchez in one morning. Showy carriages and saddle horses are the peculiar characteristics of the "moving spectacle" in the streets of south-western towns.

Every village is a nucleus of southern society, to which the least portion is generally contributed by itself. When a public ball is given by the bachelors, in one of these towns—for private parties are scarcely known—the tickets of invitation fly into the retirement of the plantations, within the prescribed circle, often to the distance of thirty miles. Thus families, who reside several leagues apart, meet together, like the inhabitants of one city. This state of things unites, in a social bond, the intelligent inhabitants of a large extent of country, who are nearly equally wealthy, and creates a state of society in the highest degree favourable to hospitality and social feeling. During the season of gayety, in the winter months, the public assemblies and private coteries of Natchez are unsurpassed by those of any other city, in the elegance, refinement, or loveliness of the individuals who compose them.

But fashion and refinement are not confined to Natchez. In nearly every county reside opulent planters, whose children enjoy precisely the same advantages as are afforded in the city. Drawn from the seclusion of their plantations, their daughters are sent to the north; whence they return, in the course of time, with cultivated minds and elegant manners. Hence every village can draw around it a polished circle of its own; for refinement and wealth do not always diminish here, as in New-England, in the inverse ration of distance from a metropolis—and elegant women may often be found blooming in the depths of forest far in the interior.

It is worthy of remark that those communities composed principally of young Mississippians, are distinguished by much less dissipation and adherence to the code of honour than such as are formed of young men principally from the northern and Atlantic southern states. The young Mississippian is not the irascible, hot-headed, and quarrelsome being he has generally been represented, although naturally warm-hearted and full of generous feelings, and governed by a high sense of honour. He is seldom a beau or a buck in the city acceptance of those terms, but dresses plainly—as often in pantaloons of Kentucky jean, a broad brimmed white hat, brogans and a blanket coat, as in any other style of vesture. Nevertheless he knows how to be well-dressed; and the public assemblies of the south-west boast more richly attired young gentlemen than are often found in the assembly-rooms of the Atlantic cities. He is educated to become a farmer—an occupation which requires and originates plainness of manners—and not to shine in the circles of a city.

I made several excursions to plantations two hour's ride from the city of Natchez. In the first mile a huge colonnaded structure, crowning an abrupt eminence near the road, struck my eyes with an imposing effect. It was the abode of one of the wealthiest planters of this state; who, like the majority of those families who now roll in their splendid equipages, has been the maker of his fortune. The grounds about this edifice were neglected; horses were grazing around the piazzas, over which were strewed saddles, whips, horse blankets, and the motley paraphernalia with which planters love to lumber their galleries. On nearly every piazza in Mississippi may be found a wash-stand, bowl, pitcher, towel, and water-bucket, for general accommodation. But the southern gallery is not constructed, like those at the north, for orna-ment or ostentation, but for use. Here they wash, lounge, often sleep, and take their meals.—Here will the stranger or visitor be invited to take a chair, or recline upon a sofa, settee, or form, as the taste and ability of the host may have furnished this important portion of a planter's house.

I once called on a planter within an hour's ride of Natchez, whose income would constitute a fortune for five or six modest Yankees. I entered the front yard—a green level, shaded with the relics of a forest—the live oak, sycamore, and gum trees—through a narrow wicket in a white-washed paling, the most common fence around southern dwellings. In the front yard were several sheep, colts, calves, two or three saddle and a fine pair of carriage-horses, negro children, and every variety of domestic fowl. The planter was sitting upon the gallery, divested of coat, vest, and shoes, with his feet on the railing, playing, in high glee, with a little dark-eyed boy and two young negroes, who were chasing each other under the bridge formed by his extended limbs. Three or four noble dogs, which his voice and the presence of his servant, who accompanied me to the house, kept submissive, were couching like leopards around his chair. A litter of young bull-headed pups lay upon a blanket under a window opening into a bed-room, white with curtains and valances; while a domestic tabby sat upon the window-sill, gazing musingly down upon the rising generation of her hereditary foes, perhaps with reflec-tions not of the most pleasing cast. A hammock, suspended between an iron hook driven into the side of the house and one of the slender columns which supported the sloping roof of the gallery, contained a youth of fourteen, a nephew of the planter, fast locked in the embraces of Morpheus; whose *aid-de-camp,* in the shape of a strapping negress, stood by the hammock, waving over the sleeper a long plume of gorgeous feathers of the pea-fowl—that magnificent bird of the south, which struts about the ground of the planter, gratifying the eye with the glorious emblazonry upon his plumage by day, and torturing the ear with his loud clamours by night. A pair of noble antlers was secured to one of the pillars, from whose branches hung broad-brimmed hats, bridles, a sheep-skin covering to a saddle, which reposed in one corner of the piazza, a riding whip, a blanket coat or capote, spurs, surcingle, and part of a coach harness. A rifle and a shot-gun with an incredibly large bore, were suspended in beckets near the hall entrance; while a couple of shot-pouches, a game-bag, and other sporting apparatus, hung beside them. Slippers, brogans, a pillow, indented as though recently deserted, a gourd, and a broken "cotton slate," filled up the picture, whose original, in some one or other of its features, may be found in nearly every planter's dwelling in this state.

There are many private residences, in the vicinity of Natchez, of an equally expensive character with the one which furnished the above description, whose elegant interiors, contrasting with the neglected grounds about them, suggest the idea of a handsome city residence, accidentally dropped upon a bleak hill, or into the midst of a partially cleared forest, and there remaining, with its noble roof grasped by the arms of an oak, and its windows and columns festooned by the drooping moss, heavily waving in the wind. Thus are situated many of the planters' dwellings, separated from the adjacent forests by a rude, white-washed picket, enclosing around the house an un-ornamented green, or grazing lot, for the saddle and carriage-horses, which can regale their eyes at pleasure, by walking up to the parlour windows and gazing in upon handsome carpets, elegant furniture, costly mantel ornaments, and side-boards loaded with massive plate; and, no doubt, ruminate phi-losophically upon the reflection of their figures at full-length in long, richly-framed mirrors. Very few of the planters' villas, even within a few miles of Natchez, are adorned with surrounding ornamental shrubbery walks, or any other artificial auxiliaries of the natural scenery, except a few shade trees and a narrow, gravelled avenue from the gate to the house. A long avenue of trees, ornamenting and sheltering the approach to a dwelling, is a rare sight in this state, though very frequently seen in Louisiana. Every plantation residence is approached by an avenue, often nearly a mile in length; yet so little attention is paid to this species of ornament and comfort, in a climate where shade is a synonym for luxury, that scarcely one of them is shaded, except where, in their course through a forest, nature has flung the broad arms of majestic trees across the path.

You will judge from this state of things, that the Mississippi planters are not a showy and stylish class, but a plain, practical body of men, who, in general, regard comfort, and conformity to old habits, rather than display and fashionable innovations; and who would gaze with more complacency upon an acre of their domain, whitened, like a newly-washed flock, with cotton, than were it spread out before them magnificent with horticulture, or beautifully velveted with green. They never relax their exertions to add to their incomes; and this ever will be the case with the planter, so long as he can, by his efforts, annually increase his revenue ten or twenty thousand dollars. To the immense profit which every acre and the labour of every slave yield the planter, and to no other cause, is to be referred the anomalous result manifested in neglecting to improve their estates: for an acre, that will yield them sixty dollars per annum, and a slave, whose annual labour will yield from two to five hundred dollars, are, by the laws which regulate the empire of money, to be appropriated to the service of interest, to the entire exclusion of the claims of taste.

A plantation well stocked with hands, is the *ne plus ultra* of every man's ambition who resides at the south. Young men who come to this country, "to make money," soon catch the mania, and nothing less than a broad plantation, waving with the snow white cotton bolls, can fill their mental vision, as they anticipate by a few years in their dreams of the future, the result of their plans and labours. Hence, the great number of planters and the few professional men of long or eminent standing in their several professions. In such a state of things no men grow old or gray in their profession if at all successful. As soon as the young lawyer acquires sufficient to purchase a few hundred acres of the rich alluvial lands, and a few slaves, he quits his profession at once, though perhaps just rising into eminence, and turns cotton planter. The bar at Natchez is composed, with but few exceptions, entirely of young men. Ten years hence, probably not four out of five of these, if living, will remain in their profession. To the prevalence of this custom of retiring so early from the bar, and not to want of talent, is to be attributed its deficiency of distinguished names. There is much talent now concentrated at this bar, and throughout the state. But its possessors are young men; and this mania for planting will soon deprive the state of any benefit from it in a professional point of view. As the lawyers are young, the judges cannot of course be much stricken in years. The northerner, naturally associates with the title of "Judge," a venerable, dignified personage, with locks of snow, a suit of sober black, and powdered queue, shoe-buckles, and black silk stockings. Judge my surprise at hearing at the public table a few days since, a young gentleman, apparently not more than four or five and twenty, addressed as "judge"! I at first thought it applied as a mere *"soubriquet,"* till subsequently assured that he was really on the bench.

Physicians make money much more rapidly than lawyers, and sooner retire from practice and assume the planter. They, however, retain their titles, so that medico-planters are now numerous, far out-numbering the regular practitioners, who have not yet climbed high enough up the wall to leap down into a cotton field on the other side. Ministers, who constitute the third item of the diploma'd triad, are not free from the universal mania, and as writing sermons is not coining money, the plantations are like the vocative in Latin pronouns. The merchant moves onward floundering through invoices, ledgers, packages, and boxes. The gin-wright and overseer, also have an eye upon this Ultima Thule, while the more wealthy mechanics begin to form visions of cotton fields, and talk knowingly upon the "staple." Even editors have an eye that way!

Cotton and negroes are the constant theme—the ever harped upon, never worn out subject of conversation among all classes. But a small portion of the broad rich lands of this thriving state is yet appropriated. Not till every acre is purchased and cultivated—not till Mississippi becomes one vast cotton field, will this mania, which has entered into the very marrow, bone and sinew of a Mississippian's system, pass away. And not then, till the lands become exhausted and wholly unfit for farther cultivation. The rich loam which forms the upland soil of this state is of a very slight depth—and after a few years is worn away by constant culture and the action of the winds and rain. The fields are then "thrown out" as useless. Every plough-furrow becomes the bed of a rivulet after heavy rains—these uniting are increased into torrents, before which the impalpable soil dissolves like ice under a summer's sun. By degrees, acre after acre, of what was a few years previous beautifully undulating ground, waving with the dark green, snow-crested cotton, presents a wild scene of frightful precipices, and yawning chasms, which are increased in depth and destructively enlarged after every rain. There are many thousand acres within twenty miles of the city of Natchez, being the earliest cultivated portions of the country, which are now lying in this condition, presenting appearance of wild desolation, and not unfrequently, of sublimity. This peculiar feature of the country intrudes itself into every rural prospect, painfully marring the loveliest country that ever came from the hand of nature. Natchez itself is nearly isolated by a deep ravine, which forms a natural moat around the town. It has been formed by "washing," and though serpentine and irregular in its depth, it is cut with the accuracy of a canal. It is spanned by bridges along the several roads that issue from the town.

From the loose and friable nature of this soil, which renders it so liable to "wash," as is the expressive technical term here, the southwest portion of this state must within a century become waste, barren, and wild, unless peradventure, some inventing Yankee, or other patentee may devise a way of remedying the evil and making the wilderness to "blossom like the rose." A thick bluish green grass, termed Bermuda grass, is used with great success to check the progress of a *wash* when it has first commenced. It is very tenacious of the soil, takes firm and wide root, grows and spreads rapidly, and soon forms a compact matted surface, which effectually checks any farther increase of the ravines, or "bayous," as these deep chasms are usually termed; though bayou in its original signification is applied to creeks, and deep glens, with or without running water.

When this state was first settled, tobacco was exclusively cultivated as the grand staple. But this plant was found to be a great exhauster of the soil; cotton rapidly superseded its culture, and it was shortly banished from the state, and found a home in Tennessee, where it is at present extensively cultivated. It has not for many years been cultivated here. Planters have no room for any thing but their cotton, and corn, on their plantations, and scarcely are they willing to make room even for the latter, as they buy a great part of their corn, annually, from the Kentucky and Indiana flat boats at the "Landing."[1]

Among northerners, southern planters are reputed wealthy. This idea is not far from correct—as a class they are so; perhaps more so than any other body of men in America. Like our Yankee farmers they are tillers of the soil. "But why" you may ask, "do they who are engaged in the same pursuits as the New-England farmer, so infinitely surpass him in the reward of his labours?" The northern farmer cannot at the most make more than three per cent on his farm. He labours himself, or pays for labour. He *must* do the first or he cannot live. If he does the latter, he can make nothing. If by hard labour and frugal economy, the common independent Yankee farmer, such as the traveller meets with any where in New-England, lays up annually from four to seven hundred dollars, he is a thriving man and "getting rich." His daughters are attractive, and his sons will have something "handsome" to begin the world with.

But the southern farmer can make from fifteen to thirty per cent by his farm. He works on his plantation a certain number of slaves, say thirty, which are to him what the sinewy arms of the Yankee farmer are to himself. Each slave ought to average from seven to eight bales of cotton during the season, especially on the new lands. An acre will generally average from one to two bales. Each bale averages four hundred pounds, at from twelve to

1. Near this spot is a silver mine lately re-discovered, after the lapse of a third of a century. The owner found it difficult, however, to engage the neighbouring planters in his scheme of working it, for what planter would exchange his cotton fields for a silver mine?

fifteen cents a pound. This may not be an exact estimate, but it is not far from the true one. Deducting two thousand and five hundred dollars for the expenses of the plantation, there will remain the net income of eleven thousand dollars. Now suppose this plantation and slaves to have been purchased on a credit, paying at the rate of six hundred dollars apiece for his negroes, the planter would be able to pay for nearly two-thirds of them the first year. The second year, he would pay for the remainder, and purchase ten or twelve more; and the third year, if he had obtained his plantation on a credit of that length of time, he would pay for that also, and commence his fourth year with a valuable plantation, and thirty-five or forty slaves, all his own property, with an increased income for the ensuing year of some thousands of dollars. Henceforward, if prudent, he will rank as an opulent planter.

Success is not however always in proportion to the outlay or expectations of the aspirant for wealth. It is modified and varied by the wear and tear, sickness and death, fluctuations of the market, and many other ills to which all who adventure in the great lottery of life are heirs. In the way above alluded to, numerous plantations in this state have been commenced, and thus the wealth of a great number of the opulent planters of this region has originated. Incomes of twenty thousand dollars are common here. Several individuals possess incomes of from forty to fifty thousand dollars, and live in a style commensurate with their wealth. The amount is generally expressed by the number of their negroes, and the number of "bales" they make at a crop. To know the number of either is to know accurately their incomes. And as this is easily ascertained, it is not difficult to form a prompt estimate of individual wealth. So you perceive that a Yankee farmer and a southern planter are birds of a very different feather.

Men here seem to feel the truth of the maxim of Bacon, that "territory newly acquired and not settled, is a matter of burthen rather than of strength": for they are spreading over it like a cloud, and occupying the vast tracts called "the Purchase," recently obtained from the Indians, previous to their removal to the west. The tide of emigration is rapidly setting to the north and east portions of the state. Planters, who have exhausted their old lands in this vicinity, are settling and removing to these new lands, which will soon become the richest cotton growing part of Mississippi. Parents do not now think of settling their children on plantations near Natchez, but purchase for them in the upper part of the state. Small towns, with "mighty names," plucked from the ruins of some long since mouldered city of classic fame and memory, are springing up here and there, like mushrooms, amidst the affrighted forests. Sixteen new counties have lately been created in this portion of the state, where so recently the Indian tracked his game and shrieked his warwhoop; and as an agricultural state, the strength and sinew of Mississippi must be hereafter concentrated in this fresher and younger portion of her territory.

THE MISSISSIPPI SLAVE TRADE

"Will you ride with me into the country?" said a young planter. "I am about purchasing a few negroes, and a peep into a slave-mart may not be uninteresting to you." I readily embraced the opportunity and in a few minutes our horses were at the door.

Crossing Cotton Square we entered upon the great northern road leading to Jackson. Here a sudden clanking of chains, startled our horses, and the next instant a gang of negroes, in straggling procession, followed by an ordinary looking white man armed with a whip, emerged from one of the streets. Each negro carried slung over his shoulder a polished iron ball, suspended by a heavy ox chain five or six feet in length and secured to the right ancle by a massive ring. They moved along under their burthen—some with idealess faces, looking the mere animal, others with sullen and dogged looks, and others again talking and laughing. This galley-looking procession was what is very appropriately termed the "Chain gang," a fraternity well known in New-Orleans and Natchez, and valued for its services in cleaning and repairing the streets. In the former city however there is one for whites as well as blacks. These gangs are merely moving penitentiaries, appropriating that amount of labour, which at the north is expended within four walls, to the broader limits of the city. In Natchez, negro criminals only are thus honoured—a "coat of tar and feathers" being applied to those white men who may require discipline not provided by the courts.

"The Chain gang," consists of insubordinate negroes and slaves, who, having run away from their masters, have been taken up and confined in jail, to await the reclamation of their owners; during the interval elapsing between their arrest and the time of their liberation by their masters, they are daily led forth from the prison to work on the streets, under the charge of an overseer. The punishment is considered very degrading, and merely the threat of the Calaboose, or the "ball and chain," will often intimidate and render submissive the most incorrigible.

When a runaway is apprehended he is committed to jail, and an advertisement describing his person and wearing apparel, is inserted in the newspaper for six months, if he is not claimed in the interim; at the expiration of which period he may be sold at auction, and the proceeds, after deducting all expenses, go to the use of the county. Should the owner subsequently claim and prove his property, the amount paid into the treasury, on account of the sale, is refunded to him. An owner, making his claim before the six months have expired, and proving his property before a justice of the peace, is allowed to take him away on producing a certificate to that effect from the justice, and paying the expenses incurred in the apprehension and securing of his slave. All runaways, or suspected runaways, may lawfully be apprehended, and carried before a justice of the peace, who at his discretion may either commit them to jail, or send them to the owner, and the person by whom the arrest was made, is entitled to six dollars for each, on delivering him to his master.

A mile from Natchez we came to a cluster of rough wooden buildings, in the angle of two roads, in front of which several saddle-horses, either tied or held by servants, indicated a place of popular resort.

"This is the slave market," said my companion, pointing to a building in the rear; and alighting, we left our horses in charge of a neatly dressed yellow boy belonging to the establishment. Entering through a wide gate into a narrow court-yard, partially enclosed by low buildings, a scene of a novel character was at once presented. A line of negroes, commencing at the entrance with the tallest, who was not more than five feet eight or nine inches in height—for negroes are a low rather than a tall race of men—down to a little fellow about ten years of age, extended in a semicircle around the right side of the yard. There were in all about forty. Each was dressed in the usual uniform of slaves, when in market, consisting of a fashionably shaped, black fur hat, roundabout and trowsers of coarse corduroy velvet, precisely such as are worn by Irish labourers, when they first "come over the water"; good vests, strong shoes, and white cotton shirts, completed their equipment. This dress they lay aside after they are sold, or wear out as soon as may be; for the negro dislikes to retain the indication of his having recently been in the market. With their hats in their hands, which hung down by their sides, they stood perfectly still, and in close order, while some gentlemen were passing from one to another examining for the purpose of buying. With the exception of displaying their teeth when addressed, and rolling their great white eyes about the court—they were so many statues of the most glossy ebony.

As we entered the mart, one of the slave merchants—for a "lot" of slaves is usually accompanied, if not owned, by two or three individuals—approached us, saying "Good morning, gentlemen! Would you like to examine my lot of boys? I have as fine a lot as ever came into market."—We approached them, one of us as a curious spectator, the other as a purchaser; and as my friend passed along the line, with a scrutinizing eye—giving that singular look, peculiar to the buyer of slaves as he glances from head to foot over each individual—the passive subjects of his observations betrayed no other signs of curiosity than that evinced by an occasional glance. The entrance of a stranger into a mart is by no means an unimportant event to the slave, for every stranger may soon become his master and command his future destinies. But negroes are seldom strongly affected by any circumstances, and their reflections never give them much uneasiness. To the generality of them, life is mere animal existence, passed in physical exertion or enjoyment. This is the case with the field hands in particular, and more so with the females than the males, who through a long life seldom see any other white person than their master or overseer, or any other gentleman's dwelling than the "great hus," the "white house" of these little domestic empires in which they are the subjects. To this class a change of masters is a matter of indifference;—they are handed from one to another with the passiveness of a purchased horse. These constitute the lowest rank of slaves, and lowest grade in the scale of the human species. Domestic and city slaves form classes of a superior order, though each constitutes a distinct class by itself. I shall speak of these more fully hereafter.

"For what service in particular did you want to buy?" inquired the trader of my friend, "A coachman." "There is one I think may suit you, sir," said he; "George, step out here." Forthwith a light-coloured negro, with a fine figure and good face, bating an enormous pair of lips, advanced a step from the line, and looked with some degree of intelligence, though with an air of indifference, upon his intended purchaser.

"How old are you, George?" he inquired. "I don't recollect, sir, 'zactly—b'lieve I'm somewere 'bout twenty-dree.'" "Where were you raised?" "On master R——'s farm in Wirginny." "Then you are a Virginia negro." "Yes, master, me full blood Wirginny." "Did you drive your master's carriage?" "Yes, master, I drove ole missus' carage, more dan four year." "Have you a wife?" "Yes, master, I lef' young wife in Richmond, but I got new wife here in de lot. I wishy you buy her, master, if you gwine to buy me."

Then came a series of the usual questions from the intended purchaser. "Let me see your teeth—your tongue—open your hands—roll up your sleeves—have you a good appetite? are you good tempered? "Me get mad some-time," replied George to the last query, "but neber wid my horses." "What do you ask for this boy, sir?" inquired the planter, after putting a few more questions to the unusually loquacious slave. "I have held him at one thousand dollars, but I will take nine hundred and seventy-five cash. The bargain was in a few minutes concluded, and my companion took the negro at nine hundred and fifty, giving negotiable paper—the customary way of paying for slaves—at four months. It is, however, generally understood, that if servants prove unqualified for the particular service for which they are bought, the sale is dissolved. So there is in general perfect safety in purchasing servants untried, and merely on the warrant of the seller.

George, in the meanwhile, stood by, with his hat in his hand, apparently unconcerned in the negotiations going on, and when the trader said to him, "George, the gentleman has bought you; get ready to go with him," he appeared gratified at the tidings, and smiled upon his companions apparently quite pleased, and then bounded off to the buildings for his little bundle. In a few minutes he returned and took leave of several of his companions, who, having been drawn up into line only to be shown to purchasers, were now once more at liberty, and moving about the court, all the visiters having left except my friend and myself. "You mighty lucky, George," said one, congratulating him, "to get sol so quick," "Oh, you neber min', Charly," replied the delighted George; "your turn come soon too."

"You know who you' master be—whar he live?" said another. "No, not zactly; he lib on plantation some whar here 'bout." After taking leave of his companions, George came, hat in hand, very respectfully, to his purchaser, and said, "Young master, you never be sorry for buy George; I make you a good servant. But—beg pardon, master—but—if master would be so good as buy Jane—" "Who is Jane?"—"My wife, since I come from Wirginny. She good wife and a good girl—she good seamstress an' good nurse—mek de nice shirts and ebery ting."

"Where is she, George?" "Here she be, master," said he, pointing to a bright mulatto girl, about eighteen, with a genteel figure and a lively countenance, who was waiting with anxiety the reply of the planter. Opposite to the line of males was also a line of females, extended along the left side of the court. They were about twenty in number, dressed in neat calico frocks, white aprons and capes, and fancy kerchiefs, tied in a mode peculiar to the negress, upon their heads. Their whole appearance was extremely neat and "tidy." They could not be disciplined to the grave silence observed by the males, but were constantly laughing and chattering with each other in suppressed voices, and appeared to take, generally, a livelier interest in the transactions in which all were equally concerned. The planter approached this line of female slaves, and inquired of the girl her capabilities as seamstress, nurse, and ironer. Her price was seven hundred and fifty dollars. He said he would take her to his family; and if the ladies were pleased with her, he would purchase her. The poor girl was as much delighted as though already purchased; and, at the command of the trader, went to prepare herself to leave the mart. Some other negroes were purchased, several of whom appeared merely powerful combinations of bone and muscle, and the only idea suggested to the mind, in gazing upon them, was of remarkable physical energy. In the dull eye and fleshy mouth there was no expression indicative of intellect.

The increased demand for slaves led many farmers in Virginia, whose lands were unavailable, to turn their attention to raising slaves, if I may so term it, for the south-western market. Hence a nursery for slaves has been imperceptibly forming in that state, till now, by a sort of necessity, a vast amount of its capital is involved in this trade, the discontinuance of which would be as injurious in a pecuniary point of view, to those who raise them, as the want of the facilities which the trade affords, would be to the planter. Thus Virginia has become the field for the purchaser, and the phrase—"he is gone to Virginia to buy negroes," or "niggers," as is the elegant and equally common phraseology, is as often applied to a temporarily absent planter, as "he is gone to Boston to buy goods," to a New-England country merchant.

Negroes are transported here both by sea and land. Alexandria and Norfolk are the principal depots of slaves, previous to their being shipped. To these cities they are brought from the surrounding country, and sold to the slave-trader, who purchases them for about one-half or one-third less than he expects to obtain for them in the southern market. After the resident slave-dealer has collected a sufficient number, he places them under the care of an agent. They are then shipped for New-Orleans, with as comfortable accommodations as can be expected, where one or two hundred are congregated in a single merchant vessel. I have seen more than one hundred landing from a brig, on the Levée, in New-Orleans, in fine condition, looking as lively and hearty as though a sea voyage agreed well with them. They are transferred, if destined for the Mississippi market, to a steamboat, and landed at Natchez. The debarkation of a hundred slaves, of both sexes and all ages, is a novel spectacle to a northerner. Landing on the Levée, they proceed, each with his bundle, under the charge of their temporary master or conductor, toward the city, in a long straggling line, or sometimes in double files, in well-ordered procession, gazing about them with curiosity and wonder upon the new scenes opening before them, as they advance into the city, and speculating upon the advantages afforded as their home, by the beautiful country to which they find themselves transplanted. Nothing seems to escape their attention, and every few steps offer subjects for remark or laughter; for the risible muscles of the negro are uncommonly excitable.

On arriving on the "Hill," in view of the city, and obtaining a glimpse of a fine country spread out around them, their delight is very great. Full of the impression, which they early imbibe, that the south is emphatically the grave of their race, and daily having it held up before their imaginations at home, *in terrorem,* to keep them in the line of duty, if insubordinate, they leave home, as they proudly and affectionately term Virginia, with something of the feelings of the soldier, allotted to a "forlorn hope." It cannot be denied that many have died shortly after being brought into this country; but this was owing to indiscretion, in transporting them at the wrong season of the year—in the spring, after a winter spent at the north; or in autumn, during the prevalence, in former years, of the epidemics, which once were almost annual visitants of this country. Experience has taught those who introduce slaves, in late years, to bring them quite late in autumn. Hence, the two great causes of mortality being removed, the effects have, in a great measure, ceased; and slaves, when they arrive here, and gaze with surprise upon the athletic figures and gray heads of their fellows, who meet them at every step, as they advance into the city—find that they can live even in the south, and grow old on other plantations than those in "Ol' Wirginny." "I see no dead nigger yet, Jef."—"No—nor no coffin pile up neider in de street,"—said another of a gang of negroes passing through the streets, peering on all sides for these ominous signs of this "fatal" climate, as they trudged along to their quarters in the slave-market.

Passing through the city in procession, sometimes dressed in a new uniform, purchased for them in New-Orleans, but often in the brown rags in which they left Virginia, preceded by a large wagon, carrying the surplus baggage; they are marched beyond the city limits, within which, till recently, they were publicly sold, the marts being on nearly every street. Arriving at their quarters, which are usually old unoccupied buildings, and often tents or booths, pitched upon the common, beside some stream of water, and under the shade of trees, they resort, in the first place, to a general ablution, preparatory to being exposed for sale. The toilet arrangements of one hundred negroes, just from a long voyage, are a formidable affair. Both the rivers, Alpheus and Peneus, would hardly suffice for the process. Two or three days are consumed in it; after which, all appear in new, comfortable, uniform dresses, with shining faces, and refreshed after the fatigue of travel. They are now ready for inspection and sale. To this important period, the day of sale, they cheerfully look forward, manifesting not a little emulation to be "sol' fust." The interim between their arrival and sale—for they are not sold at auction, or all at once, but singly, or in parties, as purchasers may be inclined to buy—is passed in an *otium cum dignitate* of a peculiarly African character, involving eating, drinking, playing, and sleeping. The interval of ease enjoyed in the slave-market is an oasis of luxury in their existence, which they seldom know how to appreciate, if we may judge from the wishful manner in which they gaze upon gentlemen who enter the mart, as though anxious to put a period to this kind of enjoyment, so congenial to their feelings and temperament.

Probably two-thirds of the first slaves came into this state from Virginia; and nearly all now introduced, of whom there are several thousands annually, are brought from that state. Kentucky contributes a small number, which is yearly increasing; and since the late passage of the slave law in Missouri, a new market is there opened for this trade. It is computed that more than two hundred thousand dollars' worth of slaves will be purchased in Missouri this season, for the Natchez market. A single individual has recently left Natchez with one hundred thousand dollars, for the purpose of buying up negroes in that state to sell in Mississippi.

The usual way of transporting slaves is by land, although they are frequently brought round by sea; but the last is the most expensive method, and therefore, to "bring them through," is accounted preferable. This is done by forming them into a caravan at the place where they are purchased, and conducting them by land through the Indian nations to this state. The route is for the most part through a continuous forest, and is usually performed by the negroes, on foot, in seven or eight weeks. Their personal appearance, when they arrive at Natchez, is by no means improved, although they are usually stouter and in better condition than when they leave home, for they are generally well fed, and their health is otherwise carefully attended to, while on the route. Arrived within two or three miles of Natchez, they encamp in some romantic spot near a rivulet, and like their brethren transported by sea, commence polishing their skins, and arraying themselves in the coarse but neat uniform, which their master has purchased for them in Natchez.

A few Sabbaths ago, while standing before a village church in the country, my attention was drawn to a long procession at the extremity of the street, slowly approaching like a troop of wearied pilgrims. There were several gentlemen in company, some of them planters, who gazed upon the singular spectacle with unusual interest. One sooty brown hue was cast over the whole horde, by the sombre colour of their tattered garments, which, combined with the slow pace and fatigued air of most of those who composed it, gave to the whole train a sad and funereal appearance.

First came half a dozen boys and girls, with fragments of blankets and ragged pantaloons and frocks, hanging upon, but not covering their glossy limbs. They passed along in high spirits, glad to be once more in a village, after their weary way through the wilderness; capering and practising jokes upon each other, while their even rows of teeth, and the whites of their eyes— the most expressive features in the African physiognomy—were displayed in striking contrast to their ebony skins.

These were followed by a tall mulatto, with high cheek-bones, and lean and hungry looks, making rapid inroads into a huge loaf of bread, whose twin brother was secured under his left arm. A woman, very black, very short, and very pursy, who breathed like a porpoise, and whose capacity for rapid movement was equal to that of a puncheon, trudged along behind, evidently endeavouring to come up with the mulatto, as her eye was fixed very resolutely on the spare loaf; but its owner strode forward deliberately and with perfect impunity. She was followed by another female, bearing an infant in her arms, probably born in the wilderness. Close behind her came a covered wagon, from which she had just descended to walk, drawn by two fine horses, and loaded with young negroes, who were permitted to ride and walk alternately on the journey. Behind the wagon, at a long distance, came an old patriarch, at least eighty years of age, bent nearly double with the weight of years and infirmity. By his side moved an old negress, nearly coeval with him, who supported her decrepit form by a staff. They were the venerable progenitors of the children and grandchildren who preceded them. This aged couple, who were at liberty to ride when they chose, in a covered wagon behind them, were followed by a mixed crowd of negroes of all ages, and of both sexes, with and without staff, hatless and barefooted. The office of the negro's hat is a mere sinecure—they love the warm sun upon their heads—but they like to be well shod, and that with boots, for the lower region of their limbs about the ancles is very sensitive.

Behind these came a wretched cart, covered with torn, red-painted canvass, and drawn by a mule and a horse;—Sancho Panza's mule and Rosinante—I mean no insult to the worthy knight or his squire—if coupled together, would have made precisely such a pair. This vehicle contained several invalids, two of whom were reclining on a matrass laid along the bottom. Around it were many young slaves of both sexes, talking and marching along in gleeful mood. Two or three old people followed, one of whom, who walked with both hands grasping a long staff, stopped as he passed us, and with an air of affecting humility, and with his venerable forehead bowed to the earth, addressed us, "hab massas got piece 'bacca' for ol' nigger?" An old gentleman standing by, whose locks were whitened with the snows of sixty winters, having first obtained leave to do so from the owner of the drove, mounted on a fine blooded horse, rode carelessly along behind them, gave the old slave all he had about him, which, fortunately for the petitioner, happened to be a large quantity, and for which he appeared extremely grateful. Several other negroes, walking along with vigorous steps, and another white conductor, with a couple of delicately limbed race-horses, enveloped in broidered mantles, and ridden by bright-eyed little mulatto boys, and two or three leashes of hounds, led by a slave, completed the train. They had been seven weeks on the road, travelling by easy stages, and encamping at night. Old people are seldom seen in these "droves." The young and athletic usually compose them. But as in this instance, the old people are sometimes allowed to come with the younger portion of their families, as a favour; and if sold at all, they are sold with their children, who can take care of them in their old age, which they well do—for negroes have a peculiarly strong affection for the old people of their own colour.

Probably of the two ways of bringing slaves here, that by land is preferable; not only because attended with less expense, but by gradually advancing them into the climate, it in a measure precludes the effect which a sudden transition from one state to the other might produce. All slaves, however, are not brought here by negro traders. Many of the planters prefer going on and purchasing for themselves, for which purpose it is not unusual for them to take on from twenty to forty and fifty thousand dollars, lay out the whole in slaves, and either accompany through the wilderness themselves on horse-back, or engage a conductor. By adopting this method they purchase them at a much greater advantage, than at second-hand from the professional trader, as slaves can be bought for fifty per cent less there, than after they are once brought into this market. The number of slaves introduced into the south-western market is annually increasing. Last year more than four thousand were brought into the state. The prices of slaves vary with the prices of cotton and sugar. At this time, when cotton brings a good price, a good "field hand" cannot be bought for less than eight hundred dollars, if a male; if a female, for six hundred. "Body servants" sell much higher, one thousand dollars being a common price for them. Children are valued in proportion to their ages. An infant adds one hundred dollars to the price of the mother; and from infancy the children of the slaves increase in value about one hundred dollars for every three years. All domestic servants, or "house servants," which class includes coachmen, nurses, hostlers, gardeners, footmen, cooks, waiting-maids, &c.,—all indispensable to the *menage* of a wealthy planter—are always in great demand, and often sell for eighteen hundred and two thousand dollars apiece, of either sex. But these are exceptions, where the slave possesses some peculiarly valuable trait as a domestic.

Negro traders soon accumulate great wealth, from the immense profit they make on their merchandise. Certainly if any earn their gold, it is the slave-dealer. One of their number, who, for the last fifteen years, has supplied this country with two-thirds of the slaves brought into it, has amassed a fortune of more than a million dollars by this traffic alone. He is a bachelor, and a man of gentlemanly address, as are many of these merchants, and not the ferocious fellows, we Yankees have been apt to imagine them. Their admission into society, however, is not recognized. Planters associate with them freely enough, in the way of business, but notice them no further.

A CLASS SYSTEM AMONG THE NEGROES

There are properly three distinct classes of slaves in the south. The first, and most intelligent class, is composed of the domestic slaves, or "servants," as they are properly termed, of the planters. Some of these both read and write, and possess a great degree of intelligence: and as the negro, of all varieties of the human species, is the most imitative, they soon learn the language, and readily adopt the manners, of the family to which they are attached.

In the more fashionable families, negroes feel it their duty—to show their aristocratic breeding—to ape manners, and to use language, to which the common herd cannot aspire. An aristocratic negro, full of his master's wealth and importance, which he feels to be reflected upon himself, is the most aristocratic personage in existence. He supports his own dignity, and that of his master, or *"family,"* as he phrases it, which he deems inseparable, by a course of conduct befitting coloured gentlemen. Always about the persons of their masters or mistresses, the domestic slaves obtain a better knowledge of the modes of civilized life than they could do in the field, where negroes can rise but little above their original African state. It is from this class that the friends of wisely-regulated emancipation are to seek material for carrying their plans into effect.

The second class is composed of town slaves; which not only includes domestic slaves, but also all negro mechanics, draymen, hostlers, labourers, hucksters, and washwomen, and the heterogeneous multitude of every other occupation—for slaves are trained to every kind of labour. The blacksmith, cabinet-maker, carpenter, wheelwright—all have one or more slaves labouring at their trades. The negro is a third arm to every working man, who can possibly save enough money to purchase one. Even free negroes cannot do without them: some of them own several, to whom they are the severest masters.

"To whom do you belong?" I once inquired of a negro whom I had employed. "There's my master," he replied; pointing to a steady old negro, who had purchased himself, then his wife, and subsequently his three children, by his own manual exertions and persevering industry. He was now the owner of a comfortable house, a piece of land, and two or three slaves, to whom he could add one every three years. It is worthy of remark, and serves to illustrate one of the many singularities characteristic of the race, that the free negro, who "buys his wife's freedom," as they term it, from her master, by paying him her full value, ever afterward considers her in the light of property.

"Thomas, you are a free man," I remarked to one who had purchased himself and wife from his master, by the profits of a poultry yard and vegetable garden, industriously attended to for many years, in his leisure hours and on Sunday. "You are a free man; I suppose you will soon have negroes of your own."

"Hi! Hab one now, master." "Who, Tom?"—"Ol' Sarah, master." "Old Sarah! she is your wife." "She my nigger too; I pay master five hun'red dollar for her."

Many of the negroes who swarm in the cities are what are called "hired servants." They belong to planters, or others, who, finding them qualified for some occupation in which they cannot afford to employ them, hire them to citizens, as mechanics, cooks, waiters, nurses, &c., and receive the monthly wages for their services. Some steady slaves are permitted to "hire their own time;" that is, to go into town and earn what they can, as porters, labourers, gardeners, or in other ways, and pay a stipulated sum weekly to their owners, which will be regulated according to the supposed value of the slave's labour. Masters, however, who are sufficiently indulgent to allow them to "hire their time," are seldom rigorous in rating their labour very high. But whether the slave earn less or more than the specified sum, he must always pay that, and neither more nor less than that to his master at the close of each week, as the condition of this privilege. Few fail in making up the sum; and generally they earn more, if industrious, which is expended in little luxuries, or laid by in an old rag among the rafters of their houses, till a sufficient sum is thus accumulated to purchase their freedom. This they are seldom refused, and if a small amount is wanting to reach their value, the master makes it up out of his own purse, or rather, takes no notice of the deficiency. I have never known a planter to refuse to aid, by peculiar indulgences, any of his steady and well-disposed slaves, who desired to purchase their freedom. On the contrary, they often endeavor to excite emulation in them to the attainment of this end. This custom of allowing slaves to "hire their time," ensuring the master a certain sum weekly, and the slave a small surplus, is mutually advantageous to both.

The majority of town servants are those who are hired to families by planters, or by those living in town who own more than they have employment for, or who can make more by hiring them out than by keeping them at home. Some families, who possess not an acre of land, but own many slaves, hire them out to different individuals; the wages constituting their only income, which is often very large. There are indeed few families, however wealthy, whose incomes are not increased by the wages of hired slaves, and there are many poor people, who own one or two slaves, whose hire enables them to live comfortably. From three to five dollars a week is the hire of a female, and seventy-five cents or a dollar a day for a male. Thus, contrary to the opinion at the north, families may have good servants, and yet not own one, if they are unable to buy, or are conscientious upon that ground, though there is not a shade of difference between hiring a slave, where prejudices are concerned, and owning one. Those who think otherwise, and thus compound with conscience, are only making a distinction without a difference. Northern people, when they come to this country, who dislike either to hire or purchase, often bring free coloured, or white servants (helps) with them. The first soon marry with the free blacks, or become too lofty in their conceptions of things, in contrasting the situation of their fellows around them, with their own, to be retained. The latter, if they are young and pretty, or even old and ugly, assume the fine lady at once, disdaining to be servants among slaves, and Hymen, in the person of some spruce overseer, soon fulfils their expectations. I have seen but one white servant, or domestic, of either sex, in this country, and this was the body servant of an Englishman who remained a few days in Natchez, during which time, John sturdily refused to perform a single duty of his station.

The expense of a domestic establishment at the south, would appear very great in the estimation of a New-Englander. A gardener, coachman, nurse, cook, seamstress, and a house-maid, are indispensable. Some of the more fashionable families add footmen, chamber-maids, hostler, an additional nurse, if there be many children, and another seamstress. To each of these officials is generally attached a young neophyte, while one constantly stumbles over useless little negroes scattered all about the house and court-yard. Necessary as custom has made so great a number of servants, there seems to be much less domestic labour performed in a family of five, such perfect "eye-servants" are they, than in a northern family, with only one "maid of all work." There are some Yankee "kitchen girls"—I beg their ladyships' pardon for so styling them—who can do more house-work, and do it better, than three or four negro servants, unless the eye of their mistress is upon them. As nearly all manual labour is performed by slaves, there must be one to each department, and hence originates a state of domestic manners and individual character, which affords an interesting field of contemplation to the severer northerner. The city slaves are distinguished as a class, by superior intelligence, acuteness, and deeper moral degradation. A great proportion of them are hired, and, free from restraint in a great degree, compared with their situations under their own masters, or in the country, they soon become corrupted by the vices of the city, and in associating indiscriminately with each other, and the refuse of the white population. Soon the vices of the city, divested of their refinement, become their own unmasked. Although they may once have ranked under the first class, and possessed the characteristics which designate the decent, well-behaved domestic of the planter, they soon lose their identity. There are of course exceptions to these characteristics, as also in the other classes. Some of these exceptions have come within my knowledge, of a highly meritorious character.

The third and lowest class consists of those slaves, who are termed "field hands." Many of them rank but little higher than the brutes that perish, in the scale of intellect, and they are in general, as a class, the last and lowest link in the chain of the human species. Secluded in the solitude of an extensive plantation, which is their world, beyond whose horizon they know nothing—their walks limited by the "quarters" and the field—their knowledge and information derived from the rude gossip of their fellows, straggling runaways, or house servants, and without seeing a white person except their master or overseer, as they ride over the estate, with whom they seldom hold any conversation—they present the singular feature of African savages, disciplined to subordination, and placed in the heart of a civilized community. Mere change of place will not change the savage. Moral and intellectual culture alone, will elevate him to an equality with his civilized brethren. The African transplanted from the arid soil of Ebo, Sene-Gambia, or Guinea, to the green fields of American, without mental culture, will remain still the wild African, though he may wield his ox-whip, whistle after his plough, and lift his hat, when addressed, like his more civilized fellows. His children, born on the plantation to which he is attached, and suffered to grow up as ignorant as himself, will not be one degree higher in the scale of civilization. The next generation, though they may have thrown away the idols of their country, and been taught some vague notions of God, are in almost every sense of the word Africans. This has been, till within a few years, the general condition of "field hands" in this country, though there have been exceptions on some plantations highly honourable to their proprietors.

THE MISSISSIPPI POOR WHITE

Cotton is often conveyed to Vicksburg from a distance of one hundred miles in the interior. The teamsters camp every night, in an enclosure formed by their waggons and cattle, with a bright fire burning. Many are small farmers who form a peculiar class, and include the majority of the inhabitants in the east part of this state. With the awkwardness of the Yankee countryman, they are destitute of his morals, education, and reverence for religion. With the rude and bold qualities of the chivalrous Kentuckian, they are destitute of his intelligence, and the humour which tempers and renders amusing his very vices. They are in general uneducated, and their apparel consists of a coarse linsey-woolsey, of a dingy yellow or blue, with broad-brimmed hats; though they usually follow their teams barefooted and bare-headed, with their long locks hanging over their eyes and shoulders, giving them a wild appearance. Accost them as they pass you, one after another, in long lines, cracking their whips, which they use instead of the goad—perhaps the turn-out of a whole district, from the old, gray-headed hunter, to the youngest boy that can wield the whip, often fifteen and twenty feet in length, including the staff—and their replies will generally be sullen or insulting. There is in them a total absence of that courtesy which the country people of New-England manifest for strangers. They will seldom allow carriages to pass them, unless attended by gentlemen, who often have to do battle for the high-way. Ladies, in carriages or on horseback, if unattended by gentlemen, are most usually insulted by them. They have a decided aversion to a broad-cloth coat, and this antipathy is transferred to the wearer. There is a species of warfare kept up between them and the citizens of the shipping ports, mutually evinced by the jokes and tricks played upon them by the latter when they come into market; and their retaliation, when their hour of advantage comes, by an encounter in the back woods, which they claim as their domain.

At home they live in log-houses on partially cleared lands, labor hard in their fields, sometimes owning a few slaves, but more generally but with one or none.—They are good hunters, and expert with the rifle, which is an important article of furniture in their houses. Whiskey is their favourite beverage, which they present to the stranger with one hand, while they give him a chair with the other.

They are uneducated, and destitute of the regular administration of the gospel. As there is no common school system of education adopted in this state, their children grow up as rude and ignorant as themselves; some of whom, I have caught in the cotton market at Natchez, and questioned upon the simple principles of religion and education which every child is supposed to know, and have found them wholly uninformed. This class of men is valuable to the state, and legislative policy, at least, should recommend such measures as would secure religious instruction to the adults, and the advantages of a common education to the children, who, in thirty years, will form a large proportion of the native inhabitants of Mississippi.

21

Sensible Reflections on Southern Society, 1852–58

*F*rederick Law Olmstead possesses fame today for two diverse reasons: as the most dispassionate commentator on the South before the Civil War and as the great landscape architect of the park systems of the United States. He was born in Hartford, Connecticut, in 1822. For nearly thirty years his life seems to have been without fixed purpose while he "found himself." He was a desultory student at Yale, a sailor, a businessman, and a farmer. In 1850 he commenced his travels which, within a decade, were to make him famous. Beginning with England, he wrote Walks and Talks of an American Farmer in England *(1852) and was thereupon commissioned by the* New York Times *to travel throughout the South to report for northern readers what the Cotton Kingdom was really like. Three books were the result:* A Journey in the Seaboard States *(1856),* A Journey through Texas *(1857), and* A Journey in the Back Country *(1860).*

These three works—from which come the following extracts—comprise a thorough, unbiased description of southern life, especially in its social and economic phases, with chief attention centered upon the plantation, the Negro, and the institution of slavery. From every point of view it is a remarkable survey. The 1850's were a period of passionate controversy between North and South. Vilification was rampant on both sides of the Mason and Dixon Line. The air was filled with recriminations, denunciation, partisan politics, and economic self-interest. It was, indeed, a decade in which it would *appear that no participant could be found who would judge of the issues raging between North and South with either calmness or objectivity. Yet such an observer was Olmstead. He seldom entered into the troubled waters of the moral issue of slavery, but he did, with serenity and reason, observe what life was actually like, to white and black, in a slave society and what were the effects of that institution upon economic and social progress. His conclusions are plain. He found slavery wasteful and expensive. But he clearly saw facts, indulged in no romantic nonsense about the Negro, and opposed immediate emancipation as impractical and as likely to create more harm than good. It is a great pity that North and South alike did not derive more knowledge from the pages of Olmstead and less from the sentimental* Uncle Tom's Cabin *or the vitriolic* Impending Crisis of the South. *But if by 1860 rampant emotionalism had destroyed all rationality, it is pleasing to recognize that some few minds still kept their heads, as the classic pages of Olmstead's travels reveal.*

After the Civil War, Olmstead turned to the other of his interests. It was he who designed Central Park for New York, Prospect Park for Brooklyn, the great park systems of Boston, Buffalo, and Chicago, and launched the state and national public reservations with the Yosemite in California. He died at an advanced age in 1903.

SLAVERY IN VIRGINIA

The Negroes of Richmond

The greater part of the colored people, on Sunday, seemed to be dressed in the cast-off fine clothes of the white people, received I suppose, as presents, or purchased of the Jews, whose shops show that there must be considerable importation of such articles, probably from the North. Many, who had probably come in from the farms near the town, wore clothing of coarse gray "negro-cloth," that appeared as if made by contract, without regard to the size of the particular individual to whom it had been allotted, like penitentiary uniforms. A few had a better suit of coarse blue cloth, expressly made for them evidently, for "Sunday clothes."

Some were dressed with laughably foppish extravagance, and a great many in clothing of the most expensive materials, and in the latest style of fashion. In what I suppose to be the fashionable streets, there were many more well-dressed and highly-dressed colored people than white, and among this dark gentry the finest French cloths, embroidered waist-coats, patent-leather shoes, resplendent brooches, silk hats, kid gloves, and *eau de mille fleurs,* were quite as common as among the New York "dry-goods clerks," in their Sunday promenades, in Broadway. Nor was the fairer, or rather the softer sex, at all left in the shade of this splendor. Many of the colored ladies were dressed not only expensively, but with good taste and effect, after the latest Parisian mode. Many of them were quite attractive in appearance, and some would have produced a decided sensation in any European drawing-room. Their walk and carriage was often more stylish and graceful than that of the white ladies who were out. About one quarter seemed to me to have lost all distinguishingly African peculiarity of feature, and to have acquired, in place of it, a good deal of that voluptuousness of expression which characterizes many of the women of the south of Europe. I was especially surprised to notice the frequency of thin, aquiline noses.

There was no indication of their belonging to a subject race, but that they invariably gave the way to the white people they met. Once, when two of them, engaged in conversation and looking at each other, had not noticed his approach, I saw a Virginia gentleman lift his cane and push a woman aside with it. In the evening I saw three rowdies, arm-in-arm, taking the whole of the sidewalk, hustle a black man off it, giving him a blow, as they passed, that sent him staggering into the middle of the street. As he recovered himself he began to call out to and threaten them. Perhaps he saw me stop, and thought I should support him, as I was certainly inclined to: "can't you find anything else to do than to be knocking quiet people round! You jus' come back here, will you? Here, you! *don't care if you is white*. You jus' come back here and I'll teach you how to behave—knock' people round!—don't care if I does hab to go to der watch-house." They passed on without noticing him further, only laughing jeeringly—and he continued: "You come back here and I'll make you laugh; you is just' three white nigger cowards, dat's what *you* be."

I observe, in the newspapers, complaints of growing insolence and insubordination among the negroes, arising, it is thought, from too many privileges being permitted them by their masters, and from too merciful administration of the police laws with regard to them. Except in this instance, however, I have seen not the slightest evidence of any independent manliness on the part of the negroes towards the whites. As far as I have yet observed, they are treated very kindly and even generously as servants, but their manner to white people is invariably either sullen, jocose, or fawning.

A VIRGINIA TOBACCO PLANTATION

Half an hour beyond the main road, I arrived at the negro-quarters—a little hamlet of ten or twelve small and dilapidated cabins. Just beyond them was a plain farm-gate, at which several negroes were standing; one of them, a well-made man, with an intelligent countenance and prompt manner, directed me how to find my way to his owner's house. It was still nearly a mile distant; and yet, until I arrived in its immediate vicinity, I saw no cultivated field, and but one clearing. In the edge of this clearing, a number of negroes, male and female, lay stretched out upon the ground near a small smoking charcoal pit. Their master afterwards informed me that they were burning charcoal for the plantation blacksmith, using the time allowed them for holidays—from Christmas to New Year's—to earn a little money for themselves in this way. He paid them by the bushel for it. When I said that I supposed he allowed them to take what wood they chose for this purpose, he replied that he had five hundred acres covered with wood, which he would be very glad to have any one burn, or clear off in any way. Cannot some Yankee contrive a method of concentrating some of the valuable properties of this old-field pine, so that they may be profitably brought into use in more cultivated regions? Charcoal is now brought to New York from Virginia; but when made from pine it is not very valuable, and will only bear transportation from the banks of the navigable rivers, whence it can be shipped, at one movement, to New York. Turpentine does not flow in sufficient quantity from this variety of the pine to be profitably collected, and for lumber it is of very small value.

Mr. W.'s house was an old family mansion, which he had himself remodelled in the Grecian style, and furnished with a large wooden portico. An oak forest had originally occupied the ground where it stood; but this having been cleared and the soil worn out in cultivation by the previous proprietors, pine woods now surrounded it in every direction, a square of a few acres only being kept clear immediately about it. A number of the old oaks still stood in the rear of the house, and, until Mr. W. commenced his improvements, there had been some in its front. These, however, he had cut away, as interfering with the symmetry of his grounds, and in place of them had planted ailanthus trees in parallel rows.

On three sides of the outer part of the cleared square there was a row of large and comfortable-looking negro-quarters, stables, tobacco-houses, and other offices, built of logs.

Mr. W. was one of the few large planters, of his vicinity, who still made the culture of tobacco their principal business. He said there was a general prejudice against tobacco, in all the tide-water region of the State, because it was through the culture of tobacco that the once fertile soils had been impoverished; but he did not believe that, at the present value of negroes, their labor could be applied to the culture of grain, with any profit, except under peculiarly favorable circumstances. Possibly, the use of guano might make wheat a paying crop, but he still doubted. He had not used it, himself. Tobacco required fresh land, and was rapidly exhausting, but it returned more money, for the labor used upon it, than anything else; enough more, in his opinion, to pay for the wearing out of the land. If he was well-paid for it, he did not know why he should not wear out his land.

His tobacco-fields were nearly all in a distant and lower part of his plantation; land which had been neglected before his time, in a great measure, because it had been sometimes flooded, and was, much of the year, too wet for cultivation. He was draining and clearing it, and it now brought good crops.

He had had an Irish gang draining for him, by contract. He thought a negro could do twice as much work, in a day, as an Irishman. He had not stood over them and seen them at work, but judged entirely from the amount they accomplished: he thought a good gang of negroes would have got on twice as fast. He was sure they must have "trifled" a great deal, or they would have accomplished more than they had. He complained much, also, of their sprees and quarrels. I asked why he should employ Irishmen, in preference to doing the work with his own hands. "It's dangerous work (unhealthy?), and a negro's life is too valuable to risked at it. If a negro dies, it's a considerable loss, you know."

He afterwards said that his negroes never worked so hard as to tire themselves—always were lively, and ready to go off on a frolic at night. He did not think they ever did half a fair day's work. They could not be made to work hard: they never would lay out their strength freely, and it was impossible to make them do it.

This is just what I have thought when I have seen slaves at work—they seem to go through the motions of labor without putting strength into them. They keep their powers in reserve for their own use at night, perhaps.

Mr. W. also said that he cultivated only the coarser and lower-priced sorts of tobacco, because the finer sorts required more painstaking and discretion than it was possible to make a large gang of negroes use. "You can make a nigger work," he said, *"but you cannot make him think."*

Although Mr. W. was very wealthy (or, at least, would be considered so anywhere at the North), and was a gentleman of education, his style of living was very farmer-like, and thoroughly Southern. On their plantations, generally, the Virginia gentlemen seem to drop their full-dress and constrained town-habits, and to live a free, rustic, shooting-jacket life. We dined in a room that extended out, rearwardly, from the house, and which, in a Northern establishment, would have been the kitchen. The cooking was done in a detached log-cabin, and the dishes brought some distance, through the open air, by the servants. The outer door was left constantly open, though there was a fire in an enormous old fire-place, large enough, if it could have been distributed sufficiently, to have lasted a New York seamstress the best part of the winter. By the door, there was indiscriminate admittance to negro-children and fox-hounds, and, on an average, there were four of these, grinning or licking their chops, on either side of my chair, all the time I was at the table. A stout woman acted as head waitress, employing two handsome little mulatto boys as her aids in communicating with the kitchen, from which relays of hot corn-bread, of an excellence quite new to me, were brought at frequent intervals. There was no other bread, and but one vegetable served—sweet potato, roasted in ashes, and this, I thought, was the best sweet potato, also, that I ever had eaten; but there were four preparations of swine's flesh, besides fried fowls, fried eggs, cold roast turkey, and opossum, cooked, I know not how, but it somewhat resembled baked sucking-pig. The only beverages on the table were milk and whisky.

I was pressed to stay several days with Mr. W., and should have been glad to have accepted such hospitality, had not another engagement prevented.

A JAMES RIVER FARM

This morning I visited a farm, some account of which will give a good idea of the more advanced mode of agriculture in Eastern Virginia. It is situated on the bank of James River, and has ready access, by water or land-carriage, to the town of Richmond.

The labor of this farm was entirely performed by slaves. I did not inquire their number, but I judged there were from twenty to forty. Their "quarters" lined the approach-road to the mansion, and were well-made and comfortable log cabins, about thirty feet long by twenty wide, and eight feet wall, with a high loft and shingle roof. Each, divided in the middle, and having a brick chimney outside the wall at each end, was intended to be occupied by two families. There were square windows, closed by wooden ports, having a single pane of glass in the center. The house-servants were neatly dressed, but the field-hands wore very coarse and ragged garments.

During three hours, or more, in which I was in company with the proprietor, I do not think there were ten consecutive minutes uninterrupted by some of the slaves requiring his personal direction or assistance. He was even obliged, three times, to leave the dinner-table.

"You see," said he, smiling, as he came in the last time, "a farmer's life, in this country, is no sinecure." This turning the conversation to Slavery, he observed, in answer to a remark of mine, "I only wish your philanthropists would contrive some satisfactory plan to relieve us of it; the trouble and the responsibility of properly taking care of our negroes, you may judge, from what you see yourself here, is anything but enviable. But what can we do that is better? Our free negroes—and, I believe it is the same at the North as it is here—are a miserable set of vagabonds, drunken, vicious, worse off, it is my honest opinion, than those who are retained in slavery. I am satisfied, too, that our slaves are better off, as they are, than the majority of your free laboring classes at the North."

I expressed my doubts.

"Well, they certainly are better off than the English agricultural laborers or, I believe, those of any other Christian country. Free labor might be more profitable to us: I am inclined to think it would be. The slaves are excessively careless and wasteful, and, in various ways—which, without you lived among them, you could hardly be made to understand—subject us to very annoying losses.

"To make anything by farming, here, a man has got to live a hard life. You see how constantly I am called upon—and, often, it is about as bad at night as by day. Last night I did not sleep a wink till near morning; I am quite worn out with it, and my wife's health is failing. But I cannot rid myself of it."

I asked why he did not employ an overseer.

"Because I do not think it right to trust to such men as we have to use, if we use any, for overseers."

"Is the general character of overseers bad?"

"They are the curse of this country, sir; the worst men in the community. But lately, I had another sort of fellow offer—a fellow like a dancing-master, with kid gloves, and wrist-bands turned up over his coat-sleeves, and all so nice, that I was almost ashamed to talk to him in my old coat and slouched hat. Half a bushel of recommendations he had with him, too. Well, he was not the man for me—not half the gentleman, with all his airs, that Ned here is"—(a black servant, who was bursting with suppressed laughter, behind his chair).

"Oh, they are interesting creatures, sir," he continued, "and, with all their faults, have many beautiful traits. I can't help being attached to them, and I am sure they love us." In his own case, at least, I did not doubt it; his manner towards them was paternal—familiar and kind; and they came to him like children who have been given some task, and constantly are wanting to be encouraged and guided, simply and confidently. At dinner, he frequently addressed the servant familiarly, and drew him into our conversation as if he were a family friend, better informed, on some local and domestic points, than himself.

He informed me that able-bodied field-hands were hired out, in this vicinity, at the rate of one hundred dollars a year, and their board and clothing. Four able-bodied men, that I have employed the last year, on my farm in New York, I pay, on an average, one hundred and five dollars each, and board them; they clothe themselves at an expense, I think, of twenty dollars a year;—probably, slaves' clothing costs twice that. They constitute all the force of my farm, hired by the year (except a boy, who goes to school in Winter), and, in my absence, have no overseer except one of themselves, whom I appoint. I pay the fair wages of the market, more than any of my neighbors, I believe, and these are no lower than the average of what I have paid for the last five years. It is difficult to measure the labor performed in a day by one, with that of the other, on account of undefined differences in the soil, and in the bulk and weight of articles operated upon. But, here, I am shown tools that no man in his senses, with us, would allow a laborer, to whom he was paying wages, to be encumbered with; and the excessive weight and clumsiness of which, I would judge, would make work at least ten per cent. greater than those ordinarily used with us. And I am assured that, in the careless and clumsy way they must be used by the slaves, anything lighter or less rude could not be furnished them with good economy, and that such tools as we constantly give our laborers, and find our profit in giving them, would not last out a day in a Virginia corn-field—much lighter and more free from stones though it be than ours.

So, too, when I ask why mules are so universally substituted for horses on the farm, the first reason given, and confessedly the most conclusive one, is, that horses cannot bear the treatment that they always *must* get from negroes; horses are always soon foundered or crippled by them, while mules will bear cudgeling, and lose a meal or two now and then, and not be materially injured, and they do not take cold or get sick if neglected or overworked. But I do not need to go further than to the window of the room in which I am writing, to see, at almost any time, treatment of cattle that would insure the immediate discharge of the driver, by almost any farmer owning them at the North.

A SOUTH CAROLINA RICE PLANTATION

I left Charleston yesterday morning, on horseback, with a letter in my pocket to Mr. X., a rice planter, under whose roof I am now writing. Nowhere in the world could a man live more pleasantly than where I am. I was awakened this morning by a servant making a fire for me to dress by. Opening the window, I found a clear, brisk air, but without frost. There was not a sign of winter, except that a few cypress trees were leafless. A grove which surrounded the house was all in dark verdure; and there were green oranges on trees near the window; the buds were swelling on a jessamine-vine, and a number of camilia-japonicas were in full bloom. Sparrows were chirping, doves cooing, and a mocking bird whistling loudly.

Mr. X. has two plantations on the river, besides a large tract of poor pine forest land, extending some miles back upon the upland, and reaching above the malarious region. In the upper part of this pine land is a house, occupied by his overseer during the malarious season, when it is dangerous for any but negroes to remain during the night in the vicinity of the swamps or rice-fields. Even those few who have been born in the region, and have grown up subject to the malaria, are generally weakly and short-lived. The negroes do not enjoy as good health on rice plantations as elsewhere; and the greater difficulty with which their lives are preserved, through infancy especially, shows that the subtle poison of the miasma is not innocuous to them; but Mr. X. boasts a steady increase of his negro stock of five per cent. per annum, which is better than is averaged on the plantations of the interior.

As to the degree of danger to others, "I would as soon stand fifty feet from the best Kentucky rifleman and be shot at by the hour, as to spend a night on my plantation in summer," a Charleston gentleman said to me.

The plantation which contains Mr. X.'s winter residence, has but a small extent of rice land, the greater part of it being reclaimed upland swamp soil, suitable for the culture of Sea Island cotton, which, at the present market, might be grown upon it with profit. But, as his force of slaves has ordinarily been more profitably engaged in the rice-fields, all this has been for many years "turned out," and is now overgrown with pines. The other plantation contains over five hundred acres of rice-land, fitted for irrigation; the remainder is unusually fertile, reclaimed upland swamp, and some hundred acres of it are cultivated for maize and Sea Island cotton.

There is a "negro settlement" on each; but both plantations, although a mile or two apart, are worked together as one, under one overseer—the hands being drafted from one to another as their labor is required. Somewhat over seven hundred acres are at the present time under the plow in the two plantations: the whole number of negroes is two hundred, and they are reckoned to be equal to about one hundred prime hands—an unusual strength for that number of all classes. The overseer lives, in winter, near the settlement of the larger plantation, Mr. X. near that of the smaller.

It is an old family estate, inherited by Mr. X.'s wife, who, with her children, were born and brought up upon it in close intimacy with the negroes, a large proportion of whom were also included in her inheritance, or have been since born upon the estate. Mr. X. himself is a New England farmer's son, and has been a successful merchant and manufacturer. He is also a religious man, without the dementifying bigotry or self-important humility, so frequently implied by that appellation to a New Englander, but generous, composed and cheerful in disposition, as well as conscientious.

The patriarchal institution should be seen here under its most favorable aspects; not only from the ties of long family association, common traditions, common memories, and, if ever, common interest, between the slaves and their rulers, but, also, from the practical talent for organization and administration, gained among the rugged fields, the complicated looms, and the exact and comprehensive counting-houses of New England, which directs the labor.

The house-servants are more intelligent, understand and perform their duties better, and are more appropriately dressed, than any I have seen before. The labor required of them is light, and they are treated with much more consideration for their health and comfort than is usually given to that of free domestics. They live in brick cabins, adjoining the house and stables, and one of these, into which I have looked, is neatly and comfortably furnished. Several of the house-servants, as is usual, are mulattoes, and good-looking. The mulattoes are generally preferred for in-door occupations. Slaves brought up to house-work dread to be employed at field-labor; and those accustomed to the comparatively unconstrained life of the negro-settlement, detest the close control and careful movements required of the house-servants. It is a punishment for a lazy field-hand, to employ him in menial duties at the house, as it is to set a sneaking sailor to do the work of a cabin-servant; and it is equally a punishment to a neglectful house-servant, to banish him to the field-gangs. All the household economy is, of course, carried on in a style appropriate to a wealthy gentleman's residence—not more so, nor less so, that I observe, than in an establishment of similar grade at the North.

It is a custom with Mr. X., when on the estate, to look each day at all the work going on, inspect the buildings, boats, embankments and sluice-ways, and examine the sick. Yesterday I accompanied him in one of these daily rounds.

After a ride of several miles through the woods, in the rear of the plantations, we came to his largest negro-settlement. There was a street, or common, two hundred feet wide, on which the cabins of the negroes fronted. Each cabin was a framed building, the walls boarded and whitewashed on the outside, lathed and plastered within, the roof shingled; forty-two feet long, twenty-one feet wide, divided into two family tenements, each twenty-one by twenty-one; each tenement divided into three rooms—one, the common household apartment, twenty-one by ten; each of the others (bedrooms), ten by ten. There was a brick fire-place in the middle of the long side of each living room, the chimneys rising in one, in the middle of the roof. Besides these rooms, each tenement had a cock-loft, entered by steps from the household room. Each tenement is occupied, on an average, by five persons. There were in them closets, with locks and keys, and a varying quantity of rude furniture. Each cabin stood two hundred feet from the next, and the street in front of them being two hundred feet wide, they were just that distance apart each way. The people were nearly all absent at work, and had locked their outer doors, taking the keys with them. Each cabin has a front and back door, and each room a window, closed by a wooden shutter, swinging outward, on hinges. Between each tenement and the next house, is a small piece of ground, inclosed with palings, in which are coops of fowl with chickens, hovels for nests, and for sows with pig. There were a great many fowls in the street. The negroes' swine are allowed to run in the woods, each owner having his own distinguished by a peculiar mark. In the rear of the yards were gardens—a half-acre to each family. Internally the cabins appeared dirty and disordered, which was rather a pleasant indication that their home-life was not much interfered with, though I found certain police regulations were enforced.

The cabin nearest the overseer's house was used as a nursery. Having driven up to this, Mr. X. inquired first of an old nurse how the children were; whether there had been any births since his last visit; spoke of two convalescent young mothers, that were lounging on the floor of the portico, with the children, and then asked if there were any sick people.

"Nobody, oney dat boy, Sam, sar."

"What Sam is that?"

"Dat little Sam, sar; Tom's Sue's Sam, sar."

"What's the matter with him?"

"Don' 'spec dere's noting much de matter wid him now, sar. He came in Sa'dy, complainin' he had de stomach-ache, an' I gin him some ile, sar; 'spec he mus' be well, dis time, but he din go out dis mornin'."

"Well, I'll see to him."

Mr. X. went to Tom's Sue's cabin, looked at the boy, and, concluding that he was well, though he lay abed, and pretended to cry with pain, ordered him to go out to work. Then, meeting the overseer, who was just riding away, on some business off the plantation, he remained some time in conversation with him, while I occupied myself in making a sketch of the nursery and the street of the settlement in my note-book. On the verandah and the steps of the nursery, there were twenty-seven children, most of them infants, that had been left there by their mothers, while they were working their tasks in the fields. They probably make a visit to them once or twice during the day, to nurse them, and receive them to take to their cabins, or where they like, when they have finished their tasks—generally in the middle of the afternoon. The older children were fed with porridge, by the general nurse. A number of girls, eight or ten years old, were occupied in holding and tending the youngest infants. Those a little older—the crawlers—were in the pen, and those big enough to toddle were playing on the steps, or before the house. Some of these, with two or three bigger ones, were singing and dancing about a fire that they had made on the ground. They were not at all disturbed or interrupted in their amusement by the presence of their owner and myself. At twelve years of age, the children are first put to regular field-work; until then no labor is required of them, except, perhaps, occasionally, they are charged with some light kind of duty, such as frightening birds from corn. When first sent to the field, one-quarter of an able-bodied hand's day's work is ordinarily allotted to them, as their task.

But very few of the babies were in arms; such as were not, generally lay on the floor, rolling about, or sat still, sucking their thumbs. The nurse was a kind-looking old negro woman, with, no doubt, philo-progenitiveness well developed; but she paid very little attention to them, only sometimes chiding the older ones for laughing or singing too loud. I watched for half an hour, and in all that time not a baby of them began to cry; nor have I ever heard one, at two or three other plantation-nurseries which I have visited.

From the settlement, we drove to the "mill"—not a flouring mill, though I believe there is a run of stones in it—but a monster barn, with more extensive and better machinery for threshing and storing rice, driven by a steam-engine, than I have ever seen used for grain on any farm in Europe or America before. Adjoining the mill-house were shops and sheds, in which blacksmiths, carpenters, and other mechanics—all slaves, belonging to Mr. X. —were at work. He called my attention to the excellence of their workmanship, and said that they exercised as much ingenuity and skill as the ordinary mechanics that he was used to employ in New England. He pointed out to me some carpenter's work, a part of which had been executed by a New England mechanic, and a part by one of his own hands, which indicated that the latter was much the better workman.

I was gratified by this, for I had been so often told, in Virginia, by gentlemen, anxious to convince me that the negro was incapable of being educated or improved to a condition in which it would be safe to trust him with him-self—that no negro mechanic could ever be taught, or induced to work care-fully or nicely—that I had begun to believe it might be so.

We were attended through the mill-house by a respectable-looking, orderly, and gentlemanly-mannered mulatto, who was called, by his master, "the watchman." His duties, however, as they were described to me, were those of a steward, or intendant. He carried, by a strap at his waist, a very large number of keys, and had charge of all the stores of provisions, tools, and materials of the plantations, as well as of all their produce, before it was shipped to market. He weighed and measured out all the rations of the slaves and the cattle; superintended the mechanics, and himself made and repaired, as was necessary, all the machinery, including the steam-engine.

In all these departments, his authority was superior to that of the overseer. The overseer received his private allowance of family provisions from him, as did also the head-servant at the mansion, who was his brother. His responsi-bility was much greater than that of the overseer; and Mr. X. said, he would trust him with much more than he would any overseer he had ever known.

When we were leaving the house, to go to church, on Sunday, after all the white family had entered their carriages, or mounted their horses, the head house-servant also mounted a horse—as he did so, slipping a coin into the hands of the boy who had been holding him. Afterwards, we passed a family of negroes, in a light wagon—the oldest among them driving the horse. On my inquiring if the slaves were allowed to take horses to drive to church, I was informed that, in each of these three cases, the horse belonged to the negroes who were driving them. The old man was infirm, and Mr. X. had given him a horse, to enable him to move about.

But the watchman and the house-servant had bought their horses with money. The watchman was believed to own three horses; and, to account for his wealth, Mr. X.'s son told me that his father considered him a very valuable servant, and frequently encouraged him in his good behavior, with handsome gratuities. He receives, probably, considerably higher wages, in fact (in the form of presents), than the white overseer. He knew his father gave him two hundred dollars at once, a short time ago. The watchman has a private house, and, no doubt, lives in considerable luxury.

After passing through tool-rooms, corn-rooms, mule-stables, store-rooms, and a large garden, in which vegetables to be distributed among the negroes, as well as for the family, are grown, we walked to the rice-land. It is divided by embankments into fields of about twenty acres each, but varying some-what in size, according to the course of the river. The arrangements are such that each field may be flooded independently of the rest, and they are subdivided by open ditches into rectangular plats of a quarter acre each. We first proceeded to where twenty or thirty women and girls were engaged in raking together, in heaps and winrows, the stubble and rubbish left on the field after the last crop, and burning it. The main object of this operation is to kill all the seeds of weed, or of rice, on the ground. Ordinarily it is done by tasks—a certain number of the small divisions of the field being given to each hand to burn in a day; but owing to a more than usual amount of rain having fallen lately, and some other causes, making the work harder in some places than others, the women were now working by the day, under the direction of a "driver," a negro man, who walked about among them, taking care that they left nothing unburned. Mr. X. inspected the ground they had gone over, to see whether the driver had done his duty. It had been sufficiently well burned, but, not more than quarter as much ground had been gone over, he said, as was usually burned in task-work,—and he thought they had been very lazy, and reprimanded them for it. The driver made some little apology, but the women offered no reply, keeping steadily, and it seemed sullenly, on at their work.

In the next field, twenty men, or boys, for none of them looked as if they were full-grown, were plowing, each with a single mule, and a light, New-York-made plow. The soil was very friable, the plowing easy, and the mules proceeded at a smart pace; the furrows were straight, regular, and well turned. Their task was nominally an acre and a quarter a day; somewhat less actually, as the measure includes the space occupied by the ditches, which are two to three feet wide, running around each quarter of an acre. The plowing gang was superintended by a driver who was provided with a watch; and while we were looking at them he called out that it was twelve o'clock. The mules were immediately taken from the plows, and the plow-boys mounting them, leapt the ditches, and cantered off to the stables, to feed them. One or two were ordered to take their plows to the blacksmith, for repairs.

The plowmen got their dinner at this time: those not using horses do not usually dine till they have finished their tasks; but this, I believe, is optional with them. They commence work at sunrise, and at about eight o'clock have breakfast brought to them in the field, each hand having left a bucket with the cook for that purpose. All who are working in connection leave their work together, and gather in a social company about a fire, where they generally spend about half an hour, at breakfast time. The provisions furnished them consist mainly of meal, rice and vegetables, with salt and molasses, and occasionally bacon, fish, and coffee. The allowance is a peck of meal, or an equivalent quantity of rice per week, to each working hand, old or young, besides small stores. Mr. X. says that he has lately given a less amount of meat than is now usual on plantations, having observed that the general health of the negroes is not as good as formerly, when no meat at all was customarily given them. The general impression among planters is, that the negroes work much better for being supplied with three or four pounds of bacon a week.

Leaving the rice-land, we went next to some of the upland fields, where we found several other gangs of negroes at work; one entirely of men engaged in ditching; another of women, and another of boys and girls, "listing" an old corn-field with hoes. All of them were working by tasks, and were overlooked by negro drivers. They all labored with greater rapidity and cheerfulness than any slaves I have before seen; and the women struck their hoes as if they were strong, and well able to engage in muscular labor. The expression of their faces was generally repulsive, and their *tout ensemble* anything but agreeable to the eye. The dress of most of them was uncouth and cumbrous, dirty and ragged; reefed up, at the hips, so as to show their heavy legs, wrapped round with a piece of old blanket, in lieu of leggings or stockings. Most of them worked with bare arms, but wore strong shoes on their feet, and handkerchiefs on their heads; some of them were smoking, and each gang had a fire burning on the ground, near where they were at work, to light their pipes and warm their breakfast by. Mr. X. said this was always their custom, even in summer. To each gang a boy or girl was also attached, whose business it was to bring water for them to drink, and to go for anything required by the driver. The drivers would frequently call back a hand to go over again some piece of his or her task that had not been worked to his satisfaction, and were constantly calling to one or another, with a harsh and peremptory voice, to strike harder or hoe deeper, and otherwise taking care that the work was well done. Mr. X. asked if Little Sam ("Tom's Sue's Sam") worked yet with the "three-quarter" hands, and learning that he did, ordered him to be put with the field-hands, observing that though rather short, he was strong and stout, and, being twenty years old, well able to do a man's work.

The field-hands are all divided into four classes, according to their physical capacities. The children beginning as "quarter-hands," advancing to "half-hands," and then to "three-quarter hands"; and, finally, when mature, and able-bodied, healthy and strong, to "full hands." As they decline in strength, from age, sickness, or other cause, they retrograde in the scale, and proportionately less labor is required of them. Many, of naturally weak frame, never are put among the full hands. Finally, the aged are left out at the annual classification, and no more regular field-work is required of them, although they are generally provided with some light, sedentary occupation. I saw one old woman picking "tailings" of rice out of a heap of chaff, an occupation at which she was literally not earning her salt. Mr. X. told me she was a native African, having been brought when a girl from the Guinea coast. She spoke almost unintelligibly; but after some other conversation, in which I had not been able to understand a word she said, he jokingly proposed to send her back to Africa. She expressed her preference to remain where she was, very emphatically. "Why?" She did not answer readily, but being pressed, threw up her palsied hands, and said furiously, "I lubs 'ou mas'r, oh, I lubs 'ou. I don't want go 'way from 'ou."

The field hands are nearly always worked in gangs, the strength of a gang varying according to the work that engages it; usually it numbers twenty or more, and is directed by a driver. As on most large plantations, whether of rice or cotton, in Eastern Georgia and South Carolina, nearly all ordinary and regular work is performed *by tasks:* that is to say, each hand has his labor for the day marked out before him, and can take his own time to do it in. For instance, in making drains in light, clean meadow land, each man or woman of the full hands is required to dig one thousand cubic feet; in swamp-land that is being prepared for rice culture, where there are not many stumps, the task for a ditcher is five hundred feet; while in a very strong cypress swamp, only two hundred feet is required; in hoeing rice, a certain number of rows, equal to one-half or two-thirds of an acre, according to the condition of the land; in sowing rice (strewing in drills), two acres; in reaping rice (if it stands well), three-quarters of an acre; or, sometimes a gang will be required to reap, tie in sheaves, and carry to the stack-yard the produce of a certain area, commonly equal to one fourth the number of acres that there are hands working together.

These tasks certainly would not be considered excessively hard, by a Northern laborer; and, in point of fact, the more industrious and active hands finish them often by two o'clock. I saw one or two leaving the field soon after one o'clock, several about two; and between three and four, I met a dozen women and several men coming home to their cabins, having finished their day's work.

Under this "Organization of Labor," most of the slaves work rapidly and well. In nearly all ordinary work, custom has settled the extent of the task, and it is difficult to increase it. The driver who marks it out, has to remain on the ground until it is finished, and has no interest in over-measuring it; and if it should be systematically increased very much, there is danger of a general stampede to the "swamp"—a danger the slave can always hold before his master's cupidity. In fact, it is looked upon in this region as a

TWO SLAVE DRIVERS AND A BACKWOODSMAN

proscriptive right of the negroes to have this incitement to diligence offered them; and the man who denied it, or who attempted to lessen it, would, it is said, suffer in his reputation, as well as experience much annoyance from the obstinate "rascality" of his negroes. Notwithstanding this, I have heard a man assert, boastingly, that he made his negroes habitually perform double the customary tasks. Thus we get a glimpse again of the black side. If he is allowed the power to do this, what may not a man do?

It is the driver's duty to make the tasked hands do their work well. If, in their haste to finish it, they neglect to do it properly, he "sets them back," so that carelessness will hinder more than it will hasten the completion of their tasks.

In the selection of drivers, regard seems to be had to size and strength—at least, nearly all the drivers I have seen are tall and strong men—but a great deal of judgment, requiring greater capacity of mind than the ordinary slave is often supposed to be possessed of, is certainly needed in them. A good driver is very valuable and usually holds office for life. His authority is not limited to the direction of labor in the field, but extends to the general deportment of the negroes. He is made to do the duties of policeman, and even of police magistrate. It is his duty, for instance, on Mr. X.'s estate, to keep order in the settlement; and, if two persons, men or women, are fighting, it is his duty to immediately separate them, and then to "whip them both."

Before any field of work is entered upon by a gang, the driver who is to superintend them has to measure and stake off the tasks. To do this at all accurately, in irregular-shaped fields, must require considerable powers of calculation. A driver, with a boy to set the stakes, I was told, would accurately lay out forty acres a day, in half-acre tasks. The only instrument used is a five-foot measuring rod. When the gang comes to the field, he points out to each person his or her duty for the day, and then walks about among them, looking out that each proceeds properly. If, after a hard day's labor, he sees that the gang has been overtasked, owing to a miscalculation of the difficulty of the work, he may excuse the completion of the tasks; but he is not allowed to extend them. In the case of uncompleted tasks, the body of the gang begin new tasks the next day, and only a sufficient number are detailed from it to complete, during the day, the unfinished tasks of the day before. The relation of the driver to the working hands seems to be similar to that of the boatswain to the seamen in the navy, or of the sergeant to the privates in the army.

Having generally had long experience on the plantation, the advice of the drivers is commonly taken in nearly all the administration, and frequently they are, *de facto,* the managers. Orders on important points of the plantation economy, I have heard given by the proprietor directly to them, without the overseer's being consulted or informed of them; and it is often left with them to decide when and how long to flow the rice-grounds—the proprietor and overseer deferring to their more experienced judgment. Where the drivers are discreet, experienced and trusty, the overseer is frequently employed merely as a matter of form, to comply with the laws requiring the superintendence or presence of a white man among every body of slaves; and his duty is rather to inspect and report, than to govern. Mr. X. considers his overseer an uncommonly efficient and faithful one, but he would not employ him, even during the summer, when he is absent for several months, if the law did not require it. He has sometimes left his plantation in care of one of the drivers for a considerable length of time, after having discharged an overseer; and he thinks it has then been quite as well conducted as ever. His overseer consults the drivers on all important points, and is governed by their advice.

Mr. X. said, that though overseers sometimes punished the negroes severely, and otherwise ill-treated them, it is their more common fault to indulge them foolishly in their disposition to idleness, or in other ways to curry favor with them, so they may not inform the proprietor of their own misconduct or neglect. He has his overseer bound to certain rules, by written contract; and it is stipulated that he can discharge him at any moment, without remuneration for his loss of time and inconvenience, if he should at any time be dissatisfied with him. One of the rules is, that he shall never punish a negro with his own hands, and that corporeal punishment, when necessary, shall be inflicted by the drivers. The advantage of this is, that it secures time for deliberation, and prevents punishment being made in sudden passion. His drivers are not allowed to carry their whips with them in the field; so that if the overseer wishes a hand punished, it is necessary to call a driver; and the driver has then to go to his cabin, which is, perhaps, a mile or two distant, to get his whip, before it can be applied.

I asked how often the necessity of punishment occurred?

"Sometimes, perhaps, not once for two or three weeks; then it will seem as if the devil had got into them all, and there is a good deal of it."

As the negroes finish the labor, required of them by Mr. X., at three or four o'clock in the afternoon, they can employ the remainder of the day in laboring for themselves, if they choose. Each family has a half-acre of land allotted to it, for a garden; besides which, there is a large vegetable garden, from which they are supplied. They are at liberty to sell whatever they choose from the products of their own garden, and to make what they can by keeping swine and fowls. Mr. X.'s family have no other supply of poultry and eggs than what is obtained by purchase from his own negroes; they frequently, also, purchase game from them. The only restriction upon their traffic is a "liquor law." They are not allowed to buy or sell ardent spirits. This prohibition, like liquor laws elsewhere, unfortunately, cannot be enforced; and, of late years, grog shops, at which stolen goods are bought from the slaves, and poisonous liquors—chiefly the worse whiskey, much watered and made stupefying by an infusion of tobacco—are clandestinely sold to them, have become an established evil, and the planters find themselves almost powerless to cope with it.

So far as I have observed, slaves show themselves worthy of trust most, where their masters are most considerate and liberal towards them. Mr. X.'s slaves are permitted to purchase fire-arms and ammunition, and to keep them in their cabins; and his wife and daughters reside with him, among them, the doors of the house never locked, or windows closed, perfectly defenseless, and miles distant from any other white family.

I do not think, after all I have heard to favor it, that there is any good reason to consider the negro the moral inferior of the white; or, that if he is so, it is in those elements of character which should prevent us from trusting him with equal social munities with ourselves.

MOUNTAIN WHITES

Extreme poverty is rare in the mountains, but a smaller proportion of the people live in a style corresponding to that customary among what are called in New England "fore-handed folks," than in any other part of the civilized world which I have visited. The number who can be classed as moderately well-informed, using the New England rural standard, is extremely small. I did not meet in a whole month more than two or three natives who seemed to have enjoyed equal advantages of education with the lowest class of New England (native) working people. Each of those above the average in this respect I shall speak of distinctly.

The great majority live in small and comfortless log huts, two detached cabins usually forming the habitation of a family. These are rarely provided with glass windows, many are even without a port; yet the winter is more severe than that of England. The interior of one frame house, in which I spent a night, forty by thirty feet in dimensions, and two stories in height, occupied by a family of much more than the usual wealth, received light in the lower story only by the door and the occasional interstices of the boarding, and in the upper, by two loopholes, unfurnished with shutters.

The table is usually abundantly provided, its only marked difference from that of the lower country being the occasional presence of unleavened rye bread, made with saleratus and fat, unlike any rye bread I have eaten elsewhere, but more palatable to me than the usual corn bread. Butter is always offered in the mountains, and is usually good.

The women, as well as the men, generally smoke, and tobacco is grown for home use. They are more industrious than the men, often being seen at work in the fields, and at spinning wheels and hand-looms in almost every house. I was less troubled by vermin than in the low country, yet so much so that I adopted the habit of passing the night on the floor of the cabins, rather than in their beds. The furniture of the cabins is rather less meager than that of a similar class of habitations in the lower region. In the northern parts, it is common to see a square frame in which are piled a dozen bed quilts. Notwithstanding the ignorance of the people, books are more common than even in the houses of the slave owners of the planting districts. They seemed fond of reading aloud, those who were able—in a rather doleful and jolting manner. Their books are generally the cheapest and tawdriest of religious holiday books, as Mr. Sears' publications, Fox's "Martyrs," the "Biography of Distinguished Divines," with such others as "The Alarm to the Unconverted" and "The Cause and Cure of Infidelity"; not such as *Pilgrim's Progress,* or *Robinson Crusoe,* neither of which did I ever meet with.

I rode late last night, there being no cabins for several miles in which I was willing to spend the night, until I came to one of larger size than usual, with a gallery on the side toward the road and a good stable opposite it. A man on the gallery was about to answer (as I judged from his countenance), "I reckon you can," to my inquiry if I could stay, when the cracked voice of a worryful woman screeched out from within, "We don't foller takin' in people."

"No, sir," said the man, "we don't foller it."

"How far shall I have to go?"

"There's another house a little better than three quarters of a mile further on."

To this house I proceeded—a cabin of one room and a loft, with a kitchen in a separate cabin. The owner said he never turned anybody away, and I was welcome. He did not say that he had no corn, until after supper, when I asked for it to feed my horse. The family were good-natured, intelligent people, but very ignorant. The man and his wife and the daughters slept below, the boys and I in the cock-loft. Supper and breakfast were eaten in the detached kitchen. Yet they were by no means poor people. The man told me that he had over a thousand acres of rich tillable land, besides a large extent of mountain range, the most of which latter he had bought from time to time as he was able, to prevent the settlement of squatters near his valley-land. "There were people who would be bad neighbors I knew," he said, "that would settle on most any kind of place, and every body wants to keep such as far away from them as they can." (When I took my bridle off, I hung it up by the stable door; he took it down and said he'd hang it in a safer place. "He'd never had any thing stolen from here, and he didn't mean to have—it was just as well not to put temptation before people," and he took it into the house and put it under his bed.)

Besides this large tract of land here, he owned another tract of two hundred acres with a house upon it, rented for one third the produce, and another smaller farm, similarly rented; he also owned a grist mill, which he rented to a miller for half the tolls. He had also a considerable stock of cattle and large crops of grain, so that he must be considered a very respectable capitalist for a mountaineer. He told me that he had thought a good deal formerly of moving to new countries, but he had been doing pretty well and had staid here now so long, he didn't much think he should ever budge. He reckoned he'd got enough to make him a living for the rest of his life, and he didn't know any use a man had for more'n that.

I did not see a single book in the house, nor do I think that any of the family could read. He said that many people here were talking about Iowa and Indiana; "was Iowa (Hiaway) beyond the Texies?" I opened my map to show him where it was, but he said he "wasn't scollar'd enough" to understand it, and I could not induce him to look at it. I asked him if the people here preferred Iowa and Indiana to Missouri at all because they were free States. "I reckon," he replied, "they don't have no allusion to that. Slavery is a great cuss, though, I think, the greatest there is in these United States. There ain't no account of slaves up here in the west, but down in the east part of this State about Fayetteville, there's as many as there is in South Carolina. That's the reason the West and the East don't agree in this State; people out here hates the eastern people."

"Why is that?"

"Why you see they vote on the slave basis, and there's some of them nigger counties where there ain't more'n four or five hundred white folks, that has just as much power in the Legislature as any of our mountain counties where there'll be some thousand voters."

He made further remarks against slavery and against slave-holders. When I told him that I entirely agreed with him, and said further that poor white people were usually far better off in the free States than in the slave, he seemed a little surprised and said, "New York ain't a free State, is it?"

NEW ORLEANS JUST BEFORE THE WAR

I had expected to be landed at New Orleans by the boat from New York, and had not been informed of the rail-road arrangements across the Delta, and had no idea in what part of Louisiana we might be.

I asked the name of the village.

"Note Anglische, sare," was the gruff reply.

There was a sign, *"Café du Faubourg,"* and, putting my head out of the window, I saw that we were thundering into New Orleans. We reached the terminus, which was surrounded with *fiacres,* in the style of Paris.

"To the hotel St. Charles," I said to the driver, confused with the loud French and quiet English of the crowd about me.

"Oui, yer 'onor," was the reply of my Irish-born fellow-citizen: another passenger was got, and away we rattled through narrow dirty streets, among grimy old stuccoed walls; high, arched windows and doors, balconies and entresols, and French noises and French smells (nothing so strong, in associations, as old smells); French signs, ten to one of English, but with funny polygomatic arrangements.

The other fare, whom I had not ventured to speak to, was set down at a *salle pour la vente des* somethings, and soon after the *fiacre* turned out upon a broad place, covered with bales of cotton, and casks of sugar, and weighing scales, and disclosing an astonishing number of steam-boats, lying all close together in a line, the ends of which were lost in the midst, which still hung upon the river.

Now the signs became English, and the new brick buildings American. We turned into a broad street, in which shutters were being taken from great glass store-fronts, and clerks were exercising their ingenuity in the display of muslin, and silks, and shawls. In the middle of the broad street there was an open space of waste ground, looking as if the corporation had not been able to pave the whole at once, and had left this interval to be attended to when the treasury was better filled. Crossing through a gap in this waste, we entered a narrow street of higher buildings, French, Spanish, and English signs, the latter predominating; and at the second block, I was landed before the great Grecian portico of the stupendous, tasteless, ill-contrived and inconvenient St. Charles Hotel.[1]

1. [The St. Charles Hotel was one of the most luxurious in the nation. Most travelers gave a more favorable description of it. J. M. Mackie, at approximately the same time as Olmstead's visit, thus pictured it:

"The Englishman who, having come over in a Cunarder, takes lodgings at the St. Nicholas Hotel in New York, pronounces its drawing rooms *stunnin'*. But as much more magnificent as

After a bath and breakfast, I returned with great interest, to wander in the old French town. Among the houses, one occasionally sees a relic of ancient Spanish builders, while all the newer edifices have the characteristics of the unartistic and dollar pursuing Yankees.

I was delighted when I reached the old Place d'Armes, now a public garden, bright with the orange and lemon trees, and roses, and myrtles, and laurels, and jessamines of the south of France. Fronting upon it is the old Hotel de Ville, still the city court-house, and a quaint old French structure, with scaly and vermiculated surface, and deep-worn door-sills, and smooth-rubbed corners. Adjoining it is an old Spanish cathedral, damaged by paint, and late alterations and repairs, but still a fine thing in our desert of the reverend architecture. Enough, that while it is not new, it is not shabby, and is not tricked out with much frippery, gingerbread and confectionery work.

In the crowded market-place, there were not only the pure old Indian Americans, and the Spanish, French, English, Celtic, and African, but nearly all possible mixed varieties of these, and no doubt of some other breeds of mankind. Some of the colored women spoke French, Spanish, and English, as their customers demanded. Three taverns, bearing the sign of "The Pig

---

was its bridal chamber than its bedrooms in the fifth story, so much does one parlor of the St. Charles in New Orleans exceed in splendor the whole suite of showrooms of the New York caravansary. For, when all the cotton widows and cotton girls have bought their new dresses in Canal or Chartres street, they display them at once in the St. Charles parlor. Every chair and sofa is set out with the new silks and satins. You hear it whispered about, that the dress of white point lace worn by the young belle standing before you cost papa two thousand dollars; and that the lady by her side, from Red River, flames with twenty thousand dollars' worth of jewelry. Yonder miss has hidden herself in the corner, because, for the embroidered muslin she has on, Madame Olympe did not charge but two hundred dollars. The Mississippi widow, bent on making a sensation, will not come down to the breakfast table in anything short of diamond brooches, and lace from the high altar; while even then the dowager from Baton Rouge wins the general stare from her by planting herself *vis-à-vis* in pearls, and supplementary puffs made by the barber.

"However, it must be acknowledged that the extra ordinary things that the New Yorker will see at the St. Charles will go far toward repaying him for the trouble of his journey. He will see gentlemen in purple pantaloons. Twice in the twenty-four hours all the magnificence of Red River and Arkansas empties itself—a perfect flood of jewels, laces, painted silks, and muslins—into the parlor; for, among them, he will find some with not less than four thousand cotton bales a year, and others who run two sets of sugar kettles. "Look at 'em straight, to see if you like 'em," as the orange boy said to me on the Mississippi steamer, when I stopped him for the purpose of making an investment in the contents of his baskets. And when the gorgeous tide is out of the parlor, our New Yorker may be entertained, with the sight of a couple of lovers on a sofa, sucking each an orange, while they estimate the value of their respective crops for the next season, and speculate on the probable price of negroes. Then, when he goes to dinner, it will be an amusement for him to divine the character and occupation of the gentleman sitting opposite, with such an imposing countenance, with hair artistically combed back, with so grand an air, so much deference toward the lady sitting by his side. Is he a cotton lord, or a sugar lord?—a question which may well occupy the mind for a half hour, at the end of which time our traveller, on going down to the barroom for his *petit verre* of Cognac, gets the solution. His *vis-à-vis* is a tap-man, and mixes juleps."—ED.]

and Whistle," indicated the recent English, a cabaret to the Universal Republic, with a red flag, the French, and the Gasthaus zum Rhein platz, the Teutonic contributions to the strength of our nation. A policeman, with the richest Irish brogue, directed me back to the St. Charles.

A mechanic, English by birth, who had lived in New Orleans for several years, always going up the river in the summer, to escape the danger of fever in the city, told me that he could lay up money much more rapidly there than in New York. The expenses of living were not necessarily greater than in New York. If a man kept house, and provided for himself, he could live much cheaper than at boarding-houses. Many unmarried mechanics, therefore, lived with colored mistresses, who were commonly vile and dishonest. He was at a boarding-house, where he paid four dollars a week. In New York he had paid three dollars, but the board was not as good as in New Orleans. "The reason," said he, "that people say it costs so much more to live here than in New York is, that what they think treats in New York, they consider necessaries here. Everybody lives freer, and spend their money more willingly here."

The master mechanics, who bought up slaves, and took contracts for work, he said, made more money than any others. They did so because they did very poor work—poorer than white mechanics could generally be got to do. But nearly all work was done in New Orleans more hastily and carelessly than in New York, though he thought it was bad enough there. The slave-holding bosses could get no white men to work with their slaves, except Irishmen and Germans—no man who had any regard for his position among his fellow-craftsmen would ever let himself be seen working with a negro. He said I could see any day in Canal street, "a most revolting sight" —Irishmen waiting on negro masons. He had seen, one morning a negro carrying some mortar, when another negro hailed him with a loud laugh: "Hallo! you is turned Irishman, is 'ou?"

White working men were rapidly displacing the slaves in all sorts of work, and he hoped and believed it would not be many years before every negro would be driven out of the town. He thought acclimated white men could do more hard work than negroes, even in the hottest weather, if they were temperate, and avoided too stimulating food. That, he said, was the general opinion among those of them who staid over summer. Those who drank much whiskey and cordials, and kept up old habits of eating, were the ones who complained most of the climate, and who thought white men were not made to work in it.

It is obvious that free men have very much gained the field of labor in

New Orleans to themselves. The majority of the cartmen, hackney-coach men, porters, rail-road hands, public waiters, and common laborers, as well as of skilled mechanics, appear to be white men; and of the negroes employed in those avocations, a considerable proportion are free.

This is the case here more than in any other town in Slavery, although the climate is torrid, and inconvenient or dangerous to strangers; because New Orleans is more extensively engaged in commerce, and because there is, by the passing and sojourning immigration from Europe, constantly in the city a sufficient number of free laborers, to sustain, by competition and association with each other, the habits of free-labor communities. It is plainly perceptible that the white working men in New Orleans have more business-like manners, and more assured self-respect, than those of smaller towns. They are even not without *esprit du corps*.

As Commerce, or any high form of industry requires intelligence in its laborers, slaves can never be brought together in dense communities, but their intelligence will increase to a degree dangerous to those who enjoy the benefit of their labor. The slave must be kept dependent, day by day, upon his master for his daily bread, or he will find, and will declare his independence, in all respects, of him. This condition disqualifies the slave for any but the simplest and rudest forms of labor; and every attempt to bring his labor into competition with free labor can only be successful at the hazard of insurrection. Hundreds of slaves in New Orleans must be constantly reflecting and saying to one another, "I am as capable of taking care of myself as this Irish hod-carrier, or this German market-gardener; why can't I have the enjoyment of my labor as well as they? I am as capable of taking care of my own family as much as they of theirs; why should I be subject to have them taken from me by those other men who call themselves our owners? Our children have as much brains as the children of these white neighbors of ours, who not long ago were cooks and waiters at the hotels, why should they be turned from the school-rooms? I helped to build the school-house, and have not been paid for it. One thing I know, if I can't have my rights, I can have my pleasures; and if they won't give me wages I can take them."

First and last, I spent some weeks in New Orleans and its vicinity. I doubt if there is a city in the world, where the resident population has been so divided in its origin, or where there is such a variety in the tastes, habits, manners, and moral codes of the citizens. Although this injures civic enterprise—which the peculiar situation of the city greatly demands to be directed to means of cleanliness, convenience, comfort, and health—it also gives a greater scope to the working of individual enterprise, taste, genius, and conscience; so that nowhere are the qualities of man—as displayed in generosity, hospitality, benevolence, and courage—better developed, or the lower qualities, likening him to a beast, less interfered with, by law or the action of public opinion.

There is one, among the multitudinous classifications of society in New Orleans, which is a very peculiar and characteristic result of the prejudices, vices, and customs of the various elements of color, class, and nation, which have been brought together.

I refer to a class composed of the illegitimate offspring of white men and colored women (mulattoes or quadroons), who, from habits of early life, the advantages of education, and the use of wealth, are too much superior to the negroes, in general, to associate with them, and are not allowed by law, or the popular prejudice, to marry white people. The girls are frequently sent to Paris to be educated, and are very accomplished. They are generally pretty, and often handsome. I have rarely, if ever, met more beautiful women, than one or two of them, that I saw by chance, in the streets. They are much better formed, and have a much more graceful and elegant carriage than Americans in general, while they seem to have commonly inherited or acquired much of the taste and skill, in the selection and arrangement, and the way of wearing dresses and ornaments, that is the especial distinction of the women of Paris. Their beauty and attractiveness being their fortune, they cultivate and cherish with diligence every charm or accomplishment they are possessed of.

Of course, men are attracted by them, associate with them, are captivated, and become attached to them, and, not being able to marry them legally, and with the usual forms and securities for constancy, make such arrangements "as can be agreed upon." When a man makes a declaration of love to a girl of this class, she will admit or deny, as the case may be, her happiness in receiving it; but, supposing she is favorably disposed, she will usually refer the applicant to her mother. The mother inquires, like a Countess of Kew, into the circumstances of the suitor; ascertains whether he is able to maintain a family, and, if satisfied with him, in these and other respects, requires from him security that he will support her daughter in a style suitable to the habits she has been bred to, and that, if he should ever leave her, he will give her a certain sum for her future support, and a certain additional sum for each of the children she shall then have.

The wealth, thus secured, will, of course, vary—as in society with higher assumptions of morality—with the value of the lady in the market; that is, with her attractiveness, and the number and value of other suitors she may have, or may reasonably expect. Of course, I do not mean that love has nothing at all to do with it; but love is sedulously restrained, and held firmly in hand, until the road of competency is seen to be clear, with less humbug than our English custom requires about it. Everything being satisfactorily arranged, a tenement in a certain quarter of the town is usually hired, and the couple move into it and go to housekeeping—living as if they were married. The woman is not, of course, to be wholly deprived of the society of others—her former acquaintances are continued, and she sustains her relations as daughter, sister, and friend. Of course, too, her husband (she calls him so—why shouldn't she?) will be likely to continue, also, more or less in, and form a part of, this kind of society. There are parties and balls —*bals masqués*—and all the movements and customs of other fashionable society, which they can enjoy in it, if they wish. The women of this sort are represented to be exceedingly affectionate in disposition, and constant beyond reproach.

During all the time a man sustains this relation, he will commonly be moving, also, in reputable society on the other side of the town; not improbably, eventually he marries, and has a family establishment elsewhere. Before doing this, he may separate from his *placée* (so she is termed). If so, he pays her according to agreement, and as much more, perhaps, as his affection for her, or his sense of the cruelty of the proceeding, may lead him to; and she has the world before her again, in the position of a widow. Many men continue, for a long time, to support both establishments—particularly, if their legal marriage is one *de convenance*. But many others form so strong attachments, that the relation is never discontinued, but becomes, indeed, that of marriage, except that it is not legalized or solemnized. These men leave their estate, at death, to their children, to whom they may have previously given every advantage of education they could command. What becomes of the boys, I am not informed; the girls, sometimes, are removed to other countries, where their color does not prevent their living reputable lives; but, of course, mainly continue in the same society, and are fated to a life similar to that of their mothers.

A gentleman, of New England education, gave me the following account of his acquaintance with the quadroon society. On first coming to New Orleans, he was drawn into the social circles usually frequented by New England people, and some time afterwards was introduced by a friend to a quadroon family, in which there were three pretty and accomplished young women. They were intelligent and well informed; their musical taste was especially well cultivated; they were interested in the literature of the day, and their conversation upon it was characterized by good sense and refined discrimination. He never saw any indication of a want of purity of character or delicacy of feeling in them. He was much attracted by them, and for some time visited them very frequently. Having then discontinued his intimacy, at length one of the girls asked him why he did not come to see them as often as he had formerly done. He frankly replied that he had found their society so fascinating, that he had thought it best to restrict himself in the enjoyment of it, lest it should become necessary to his happiness; and out of regard to his general plans of life, and the feelings of his friends, he could not permit himself to indulge the purpose to be united to one of them, according to the usual custom with their class. The young woman was evidently much pained, but not at all offended, and immediately acknowledged and commended the propriety and good sense of his resolution.

One reason which leads this way of living to be frequently adopted by unmarried men, who come to New Orleans to carry on business, is, that it is much cheaper than living at hotels and boarding-houses. As no young man ordinarily dare think of marrying, until he has made a fortune to support the extravagant style of house-keeping, and gratify the expensive tastes of young women, as fashion is now educating them, many are obliged to make up their minds never to marry. Such a one undertook to show me that it was cheaper for him to *placer* than to live in any other way that he could be expected to in New Orleans. He hired, at a low rent, two apartments in the older part of the town; his placée did not, except occasionally, require a servant; she did the marketing, and performed all the ordinary duties of house-keeping herself; she took care of his clothes, and in every way was economical and saving in her habits—it being her interest, if her affection for him were not sufficient, to make him as much comfort and as little expense as possible, that he might be the more strongly attached to her, and have the less occasion to leave her. He concluded by assuring me that whatever might be said against it, it certainly was better than the way in which most young men lived who depended on salaries in New York.

A large planter told me the reason he sent his boys to the North to be educated was, that there was no possibility of their being brought up in decency at home. Another planter told me that he was intending to move to a free country on this account. He said that the practice was not occasional or general, it was universal. "There is not," he said, "a likely-looking black girl in this State, that is not the paramour of a white man. There is not an old plantation in which the grandchildren of the owner are not whipped in the field by his overseer. I cannot bear that the blood of the —— should run in the veins of slaves." He was of an old Scotch family.

The Cotton Kingdom

A MISSISSIPPI COTTON PLANTATION

As a general rule, the larger the body of negroes on a plantation or estate, the more completely are they treated as mere property, and in accordance with a policy calculated to insure the largest pecuniary returns. Hence, in part, the greater proportionate profit of such plantations, and the tendency which everywhere prevails in the planting districts to the absorption of small, and the augmentation of large estates. It may be true, that among the wealthier slaveowners, there is oftener a humane disposition, a better judgment, and a greater ability to deal with their dependents indulgently and bountifully, but the effects of this disposition are chiefly felt, even on those plantations where the proprietor resides permanently, among the slaves employed about the house and stables, and perhaps a few old favorites in the quarters. It is more than balanced by the difficulty of acquiring a personal interest in the units of a large body of slaves, and an acquaintance with the individual characteristics of each, The treatment of the mass must be reduced to a system, the ruling idea of which will be, to enable one man to force into the same channel of labor the muscles of a large number of men, of various, and often conflicting wills.

The estate I am now about to describe, was situated upon a tributary of the Mississippi, and accessible only by occasional steamboats, even this mode of communication being frequently interrupted at low stages of the rivers. The slaves upon it formed about one twentieth of the whole population of the county, in which the blacks considerably out-number the whites. At the time of my visit, the owner was sojourning upon it, with his family and several invited guests, but his usual residence was upon a small plantation, of little productive value, situated in a neighborhood somewhat noted for the luxury and hospitality of its citizens, and having a daily mail, and direct railroad and telegraphic communication with New York. This was, if I am not mistaken, his second visit in five years.

The property consisted of four adjoining plantations, each with its own negro cabins, stables and overseer, and each worked to a great extent independently of the others, but all contributing their crop to one gin-house and warehouse, and all under the general superintendence of a bailiff or manager, who constantly resided upon the estate, and in the absence of the owner, had vice-regal power over the overseers, controlling so far as he thought fit, the economy of all the plantations.

The manager was himself a gentleman of good education, generous and poetic in temperament, and possessing a capacity for the enjoyment of nature and happiness in the bucolic life. I found him a delightful companion. The gang of toiling negroes to him, however, was as essential an element of the poetry of nature as flocks of peaceful sheep and lowing kine.

The overseers were superior to most men of their class, and, with one exception, frank, honest, temperate and industrious, but their feelings toward negroes were such as naturally result from their occupation. They were all married, and lived with their families, each in a cabin or cottage, in the hamlet of the slaves of which he had especial charge. Their wages varied from $500 to $1,000 a year each.

These five men, each living more than a mile distant from either of the others, were the only white men on the estate. Of course to secure their own personal safety and to efficiently direct the labor of such a large number of ignorant, indolent, and vicious negroes, rules, or rather habits and customs, of discipline, were necessary, which would in particular cases be liable to operate unjustly and cruelly. It is apparent, also, that, as the testimony of negroes against them would not be received as evidence in court, that there was very little probability that any excessive severity would be restrained by fear of the law.

In the main, the negroes appeared to be well taken care of and abundantly supplied with the necessaries of vigorous physical existence. A large part of them lived in commodious and well-built cottages, with broad galleries in front, so that each family of five had two rooms on the lower floor, and a loft. The remainder lived in log-huts, small and mean in appearance, but those of their overseers were little better, and preparations were being made to replace all of these by neat boarded cottages. Each family had a fowl-house and hog-sty (constructed by the negroes themselves), and kept fowls and swine, feeding the latter during the summer on weeds and fattening them in the autumn on corn *stolen* (this was mentioned to me by the overseers as if it were a matter of course) from their master's corn-fields.

I several times saw gangs of them eating the dinner which they had brought, each for himself, to the field, and observed that they generally had plenty, often more than they could eat, of bacon, cornbread, and molasses. The allowance of food is weighed and measured under the eye of the manager by the drivers, and distributed to the head of each family weekly: consisting of—for each person, 3 pounds of pork, 1 peck of meal; and from January to July, 1 quart of molasses. Monthly, in addition, 1 pound of tobacco, and 4 pints of salt. No drink is ever served but water, except after unusual exposure, or to ditchers working in water, who get a glass of whiskey at night.

All hands cook for themselves after work at night, or whenever they please between night-fall and daybreak, each family in its own cabin. Each family has a garden, the products of which, together with eggs, fowls and bacon, they frequently sold, or used in addition to their regular allowance of food. Most of the families bought a barrel of flour every year. The manager endeavored to encourage this practice, and that they might spend their money for flour instead of liquor, he furnished it to them at rather less than what it cost him at wholesale. There were many poor whites within a few miles who would always sell liquor to the negroes, and encourage them to steal, to obtain the means to buy it of them. These poor whites were al-

KING COTTON

ways spoken of with anger by the overseers, and they each had a standing offer of much more than the intrinsic value of their land, from the manager, to induce them to move away.

The first morning I was on the estate, the manager invited me to ride with him on his usual daily round of inspection through the plantations. On reaching the nearest "quarters," we stopped at a house, a little larger than the ordinary cabins, which was called the loom-house, in which a dozen negroes were at work making shoes, and manufacturing coarse cotton stuff for negro clothing. One of the hands so employed was insane, and most of the others were cripples, invalids with chronic complaints, or unfitted by age, or some infirmity, for field work.

We went to another cabin and entered a room where a woman lay on a bed, groaning. It was a very dingy, comfortless room, but a musquito bar, much patched and very dirty, covered the bed. The manager asked the woman several times what was the matter, but could get no distinct reply. She appeared to be suffering great pain. The manager felt her pulse and looked at her tongue, and after making a few more inquiries, to which no intelligible reply was given, told her he did not believe she was ill at all. At this the woman's groans redoubled. "I have heard of your tricks," continued the manager; "you had a chill when I came to see you yesterday morning; you had a chill when the mistress came here, and you had a chill when the master came. I never knew a chill to last the whole day. So you'll just get up now and go to the field, and if you don't work smart, you'll get a dressing; do you hear?"

We then left. The manager said that he rarely—almost never—had occasion to employ a physician for the people. Never for accouchements; the women, from their labor in the field, were not subject to the difficulty, danger, and pain which attended women of the better classes in giving birth to their offspring.

Each overseer regulated the hours of work on his own plantation. I saw the negroes at work before sunrise and after sunset. At about eight o'clock they were allowed to stop for breakfast, and again about noon, to dine. The length of these rests was at the discretion of the overseer or drivers, usually, I should say, from half an hour to an hour. There was no rule.

The number of hands directed by each overseer was considerably over one hundred. The manager thought it would be better economy to have a white man over every fifty hands, but the difficulty of obtaining trustworthy overseers prevented it. Three of those he then had were the best he had ever known. He described the great majority as being passionate, careless, inefficient men, generally intemperate, and totally unfitted for the duties of the position. The best overseers, ordinarily, are young men, the sons of small planters, who take up the business temporarily, as a means of acquiring a little capital with which to purchase negroes for themselves.

The plowing, both with single and double mule teams, was generally performed by women, and very well performed, too. I watched with some interest for any indication that their sex unfitted them for the occupation. Twenty of them were plowing together, with double teams and heavy plows. They were superintended by a male negro driver, who carried a whip, which he frequently cracked at them, permitting no dawdling or delay at the turning; and they twitched their plows around on the head-land, jerking their reins, and yelling to their mules, with apparent ease, energy, and rapidity. Throughout the Southwest the negroes, as a rule, appear to be worked much harder than in the eastern and northern slave States. I do not think they accomplish as much daily, as agricultural laborers at the North usually do, but they certainly labor much harder, and more unremittingly. They are constantly and steadily driven up to their work, and the stupid, plodding, machine-like manner in which they labor, is painful to witness. This was especially the case with the hoe-gangs. One of them numbered nearly two hundred hands (for the force of two plantations was working together), moving across the field in parallel lines, with a considerable degree of precision. I repeatedly rode through the lines at a canter, with other horsemen, often coming upon them suddenly, without producing the smallest change or interruption in the dogged action of the laborers, or causing one of them to lift an eye from the ground. A very tall and powerful negro walked to and fro in the rear of the line, frequently cracking his whip, and calling out, in the surliest manner, to one and another, "Shove your hoe, there! shove your hoe!" But I never saw him strike any one with the whip.

The whip was evidently in constant use, however. There were no rules on the subject, that I learned; the overseers and drivers punished the negroes whenever they deemed it necessary, and in such manner, and with such severity, as they thought fit. "If you don't work faster," or "If you don't work harder," or "If you don't recollect what I tell you, I will have you flogged," are threats which I have often heard.

I said to one of the overseers, "It must be very disagreeable to have to punish them as much as you do?"

"Yes, it would be to those who are not used to it—but it's my business, and I think nothing of it. Why, sir, I wouldn't mind killing a nigger more than I would a dog."

I asked if he had ever killed a negro?

"Not quite," he said, but overseers were often obliged to. Some negroes are determined never to let a white man whip them, and will resist you, when you attempt it; of course you must kill them in that case.

Once a negro whom he was punishing, insulted and threatened him. He went to the house for his gun, and as he was returning, the negro, thinking he would be afraid to spoil so valuable a piece of property by firing, broke for the woods. He fired at once, and put six buck-shot into his hips. He always carried a bowie knife, but not a pistol, unless he anticipated some unusual act of insubordination. He always kept a pair of pistols ready loaded over the mantel-piece, however, in case they should be needed.

The severest corporeal punishment of a negro that I witnessed at the South, occurred while I was visiting this estate. I suppose however, that punishment equally severe is common—in fact, it must be necessary to the maintenance of adequate discipline on every large plantation. It is necessary because the opportunities of hiding away and shirking labor, and of wasting and injuring the owner's property without danger to themselves are great, but above all, because there is no real moral obligation on the part of the negro to do what is demanded of him.

The manner of the overseer who inflicted the punishment, and his subsequent conversation with me about it, indicated that it was by no means an unusual occurrence with him. I had accidentally encountered him, as he was showing me his plantation. In going from one side of it to the other, we had twice crossed a deep gully, at the bottom of which was a thick covert of brushwood. We were crossing it a third time, and had nearly passed through the brush, when the overseer suddenly stopped his horse exclaiming, "What's that? Hallo! who are you there?"

It was a girl lying at full length on the ground at the bottom of the gully, evidently intending to hide herself from us in the bushes.

"Who are you there?"

"Sam's Sall, sir."

"What are you skulking there for?"

The girl half rose, but gave no answer.

"Have you been here all day?"

"No sir."

"How did you get here?"

The girl made no reply.

"Where have you been all day?"

The answer was unintelligible.

After some further questioning, she said her father accidently locked her in, when he went out in the morning.

"How did you manage to get out?"

"Pushed a plank off, sir, and crawled out."

The overseer was silent for a moment, looking at the girl, and then said, "That won't do—come out here." The girl arose at once, and walked toward him; she was about eighteen years of age. A bunch of keys hung to her waist, which the overseer espied, and he said, "Ah, your father locked you in; but you have got the keys."

After a little hesitation, the girl replied that these were the keys of some other locks; her father had the door-key.

Whether her story was true or false, could have been ascertained in two minutes by riding on to the gang with which her father was at work, but the overseer had made up his mind as to the facts of the case.

"That won't do," said he, "get down on your knees."

The girl knelt on the ground; he got off his horse, and holding him with his left hand, struck her thirty or forty blows across the shoulders with his tough, flexible, "raw-hide" whip. They were well laid on, as a boatswain would thrash a skulking sailor, or as some people flog a baulking horse, but with no appearance of angry excitement on the part of the overseer.

At every stroke the girl winced, and exclaimed, "Yes, sir!" or "Ah, sir!" or "Please, sir!" not groaning or screaming.

At length he stopped and said, "Now tell me the truth."

The girl repeated the same story.

"You have not got enough yet," said he, "pull up your clothes—lie down."

The girl without any hesitation, without a word or look of remonstrance or entreaty, drew closely all her garments under her shoulders, and lay down upon the ground with her face toward the overseer, who continued to flog her with the rawhide, across her naked loins and thighs, with as much strength as before. She now shrunk away from him, not rising, but writhing, groveling, and screaming, "Oh, don't, sir! oh, please stop, master! please, sir! please, sir! oh, that's enough, master! oh, Lord! oh, master, master! oh, God, master, do stop! oh, God, master! oh, God, master!"

A young gentleman of fifteen was with us; he had ridden in front, and now, turning on his horse looked back with an expression only of impatience at the delay. It was the first time I had ever seen a woman flogged. I had seen a man cudgeled and beaten, in the heat of passion, before, but never flogged with a hundredth part of the severity used in this case. I glanced again at the perfectly passionless but rather grim business-like face of the overseer, and again at the young gentleman, who had turned away; if not indifferent he had evidently not the faintest sympathy with my emotion. Only my horse chafed with excitement. I gave him rein and spur and we plunged into the bushes and scrambled fiercely up the steep acclivity. The screaming yells and the whip strokes had ceased when I reached the top of the bank. Choking, sobbing, spasmodic groans only were heard. I rode on to where the road coming diagonally up the ravine ran out upon the cotton-field. My young companion met me there, and immediately afterward the overseer. He laughed as he joined us, and said,

"She meant to cheat me out of a day's work—and she has done it, too."

"Did you succeed in getting another story from her?"

"No; she stuck to it."

"Was it not perhaps true?"

"Oh no, sir, she slipped out of the gang when they were going to work, and she's been dodging about all day, going from one place to another as she saw me coming. She saw us crossing there a little while ago, and thought we had gone to the quarters, but we turned back so quick, we came into the gully before she knew it, and she could do nothing but lie down in the bushes."

"Was it necessary to punish her so severely?"

"Oh yes, sir," (laughing again.) "If I hadn't punished her so hard she would have done the same thing again to-morrow, and half the people on the plantation would have followed her example. Oh, you've no idea how lazy these niggers are; you northern people don't know any thing about it. They'd never do any work at all if they were not afraid of being whipped."

I inquired about the increase of the negroes on the estate, and the manager having told me of deaths and births the previous year, which gave a net increase of four per cent—on Virginia estates it is often twenty per cent.—I asked if the negroes began to have children at an early age.

"Sometimes at sixteen," said the manager.

"Yes, and at fourteen," said the overseer; "that girl's had a child"—pointing to a girl that did not appear older than fourteen.

"Is she married?"

"No."

"You see," said the manager, "negro girls are not remarkable for chastity; their habits indeed rather hinder them from having children. They'd have them sooner than they do if they would marry or live with but one man, sooner than they do. They often do not have children till they are twenty-five years old."

"Are those who are married true to each other?" I asked.

The overseer laughed heartily at the idea, and described a disgustingly "Free Love" state of things.

"Do you not try to discourage this?"

"No, not unless they quarrel."

"They get jealous and quarrel among themselves sometimes about it," the manager explained, "or come to the overseer and complain, and he has them punished."

"Give all hands a damned good hiding," said the overseer.

"You punish adultery, then, but not fornication?"

"Yes," answered the manager, but "No," replied the overseer, "we punish them for quarreling; if they don't quarrel I don't mind anything about it, but if it makes a muss, I give all four of 'em a warming."

THE TEXAS GERMANS

On entering Texas we had been so ignorant as not to know that there were larger settlements of Germans there than in any other Southern State but at Austin, we learned from Governor Pease and other acquaintances familiar with our route, that we should reach, in a day or two, the German settlements, and pass through, in fact, a German village of considerable size—Neu Braunfels.

We inquired with a good deal of interest as to the condition and social relations of the Germans, and learned, from the same sources, that the great part of them were exceedingly poor, but that, as a body, they were thriving. As to slavery, as fast as they acquired property, they followed the customs of the country and purchased slaves, like other white people. However, no one could give us any precise information about the Germans, and we had not the least idea that they were so numerous, and had so important a position in Western Texas, until we reached them, a day or two after this.

The country, next morning, continued the same in all respects as that of the day before. The first German settlers we saw, we knew at once. They lived in little log cabins, and had inclosures of ten acres of land about them. The cabins were very simple and cheap habitations, but there were many little conveniences about them, and a care to secure comfort in small ways evident, that was very agreeable to notice. So, also, the greater variety of the crops which had been grown upon their allotments, and the more clean and complete tillage they had received contrasted favorably with the patches of corn-stubble, overgrown with crab-grass, which are usually the only gardens to be seen adjoining the cabins of the poor whites and slaves. The people themselves were also to be seen, men, women, and childrn, busy at some work, and yet not so busy but that they could give a pleasant and respectful greeting to the passing traveler.

A few miles further on, we passed several much more comfortable houses, boarded over, and a good deal like the smaller class of farm-houses in New England, but some of them having exterior plaster-work, or brick, laid up between the timbers, instead of boards nailed over them. About these were large enclosures, from which extensive crops of corn had been taken; and it caused us a sensation to see a number of parallelograms of COTTON—FREE-LABOR COTTON. These were not often of more than an acre in extent. Most of them looked as if they had been judiciously cultivated, and had yielded a fine crop, differing, however, from that we had noticed on the plantations the day before, in this circumstance—the picking had been entirely completed, and that with care and exactness, so that none of the cotton, which the labor of cultivation had produced, had been left to waste.

We were entering the valley of the Guadalupe river, which is of the same general character as that of the San Marcos, and had passed a small brown house with a turret and cross upon it, which we learned was a Lutheran church, when we were overtaken by a good-natured butcher, who lived in Neu-Braunfels, whence he had ridden out early in the morning to kill and dress the hogs of one of the large farmers. He had finished his job, and was returning.

He had been in this country eight years. He liked it very much; he did not wish to go back to Germany; he much preferred to remain here. The Germans, generally, were doing well, and were contented. They had had a hard time at first, but they were all doing well now—getting rich. He knew but one German who had bought a slave; they did not think well of slavery; they thought it better that all men should be free; besides, the negroes would not work so well as the Germans. They were improving their condition very rapidly, especially within the last two years. It was sickly on the coast, but here it was very healthy. He had been as well here as he was in Germany— never had been ill. There were Catholics and Protestants among them; as for himself, he was no friend to priests, whether Catholic or Protestant. He had had enough of them in Germany. They could not tell him anything new, and he never went to any church.

We had still nearly a mile to ride before entering the town, and in this distance met eight or ten large wagons, each drawn by three or four pairs of mules, or five or six yokes of oxen, each carrying under its neck a brass bell. They were all driven by Germans, somewhat uncouthly but warmly and neatly dressed; all smoking and all good-humored, giving us "good morning" as we met. Noticing the strength of the wagons, I observed that they were made by Germans, probably.

"Yes," said the butcher, "the Germans make better wagons than the Americans; the Americans buy a great many of them. *There are seven wagon-manufactories in Braunfels.*"

The main street of Neu-Braunfels, which we soon entered upon, was very wide—three times as wide, in effect, as Broadway in New York. The houses, with which it was thickly lined on each side for a mile, were small, low cottages, of no pretensions to elegance, yet generally looking neat and comfortable. Many were furnished with verandahs and gardens, and the greater part were either stuccoed or painted. There were many workshops of mechanics and small stores, with signs oftener in English than in German; and bare-headed women, and men in caps and short jackets, with pendent pipes, were everywhere seen at work.

We had no acquaintance in the village, and no means of introduction, but, in hopes that we might better satisfy ourselves of the condition of the people, we agreed to stop at an inn and get dinner, instead of eating a cold snack in the saddle, without stopping at noon, as was our custom. "Here," said the butcher, "is my shop—indicating a small house, at the door of which hung dressed meat and beef sausages—and if you are going to stop, I will recommend you to my neighbor, there, Mr. Schmitz." It was a small cottage of a single story, having the roof extended so as to form a verandah, with a sign swinging before it, "Guadalupe Hotel, J. Schmitz."

I never in my life, except, perhaps, in awakening from a dream, met with such a sudden and complete transfer of associations. Instead of loose boarded or hewn log walls, with crevices stuffed with rags or daubed with mortar, which we have been accustomed to see during the last month, on staving in a door, where we have found any to open; instead, even, of four bare, cheerless sides of whitewashed plaster, which we have found twice or thrice only in a more aristocratic American residence, we were—in short, we were in Germany.

There was nothing wanting; there was nothing too much, for one of those delightful little inns which the pedestrian who has tramped through the Rhine land will ever remember gratefully. A long room, extending across the whole front of the cottage, the walls pink, with stenciled panels, and scroll ornaments in crimson, and with neatly-framed and glazed pretty lithographic prints hanging on all sides; a long, thick, dark oak table, with rounded ends, oak benches at its sides; chiseled oak chairs; a sofa, covered with cheap pink calico, with a small vine pattern; a stove in the corner; a little mahogany cupboard in another corner, with pitcher and glasses upon it; a smoky atmosphere; and finally, four thick-bearded men, from whom the smoke proceeds, who all bow and say "Good morning," as we lift our hats in the doorway.

The landlady enters; she does not readily understand us, and one of the smokers rises immediately to assist us. Dinner we shall have immediately, and she spreads the white cloth at an end of the table, before she leaves the room, and in two minutes' time, by which we have got off our coats and warmed our hands at the stove, we are asked to sit down. An excellent soup is set before us, and in succession there follow two courses of meat, neither of them pork, and neither of them fried, two dishes of vegetables, salad, compote of peaches, coffee with milk, wheat bread from the loaf, and beautiful and sweet butter—not only such butter as I have never tasted south of the Potomac before, but such as I have been told a hundred times it was impossible to make in a southern climate. What is the secret? I suppose it is extreme cleanliness, beginning far back of where cleanliness usually begins at the South, and careful and thorough *working*.

We then spent an hour in conversation with the gentlemen who were in the room. They were all educated, cultivated, well-bred, respectful, kind, and affable men. All were natives of Germany, and had been living several years in Texas. Some of them were travelers, their homes being in other German settlements; some of them had resided long at Braunfels.

It was so very agreeable to meet such men again, and the account they gave of the Germans in Texas was so interesting and gratifying, that we were unwilling to immediately continue our journey. We went out to look at our horses; a man in cap and jacket was rubbing their legs—the first time they had received such attention in Texas, except from ourselves, or by special and costly arrangement with a negro. They were pushing their noses into racks filled with fine mesquit hay—the first they had had in Texas. They seemed to look at us imploringly. We ought to spend the night. But there is evidently no sleeping room for us in the little inn. They must be full. But then we could sleep with more comfort on the floor here, probably, than we have been accustomed to of late. We concluded to ask if they could accommodate us for the night. Yes, with pleasure—would we be pleased to look at the room they could afford us? Doubtless in the cock-loft. No, it was another little cottage in the rear. A little room it proved, with blue walls again, and oak furniture; two beds, one of them would be for each of us— the first time we had been offered the luxury of sleeping alone in Texas; two large windows with curtains, and evergreen roses trained over them on the outside—not a pane of glass missing or broken—the first sleeping room we have had in Texas where this was the case; a sofa; a bureau, on which were a complete set of the *Conversations Lexicon;* Kendall's Santa Fé Expedition; a statuette in porcelain; plants in pots; a brass study lamp; a large ewer and basin for washing, and a couple of towels of thick stuff, full a yard and a quarter long. O, yes, it will do for us admirably; we will spend the night.

In the afternoon we called upon the German Protestant clergyman, who received us kindly, and, though speaking little English, was very ready to give all the information he could about his people, and the Germans in Texas generally. We visited some of the workshops, and called on a merchant to ascertain the quality and amount of the cotton grown by the Germans in the neighborhood. At supper, we met a dozen or more intelligent people, and spent the later evening, with several others, at the residence of one of our accidental inn acquaintances.

I will simply remark here, that the facts learned from these gentlemen, confirmed the simple good accounts of the butcher.

As I was returning to the inn, about ten o'clock, I stopped for a few moments at the gate of one of the little cottages, to listen to some of the best singing I have heard for a long time, several parts being sustained by very sweet and well-trained voices.

In the day time, I saw in the public street, at no great distance from a school-house, a tame doe, with a band on its neck, to distinguish it from the wild deer, lest it should be shot by sportsmen. It was exceedingly beautiful, and so tame that it allowed me to approach, and licked my hand. In what Texan town, through which we have passed before, could this have occurred.

In the morning we found that our horses had been bedded, for the first time in Texas.

It was delightful to meet again troops of children, with satchels and knapsacks of books, and little kettles of dinner, all with ruddy, cheerful faces, the girls especially so, with their hair braided neatly, and without caps or bonnets, smiling and saluting us—*"guten morgen"* as we met. Nothing so pleasant as that in Texas before, hardly in the South.

We now took pains to obtain some definite facts with regard to (Neu-Braunfel's) condition. The dwellings in general are small and humble in appearance, but weather-tight, and, generally, provided with galleries or verandahs, and with glazed casement windows. In the latter respect, they have the advantage over most houses we have seen in Texas, and, I have no doubt, the average comforts of life within are much greater than among the Anglo-Americans, generally, in the state.

The citizens are, however, nearly all men of very small capital. Half the men now residing in Neu-Braunfels and its vicinity, are probably agricultural laborers, or farmers, who themselves follow the plough. The majority of the latter do not, I think, own more than ten acres of land each. Within the town itself, there are master-mechanics, all of whom employ several workmen.

There are four grist-mills, and a couple of New-England men are building a sash and blind factory, and propose erecting a cotton factory.

A weekly newspaper is published—the *Neu-Braunfels Zeitung*. It is a paper of much higher character than most of the German American papers, edited by the naturalist, Lindheimer.

There are ten or twelve stores and small tradesmen's shops, two or three apothecaries, and as many physicians, lawyers, and clergymen. I do not think there is another town in the slave states in which the proportion to the whole population of mechanics, or of persons employed in the exercise of their own discretion in productive occupations, is one-quarter as large as in Neu-Braunfels, unless it be some other in which the Germans are the predominating race.

There are several organizations among the people which indicate an excellent spirit of social improvement: an Agricultural Society, a Mechanics' Institute, a Harmonic Society, a Society for Political Debates, and a "Turners'" Society. A horticultural club has expended $1,200 in one year in introducing trees and plants.

These associations are the evidence of an active intellectual life, and desire for knowledge and improvement among the masses of the people, like that which distinguishes the New-Englanders, and which is unknown wherever slavery degrades labor. Will this spirit resist the progress of slavery westward, or must it be gradually lost as the community in which it now exists becomes familiar with slavery?

In Neu-Braunfels and the surrounding German hamlets, there are five free schools for elementary education, one exclusive Roman Catholic school, a town free school of higher grades, and a private classical school. In *all* of these schools English is taught with German. The teacher of the higher department of the central town school is paid four hundred dollars a year; that of the primary department (a female), two hundred dollars.

In Neu-Braunfels and the immediate vicinity are living about three thousand Germans. The Anglo-American population of the place does not exceed twenty. Just out of the town a wealthy planter has settled, who holds one hundred negroes. He also owns a mill and water-power, and a good deal of real estate. Another American, living in the town, owns a negro girl, and one negro girl is hired by one of the Germans as a domestic. There are no other negroes in the town. The blacks of the plantation, we were told, had acquired the power of speaking in German in an extremely short time after their arrival.

Sunday was observed more thoroughly as a day of rest from labor than we had seen in any town in Texas. The stores, except one kept by a New-Englander, were closed during the day. The people who appeared in the streets were well dressed, quiet, and orderly. We saw no drunkenness. In the evening there were amusements, among them a ball, which the Lutheran pastor was expected to attend.

The health of the town is good. For several years there has been no epidemic of illness. The greater part of those of whom I made inquiry assured me their health had been better here than in Germany.

22

The Pleasures of Southern Society, 1856

The span of John Milton Mackie's life extends from 1813 to 1894. He was born in Wareham, Massachusetts, graduated from Brown University, and, after study in Berlin, taught at Brown for some years. He wrote at least four biographies, the best of which is a Life of von Leibnitz *(1845); a travel book,* Cosas de España, or Going to Madrid *(1848); and* From Cape Cod to Dixie. *This last of his works is a record of certain aspects of southern life—and the West Indies—from impressions gained in a tour just before the Civil War, though the book was not published until 1864. The account pretends to no profundities and admittedly surveys only the lighter and more superficial aspects which would normally come under the observations of a hasty traveler. Yet it possesses a certain humor and lightness of touch and recaptures the ante bellum South in its more genial aspects.*

A FASHIONABLE VIRGINIA PLEASURE RESORT

In the height of the season, there are a hundred arrivals a day at the White Sulphur Springs. Then, when nobody can get accommodations, everybody will insist on being there; for, in the month of August, the most beautiful ladies of Virginia and the South hold their court of love at this fountain; and, their fame going abroad through the mountains, the guests of the other Springs hasten to this centre of attraction. All the generals and judges of the Southern country, too, then come to drink at these waters. Nobody is of a lower grade than a colonel; and, to be called esquire, would argue a man of doubtful consideration.

But not even the being addressed by the very highest titles, will, at this part of the season, save a single man the necessity of sleeping—two in a chamber. There are no adequate accommodations for all these fine ladies and gentlemen. At night, the floors of drawing rooms and parlors are strewn with mattresses; and lucky is the guest who can secure one. Trunks are piled up, ceiling high, in the halls and passages; so that, excepting the fortunate inmates of the pretty private cottages, the thousand and one visitors are, of all men, by no means the most miserable, but probably, the most uncomfortable.

One August morning, as I was standing in the doorway of the office, a well-dressed gentleman drove up in a buggy, and, getting out, asked for a room.

"We cannot accommodate you, sir," said the clerk, looking at the stranger with an air of disinterested unconcern.

"But you can give me a mattress, or a sofa?" was the confident rejoinder.

"Impossible! not one left; and the last three chairs in the house taken half an hour ago!"

"Boy," said the rejected, but not disconcerted new comer, turning his quid from one cheek to the other, at the same time that he turned on his heel toward a servant, "unstrap my trunk."

"It really is of no use, sir," continued the clerk, calmly; "we cannot accommodate you."

"Carry my trunk under that oak tree, yonder," no less quietly added the stranger, and still addressing the black boy.

"Now," said he, sitting down on the trunk, which had been deposited under the protection of the branches, "fetch my buffalo robe; and I'll be d——d if I can't sleep here!"

This proof of pluck was an indirect appeal to the generous and hospitable sentiments which no true Virginian could withstand. There was a general clapping of hands on the utterance of this Diogenic resolution to take things as they came, and the luck of the pot with them; and one of the bystanders immediately stepping forward, politely offered to share his quarters with the tenant of the buffalo robe, who, accordingly, instead of living under an oak, like a Druid, now found himself the fortunate possessor of an apartment in one of the prettiest cottages on the grounds.

In the very height of the season there is no such thing as dining satisfactorily at some of the Springs, however well a person may fare there at all other times. Then, you fee the waiters, and still they bring you nothing. Poor fellows, they have nothing to bring! for the flour has given out; the cows have been milked dry; the mutton has run off into the mountains; and the chief cook has gone distracted! If you can manage to seize upon a bit of beef, and a slice of bread, 'tis your main chance, and hold on to it. Do not run any risks in looking about for vegetables, much less for side dishes, or pepper, or salt. For, while you are vainly endeavoring to accomplish impossibilities, some light-fingered waiter, under the pretence of changing your plate, will run off with your only chance of a dinner.

The scene presents a most ludicrous struggle for bones, and cold potatoes. Or, rather, it is fearful to witness such a desperate handling of the knife; to see so many faces red with rage at getting nothing; and ladies' cheeks pale with waiting; and starving gourmands looking stupefied into the vacuum of the platters before them; and disappointed dyspeptics leaving the table with an expression on their faces of "I'll go hang myself." Add, besides, to what one sees, that which he hears—the maledictions heaped liberally upon the heads of cook, and provider; the clatter of what knives and forks succeed in getting brought into action; the whistling and roaring of Sambo, and the rattling of his heels; with, now and then, an awful crash of chinaware, a slide of plates, or an avalanche of whips and custards; for, where there are several dozens of waiters running up and down the hall, like race horses, there must be occasional collisions; and these, again, lead to fights, at least once, or more, in the season, when a couple of strapping black boys knock each other's noses flatter, and make their mutual wool fly. Truly, the Frenchman who dines on the hair of his mustache, and the end of his toothpick, in front of the *Café de Paris,* is a lucky fellow, and has something under his jacket, compared with these boarders at two dollars per diem.

But it is still worse dining, when it rains. The ancient roofs of some of these halls and piazzas are not made of caoutchouc; and you cannot then sit at meat without two black boys at your back—one to keep off the flies, and the other to hold over your head an umbrella. There is a good excuse for the soup being thin on such days. 'Tis, in fact, mere rain water, with, possibly, a fly, or two, in it.

All the doctors lay down the rule, that the patient must drink mineral waters on an empty stomach; and, by my troth, it is easy following it, during the height of the season, at some of these Springs. That organ is rarely so much occupied in its legitimate business as to be in an unfit state to receive a glass from the fountain. It is said that Chinamen, when hard pushed for other articles of food, can subsist tolerably well on water diet; and, in spending the month of August here, one comes gradually to comprehend how the thing can be done.

Still, one likes to be at the fashionable Springs when the crowd is greatest. The more colonels, the better. The more pretty ladies, the gayer. He wants to talk upon politics with all the judges; attack or defend Sebastopol with all the generals; dance attendance on all the well-bred dames, and waltz with all their daughters. Half the pleasure is in the excitement which proceeds from the great number of persons collected together. Let the fashionable crowd dwindle down to a few dozens, and you leave also. Then you can have an entire suite of rooms, and excellent dinners, with a waiter at each elbow. But, no. When you see the trunks brought down, and hear the farewells said, you are as homesick as anybody, and crowd into the ninth place in the coach, rather than run the risk of being the last man to leave the mountains. So unreasonable are we all.

As for amusements here, do they not consist in drinking the waters, bathing, and, three times a day, supplying the wants of nature by vigorous efforts with the trencher? A few persons bring their books with them as an additional source of entertainment; but most are satisfied with occasionally looking through a newspaper, a magazine, or some learned treatise that may be lying about, on the use of mineral waters. The gentlemen sit half the morning through in easy, wicker-bottom chairs, under the trees, conversing on the subject of politics, estimating the amount of the cotton and rice crops, smoking cigars, drinking juleps, commenting on a passing lady, a horse, or a stage coach. Rarely does a Virginian propose a walk. He prefers to sit, two hours together, beneath the shade. An active, inquisitive Yankee will go out, and explore a mountain, or look at a neighboring farm, and, returning, find the Southerner in the seat where he left him. An alligator in the State from which he comes, would not lie on a log longer. The Northern-born man, rising, perhaps, not much later than the sun, racing up hill and down to get what he calls a little exercise, climbing the pathless mountains for views of the scenery, and scouring the valley without any purpose whatever, unless it be the getting rid of half a day he knows not what to do with, is thought by him of the *terra caliente* a sort of madcap, flibbertigibbet, a personification of unreason. The latter will make as much effort as may be necessary to back a horse; if there is game, he will occasionally go out with dog and gun; and, in a few instances, I have seen him wet a line for trout, or it might have been catfish. At tenpins, and at billiards, also, he will play. But, on the whole, it is an axiom with him, that too much exercise, as well as too much learning, will make a man mad. He, therefore, disparages both.

For any man living on the sunny side of the Union, to do nothing seems to be no labor; and he kills his time, apparently, without the pains of giving it a thought. After a while, indeed, all the visitors at these Springs learn more or less of the art of getting through the summer day easily. One begins with taking no note of the hour of the day, then lets his watch run down, and finally forgets the day of the week, and the month—all being alike, save Sunday. The morning papers he has ordered from town, come to hand several days old, and with such irregularity that, generally, the contradiction of the news arrives before the news itself; so that, at last, he comes to the conclusion that at the end of the watering season nothing of importance will have happened, and he sets his mind at rest.

As for the ladies, without knowing all the little ways they have of amusing themselves, one sees in their sweet faces that they are happy. They are, also, the cause of by far the greater part of the happiness there is in these watering places. If, by any strange fatality, the air of the Alleghanies should become fatal to ringlets, and the mineral waters wash the red out of the peach in the cheek, how soon would all these fair scenes revert to the original savages! But, fortunately, while woman lends a portion of her grace to the mountains, the grateful rocks repay the gift by endowing her with powers of enchantment superior even to those of old conferred on the Medea of the Caucasus. In the eyes of some man or other, every lady here is an enchantress. Scarcely was there a young man in the mountains, during the two seasons I spent there, who did not seem, at times, to be under the influence of illusions, more or less soft and roseate. Even my boy, Custopol, was obliged to confess to me, one day, that when, on the preceding Saturday night, Mary Jane came out in her yellow skirt and green bodice with a basque to it, a purple kerchief twisted round her braided hair, on her feet red morocco slippers, and gold drops pendent from her ears; and when he put his arm around her waist, and they went down the boards together, while Pompey, in the corner, "picked" his banjo, and all the "darkeys" in the place stood up and down the kitchen; and when Mary Jane, turning softly up her eyes, let him look by the half minute together into the whites of them; or, dancing round, poked her elbow in his ribs, and, grinning, pulled his whisker—even Custy was obliged to confess that he felt the tender passion.

Love-making, therefore, may fairly be set down as one of the amusements of the Virginia Springs; whether it turn out to be really diverting to the parties concerned—*cela dépend*.

Another source of pleasure upon which none of the guests can refrain from relying, more or less, is the arrival of the stage coach. Let it happen however often in the day, it is still an important event. One expects his friends; or, if not, somebody may come he has met before; at any rate he must see who is there.

Down gets the first gentleman from the coach. He is tall, with a large proportion of bone in him, and only a moderate supply of muscle. His rather long brown hair is brushed, like a Methodist minister's, off his forehead, which is a high one, but not broad. The well-tanned face indicates vigorous health, though a little sulphur water will be no disadvantage to the owner's liver. The air of calm self-possession marks the man accustomed to command; while the slow gait and quiet motions suggest the habit of overseeing work instead of performing it. The blue dress coat with brass buttons, which is neither old nor new, together with light-colored pantaloons, black satin vest, dark silk cravat, and broad-brimmed felt hat, belong evidently to a gentleman somewhat careless of personal appearance, but of independent circumstances; in short, it requires no epaulettes to convince you at a glance that the stranger is a colonel from one of the eastern counties of Virginia.

When his luggage is taken down, you will find that it consists of a leather trunk covered with small brass knobs and marked with the owner's name, in full, together with those of his county and State; on the top of it is strapped a heavy overcoat, while at one end dangle an extra pair of boots. The colonel travels without a hatbox; but has, instead, a well-worn pair of saddle bags, which are filled with the smaller articles of his wardrobe and such "traps" as he may very likely want on the journey.

On acquaintance, he proves to be a man of good plain sense, who belongs to what he denominates the Jeffersonian party in politics, tills the paternal acres very much after the fashion of his father before him, has, generally, a suit or two pending in the courts of law, but is as goodnatured as he is highminded, and really hates nobody. Once introduced, he will ask you to take a julep with him.

The general moves in more state; he arrives in his own coach and two, or even four—for this old-fashioned turnout has not yet entirely disappeared in the progress of civilization and the rail. He may, also, have two or three outriders, in the shape of sons, on ponies, and black boys riding mares. Sons, servants, mares and horses, they are all of his own raising; but the carriage, possibly, may have belonged to his father or some of his ancestors; for it is after the ancient English model, round topped, heavily timbered, and possessing the property, like Homer's heroes, of never growing old. The trunks being piled up behind, and to them attached a water pail, the footman is obliged to squeeze himself into what of the narrow seat in front is left by the driver.

When this whole affair sweeps up to the door of the hotel, the excited landlord, especially if it be a four-in-hand, rings his bell with a fury which indicates that something extraordinary has happened; and the servants come running, as if they expected to witness the arrival of a dozen stage coaches at once. But 'tis even more than that; 'tis a Virginian general, with horses and mares, black boys and maids, wife and children. The hair of every waiter in the house would stand straight on end, but for the curl in it!

The landlord opens the carriage door himself, hat in hand; and the general gets out. He is a shorter man than the colonel by a half inch, or more. He has a broader and still more open face, a wider back, and carries a respectable corporation before him. His clothes are thin, the colors light, and his face is red; while down out of his fob hangs a heavy gold chain, with two ponderous, ancestral seals, and a key between. The general takes off his white beaver courteously to the colonel, who instantly steps forward to shake him by the hand.

While these congratulations are being exchanged, down the carriage steps carefully comes Dinah. She is dressed mostly in white, and has a cotton kerchief of this color, striped with blue, tied so completely over her hair, that only enough of it remains in sight to show that it is becoming silvered o'er with the pale cast of age; while, over the kerchief and directly on the back of her head, is set a bonnet of open straw and muslin, originally made for the general's pretty daughter when she entered her teens, and so small, withal, that it serves merely to cover the good dame's cerebellum.

The baby is then handed out to Dinah; the rest follow; and when the trunks have been taken down, and the carriage pockets emptied, Cuffy, the coachman, effects his exit with a crack of the whip, such as makes not only his own horses, but all those within an eighth of a mile, jump—each one as though it were about his own ears the lash was playing.

And when, any time within the next half hour, the respectable Virginia farmer, or esquire, well-to-do at home, rides up to the hotel door on his nag, a greatcoat rolled up and tied, together with an umbrella, behind the saddle, and a pair of leathern bags, containing a scanty change of apparel, projecting beneath his thighs, the careless landlord scarcely deigns to touch the bell once. A sleepy-looking negro holds the new comer's bridle while he dismounts; another, lazily taking the saddle bags on his shoulders, and the roll under his arm, conducts him to his chamber; and there is no more noise made over the arrival, compared with the previous excitement, than might be likened to the blowing of a horn reversed.

The springs are of all waters, having for their principal ingredients sulphur, alum, iron, magnesia, or salt. They are also tri-colored, with deposits, white, red, and blue. Some are used for drinking, and some for bathing. The invalid may have his choice; and whatever his complaint, say the doctors, it makes no difference—he is sure to be cured. The cripple is set up at the Hot Springs, and the *malade imaginaire* is made whole at the Warm. The dyspeptic is put on alum water, and the Southwesterner, with bile in his blood and jaundice in his eyes, is ordered to drink of the White Sulphur or the Salt. The Healing Spring is good for the gout; ladies, weary after the winter's dancing, are strengthened by bathing in the two Sweet Waters; the Blue Sulphur, taken before eating venison steaks, is said to be excellent against all devils of the same color; and ever since the publication of the learned Dr. Burke's book, it is every man's own fault if he don't know that the Red Sulphur is a certain cure for consumption.

CHARLESTON BEFORE THE WAR

First of all I went to the races. For I had begun to hear the February races in Charleston talked of as far north as Washington, and had been told much of the fine horses, much of the beautiful women, who, in *grande toilette,* grace these festive occasions. Unfortunately, the twelve of February brought with it gentle showers of rain; but, heavy as was the course, I had rarely seen in the States better running. The horses were ridden by slips of black boys, whom, at first sight, I thought scarcely equal to the task, but who, in the end, proved themselves to be born Jehus. Like the steeds, they must have been bred specially for the race course.

As to the ladies, they were not to be cheated out of their holiday by rain. They were there in full feather; in ermine and point lace; in the light brocades and cashmeres of India. They were there in the latest *nouveautés;* gay with flowers and graceful with fringes, as well as in perfect little loves of parasols, and fans fluttering with coquetry. One or two dowagers sported their diamonds and jewels more appropriate to the ballroom. Nearly all, as it seemed to me, were rather over-dressed for the occasion; though, as it is the fashion of the Charlestonians to put on new bonnets for the February races, as the Philadelphians do at Easter, perhaps the temptation to make too much of the toilet at this time might well be irresistible. Still, bright colors do not harmonize with dark skies. But at the Charleston race course, nothing was gorgeous save the silks and ribbons; for, while heavens of lead overhung an earth scarcely yet green, even the cheeks of the fair were pale, and their eyes lacked lustre. They were, however, sufficiently pretty and high-bred.

The lords of this part of creation, likewise, were tall and fine-looking; though it struck me that their easy morning costumes, if adapted to the occasion, were not quite in harmony with the elaborate toilets of the other sex. Certain it is, that the tip-top beaux were generally dressed in overcoats, sacks, raglans, sticks, and umbrellas. I could but think, also, that many of them carried a trifle too much weight in the watch chain, and, in some instances, selected their waistcoats of a crimson slightly too emphatic for the black of their pantaloons. But, on the whole, the crowd of clubmen were well attired; and I did not see among them a single specimen of the black-satin vest gentry.

For the rest, considering that ladies came to the race in full dress, I was a little surprised at seeing that the floor of the saloon wherein they were assembled was, in places, wet with tobacco juice,[1] and sprinkled with nutshells. Lads, whose bringing up in the best families of the town should have taught them better, threw the shells on the floor as unceremoniously as if they had been in a beer garden. Even a lady arrayed in ermine, and deep frills of Chantilly lace, who was holding court, at the moment, consisting of four gentlemen, all in waxed mustaches, suffered two out of four to stand in her presence munching peanuts.

With few exceptions, the elegantly arrayed ladies present to witness the running, and receive the admiration of the handsome members of the Jockey Club, were unmarried; the presence of a somewhat larger number of matrons would have imparted a little more dignity to the festivity, without detracting too much from its grace.

To return to town. My first impression of Charleston was extremely agreeable. It was pleasant to find an American city not wearing the appearance of having all been built yesterday. The atmosphere, charged with an unusual dampness in consequence of the low position of the town on coast and river bank, helps materially to deepen the marks of years; soon discoloring the paint upon the house and facilitating the progress of the green moss, which here is ever creeping over the northern side of roofs and walls. The whole town looks picturesquely dingy, and the greater number of buildings have assumed something of the appearance of European antiquity. The

1. [Chewing and spitting tobacco was widely commented on. Mackie, a few weeks earlier, when visiting the White House, observed:

"But what is this I see before me at the threshold? Is it a spittoon? By my troth, an enormous one! A perfect monster in capacity, suggestive of quids of the very largest size, and a great many of them. A gentle hint, this, no doubt, to the stranger just arrived from Texas, or the Upper Mississippi, that he will please unpack his cheek before coming into the presence of democratic Majesty.

"But here are more spittoons in the anteroom! It would seem, then, that it is not expected that the American people, on coming to pay their respects to their chief upper servant, should for a moment relinquish their right to chew tobacco whenever and wherever it may please them; and they are accordingly provided with conveniences for expectoration within five-and-forty feet of the foot of the throne. This is as it should be—and strongly democratic. If there be anything wrong about it, it is, perhaps, that there are not vessels of this kind enough to supply the demand for them; and I would most respectfully suggest that the principal avenue to the White House should be lined with rows of them, as the approaches to European palaces are set out with rare plants and flowers."—Ed.]

heavy brick walls and the high gateways are such as one sees in London or Paris. Many front doors and piazzas had been wrought after the graceful models brought from England in the old colonial period. The verandas, story above story, and generally looking toward the south, or the sea, form another pleasant feature in the prevailing style of building. Nor less attractive are the gardens and courtyards invariably attached to the best houses, where, in winter, the hedges are green with pitosporum and the dwarf orange; and where blow the first fragrant violets and daffodils of spring. Here, in February, I beheld with delight the open rose, and camellias so numerous as to redden the ground they fell upon; also, the wild orange bursting with white buds, and the peach tree in full blossom, as well as the humble strawberry at its foot. Stopping at one of these lofty gateways, and looking through the quaint, old-fashioned gratings, I could not help repeating the lines of Goethe

> Ein sanfter Wind vom blauen Himmel weht,   10
> Die Myrte still und hoch der Lorber steht.

These charming gardens, in connection with the piazzas resting on ornamental pillars, make the whole town graceful. One sits, in the morning, in these open chambers, inhaling the refreshing air from the sea, its perfume mingled with that of the flowers below; and, at midday, closing the Venetian shutters to exclude the sun, he rests in grateful shade. Here, too, throughout the longer portion of the year, may be spread, at evening, the tea table; while the heavens still glow with the purple and amber of the sunset. And here lingers the family until the bells from the tower of St. Michael's, sweetly ringing their silver chimes through the calm, starry air, announce, at last, the hour of repose.

Many invalids from the North, delighted with these Southern balconies and these melodious evening bells, with this soft air and genial sunshine, with the lovely promenade of the ever grass-green Battery, and with the pleasing prospect of the bay, never the same with its coming and going ships, are tempted to linger here the winter through, nor go farther southward in their search for health or pleasure. But the climate of Charleston, if soft—soft, even, as that of Rome—is damp, and exceedingly variable. The consumptive invalid, therefore, should never dally long with these sea breezes, nor stay to pluck these flowers. He should proceed onward as far as St. Augustine, or inland to the dry, sandy hill country.

In winter, many of the wealthy South Carolinian planters come to Charleston to enjoy the gay season of February; and a few spend several months here for the sake of the greater advantages in educating their children. But all come to town with less parade than did the grand seigneurs of the generation preceding. For a quarter of a century, the number of coaches and four has been gradually diminishing. Fewer outriders herald the planter's advance. The family carriage has grown a little rickety, and the worse for wear; though the horses are still well blooded, and Sambo holds the reins with cheeks as full, and shoulders as widely spreading. Comparatively few are the masters who nowadays pass through the country with a retinue of from fifteen to twenty servants; who, at a wedding, or other festive oc-

STAGE COACH AND TEAM

casion, open wide their doors to all comers, entertaining troops of friends, twoscore and more, with for every one a couch, as well as for every one a month's welcome. Fiddling, indeed, has not died out; and Pompey still draws his bow, and beats his banjo with as much ardor as in the days of yore. At the merry-makings, there is dancing every night in the parlor, as well as plenty of giggling and roaring in the kitchen. Five-and-twenty varieties of corn cake may be served at breakfast; the pot of hominy, like the widow's cruse, is inexhaustible; the bacon makes the table groan; though certainly the number of pipes of wine annually laid down is getting every year less; nor do I believe there can be many nabobs left, who, in purchasing their supplies in town at the beginning of the season, do not fail to include a hogshead of caster oil for their little negroes.

The February balls in Charleston are scarcely less known to fame than the races. The most select and fashionable are those of the Saint Cecilian, and they have been given here from times running back past the memory of all the dancers now living. Only the gentry and the more favored strangers are admitted. They go at ten o'clock, and stay until three. The attendance, however, is principally confined to the younger portion of the fashionable community, who, before setting off for the dance, see the mammas and papas comfortably to bed. I observed that even the young married ladies attracted but little attention from the beaux; and, in fact, I was repeatedly told, that whenever a bride was led to the altar, she, afterward, went in society, as a matter of course, to the wall. Even the bride, who comes from other parts of the country to find in this hospitable city a home, runs imminent risk of receiving but few marks of courtesy from any gentleman not married. She may be beautiful, accomplished, and elegantly dressed; but the beaux will look at her, if they deign to look at her at all, with blank, mute admiration. This, in a city so famed as Charleston is for gallantry of manners, struck me as a little singular. I saw many fair young ladies among the dancers, and the prevailing style of toilet was characterized by simplicity as well as elegance. Some waltzing, also, I noticed, as graceful as that which may be seen in the countries where the waltz is at home. Of flowers, however, whether as an ornament for the person, or the apartments, there were quite too few; and it seemed as though the profusion with which nature, in the more genial seasons of the year, furnishes these decorations, had led to the neglect of their cultivation by artificial means in winter.

From the presence of two races, the streets of Charleston have a pepper-and-salt aspect. The blacks are almost as numerous as the whites, but are generally of smaller stature. I saw very few slaves, either male or female, who were of large size; still fewer who were good-looking. As an exception, however, in the matter of size, I noticed one portly dame striding down the street in broad-brimmed hat, and staff, who appropriated to her own use nearly the whole of the sidewalk, and swaggered with an importance which plainly marked her as having authority in the kitchen of one of the proudest families of Charleston. On Sunday, the negroes I saw airing themselves on their way to church appeared to good advantage, being respectful in manners, and, for the most part, becomingly plain in dress. The aged dames were in turbans containing only a few modest stripes, though worn pretty high. The younger damsels showed, of course, more love for dressing like white folks. One dainty miss, with large, liquid eyes, and the deep red breaking through her colored cheek, like the vermilion streaming through dark clouds that lie athwart the sunset, made herself gay in a French cashmere; another displayed her jaunty modesty in Canton crape; while the principal colored belle of the promenade held up her rich black silk to exhibit an elaborately embroidered petticoat. The other sex were decently clad, and scarcely in a single instance that came under my observation, grotesquely. They showed, occasionally, a little red in their cravats—sometimes a little buff. But not even on the coach box did Pompey go much beyond a brass buckle in his hat, and purple plush in his waistcoat. On the whole, therefore, the colored palmetto gentry seemed to me to have learned demureness from their betters; though there was, perhaps, as much grinning and giggling as was decent on a Sunday.

It was but a sorry entertainment to visit the slave market; yet, one fine morning, attracted by the auctioneer's flag, I dropped in. There was but one small lot on the block, evidently a badly damaged lot of merchandise; and I did not hear a single bid for them. One old woman, however, by trade a cook, was put up for sale separately. She was, at the time, half seas over, and might very likely have been thus exposed by her master for the sake of frightening her into better behavior. But, if such had been the purpose, the failure of the experiment was complete; for, when she saw that not a single bid was made for such a sinner, she exclaimed, with a prodigiously broad leer of satisfaction, "Nobody want dis ole nigger? Well, I goes back to massa."

We passed along the Battery, the principal promenade of the Charlestonians, and a truly beautiful one. Two rivers, the Cooper and the Ashley, flow past it into the bay, which here spreads out to view a pleasant expanse of waters. Almost entirely landlocked, the Palmetto Islands bound it on the south; to the eastward project into the water the two salient points of Forts Sumter and Moultrie; while in the west, when I first saw it, lay diffused over all the beautiful tints of the sunset. And, night after night, as I returned to the Battery at that hour, the sky was ever aglow with the same hues of purple and salmon color, of saffron, rose, and green. On the first evening, too, the full moon, rising above the eastern horizon, scattered innumerable sparkling points of light in a line across the dancing waves, laying a necklace of diamonds on the bosom of the bay. A little later in the year, all the fashion of Charleston will be met, at the hour of twilight, promenading on this smoothly laid sea wall. Nightly the cool breeze from the water fans them, and refreshes their languid spirits, when May-day introduces the season of hot weather. And hence has grown up the proverb, that the Charlestonians live but during two months of the year—in February, for the sake of the races, and in May, for that of the promenade upon the Battery.

23

An Adverse View of Slavery, 1859

John S. C. Abbott, a brother of Jacob Abbott, the creator of the popular "Rollo" books, was born in Brunswick, Maine, in 1805. A graduate of Bowdoin College, his life was devoted to teaching, the ministry, and literature. What he wrote was extremely readable but, unhappily, was polemical in character and partisan in spirit. He covered a wide range of subjects: history, biography—A History of Napoleon Bonaparte (1855) was perhaps his most famous work—juveniles, family hints, religion, and travel. His account of a brief tour in the South in December, 1859, is no better and no worse than his other writings. Though he endeavored to maintain a certain impartiality, he found on his travels pretty much what his antislavery sentiments expected to find. The account is interesting, however, because it reflects attitudes in the last months before war broke out between the sections. Two observations of his are worthy of note—that slavery could not maintain itself in urban conditions (a point which other observers had noted) and that on the very eve of secession he could find no one in the South who supported the idea. During the Civil War, Abbot was a rabid Unionist writer. He died in 1877.

Dec. 9.—The houses of the planters in Louisiana were generally plain, square, substantial mansions, surrounded with verandahs, embowered in groves of the ever-verdant orange and live oak, and presenting an aspect of much comfort. Some of these dwellings were of considerable architectural beauty, though I saw none which vied with the villas and palaces which opulence is rearing at the North.

At a little distance from the planter's mansion, were to be seen, almost invariably, in two parallel rows, the neat white-washed cabins of the negroes. We would generally count from ten, to forty or fifty. They looked, in the distance, very neat and pretty. They were of one story, apparently contained but one room, seemed to be well guarded from the rain, and very frequently, had either in front or rear, a projection of the roof, where the children could play, or the old people sit, protected from the sun. Some ladies at my side said: "How pleasant these plantations look! How comfortable these servants are provided for! How can people say that the slaves are cruelly treated!" This is the South side view. I have endeavored to give it fairly.

I enter the cabin of the slave. I see in many, perhaps most cases, but one single room where, without a shadow of delicacy, old and young, males and females, sleep promiscuously. Some one with a smile, says: "Talk of the delicacy of slaves!" Alas! Alas! there is none. In the cabin of the slave I see no book, no culture of taste, no thought. He is an animal well cared for, that he may do good service.

Were I to take any tiller of the soil in New England, to the cabin of the negro, show him the sons and daughters of this bondage, and say to him: "Are you willing to accept this as your home for life, and this as the position of your boys and girls?" with indignation he would spurn the insulting question. Absolutely no one believes that the bondsman is treated well as a *man,* but only as a *slave.*

Dec. 11.—This—Sunday—is the great market day in the French quarter in New-Orleans. As I was anxious to witness the novel scene, which brings in a large number of plantation negroes with their little ventures for sale, I went down at an early hour of the morning, to market. The whole scene is most decidedly French. Still I saw very many less of the plantation negroes than I had expected to see, and very many less than I should have seen a few years ago. Nothing has surprised me more in New-Orleans than the small number of the colored population. When the De Soto was made fast to the levee, the wide and extended plateau was thronged with laborers, but they were nearly all Germans or Irish. Rarely could I see a dark skin. It was the same in the streets as we drove through them. Upon speaking of this to a very intelligent gentleman, he observed that the slaves were becoming so exceedingly profitable upon the plantations, that large numbers had been sold from the city for that purpose; and that also it was found not well to have them associated with free laborers, as they acquired bad notions and restless habits.

Clearly it must be so. The cities, especially the commercial ones, will soon be drained, and the powerful tendency now must be to gather the slaves upon the remote plantations, where they can be excluded from popular view, and no longer be agitated by the sights and the sounds of freedom. There are many secluded plantations now, where there are from five hundred to a thousand slaves. They are never permitted to leave the plantations—never. And no one is permitted to visit them from another plantation—not one. Thus they are buried from the world, and toil in darkness from the cradle to the grave.

I am struck with the kindness with which the white population address the negroes, and the manifestly friendly relations which generally exist between the two classes. The negrophobia at the North is unknown at the South.

Dec. 12.—I met a Northern gentleman this morning, and almost his first words were: "As to this peculiar institution, I was always in favor of slavery when in the North, and I am still more so now that I have come South. The slaves are much better off than the laboring classes at the North." Noticing, perhaps, my look of surprise, he added: "The *poor* laboring classes I mean, the *poor* ones."

The condition of the slave, under a humane master, is undoubtedly preferable to that of the prostitutes, vagabonds, and thieves at the Five Points in New-York. If this be the eulogy slavery demands, let it not be withheld. But to compare the homes of the farmers, mechanics or day-laborers, in any village of New-England with the cabins of the negroes, is simply absurd.

I observe in this morning's paper that a law has just passed the Legislature of Mississippi, declaring that all the free colored people therein, who do not leave the State by the first of next July, shall be sold into perpetual slavery. I turn to the census and find that there are about a thousand free colored persons in Mississippi. Many of these people, of remote African descent, are as white as any persons in the State; not a few are the sons and daughters of opulent and intelligent planters. And how are these poor people, guilty of no crime, to escape their awful doom?

Here is a little family, perhaps a Christian family, consisting of father, mother, a son, and a daughter; they are poor and friendless and uninstructed. They must traverse on foot, for they have no means to pay their fare in boat or car, a distance of nearly a thousand miles to reach a Free State. They must run the gauntlet of the Slave States, Alabama, Georgia, the Carolinas, and

Virginia, where they are liable at every step to be arrested as fugitive slaves. When they arrive in Virginia they are certain to be thus arrested, for the laws imperiously require their arrest as vagabonds, if not slaves. They are thrown into jail and advertised as runaways. After a few months, no one appearing to claim them, they are sold at auction, to the highest bidder, *to pay their jail expenses!*

Arkansas has passed a similar law with a free colored population of about six hundred. And the same law has just passed, by an overwhelming majority, the Senate of Missouri, where there is a free colored population of over twenty-six hundred. Thus in the nineteenth century, and in Christian, republican America, more than four thousand free people, guilty of no crime, and accused of no crime, must in dismay, and through sufferings inconceivable, force their way to a cold, distant land, where they have no friends, no employment—or they, and their children, must be sold into perpetual slavery.

It is difficult for me to account for such a state of public opinion as will tolerate legislation so utterly infamous. There will be but one thought, and that will be that those States which can pass such enactments not only are lapsing, but have already lapsed into utter barbarism.

And yet, strangely, I do not meet with this spirit in the homes I visit. Who are these legislators? Where do they come from? Who are their constituents? I meet with no one here in the South, who does not regard such legislation essentially as I regard it—who will not say that it is inhuman and unpardonable. Never have I met more fervent and earnest piety than I am continually meeting at the South.

I should like to live with this people as I meet them. They seem kind, generous, warm-hearted. I constantly see indications of genuine sympathy with the colored race, such as I rarely see at the North. I find Christians here, and those not few in number, as devoted and self-denying as any who can be found on the earth.

Perhaps one explanation is found in the fact that I frequently hear Christians here say: "I am disgusted with politics, and for years have had nothing to do with them." Is it possible that the worse part of the slave-holders, with bowie-knives and revolvers, have over-awed the conscientious portion of the community and taken the affairs of state into their own hands? That they edit the papers, attend the conventions, fill the legislative halls, and send their own men to Congress?

Dec. 13.—After an exceedingly pleasant visit in New-Orleans, a visit so pleasant that, with great reluctance, I brought it to a speedy close, I took the cars this afternoon for Lake Pontchartrain, eight miles distant from the city. At four o'clock, a very beautiful and well-managed steamer, the Florida, left the pier, which extended far out into the shallow waters of the lake, to run along the shores of this quiet inland sea, and along Mississippi sound, a hundred and sixty miles, to Mobile.

During the night, at one of the little, obscure landing-places on the lake, a young planter, about twenty-five years of age, came on board, apparently from a plantation not far back from the shore. He soon rendered himself revoltingly conspicuous by his profaneness and rowdyism. Boon companions speedily gathered around him, and, for some hours, night was rendered hideous by their revelry. In the morning I found him on deck, still in the flush of his debauch. In loud tones, and with a swaggering air, He said:

"When I am dry, I drink whiskey; when I am hungry, I drink whiskey; when I am hot, I drink whiskey; when I am cold, I drink whiskey. I just keep pouring it down all the while. I had rather drink whiskey than eat or sleep!

"I am going to Mobile for a *bust*. I never expect to get nearer to heaven than I am when I get to Mobile. *If* I don't *bust* it there this afternoon and to-night!

"The damned niggers, if they don't work well while I'm gone, they'll get it. I tell you what I do, when I've been gone on a spree. When I go home, if I find the damned niggers have not done a good week's work, I just take 'em and lick 'em like hell—yes, I lick 'em like hell. God Almighty never yet made a nigger that could come it over me!"

These utterances were interlarded with the most horrible oaths imaginable. From various remarks I inferred, that this young man had recently come into the possession of his estate, somewhere in the vicinity, by the death of his father, and that his mother was still living. He has perhaps a hundred slaves, of all varieties of color, men and women, boys and girls, under his sway, in a remote plantation which no eye of civilization ever sees, and where the cry of his victims can reach no Christian ear. After spending a week in Mobile, losing all his money in gambling, his nerves irritated by debauchery, and his spirit maddened by disappointment, he returns to his helpless slaves to wreak his wrath upon them, and to goad them to severer toil to replenish his purse. Their doom is one which it is awful to contemplate.

Now this case is doubtless an exception. There were perhaps twenty other planters on board, and I did not see another one, who did not seem to me to be a mild and humane man. Still there must be not a few of such exceptions. Good men at the South abhor this, as do good men at the North. We read of the beauties of the Patriarchal Institution, but I think all must admit

that this young planter, to whom I have referred, is a rather curious specimen of one of the descendants of the Patriarch.

Dec. 15.—At eleven o'clock yesterday I reached Mobile. Hospitable friends
there took me to their house to dine, and in the afternoon I rode through
the city and its suburbs. The day was unusually fine, and to me the city
looked exceedingly attractive. Here, as in New-Orleans, I was surprised to
see how effectually free labor seems to have driven slave labor from the
wharves and the streets. The city, with its intelligence and its enterprise, is a
dangerous place for the slave. He acquires knowledge of human rights, by
working with others who receive wages when he receives none; who can
come and go at their pleasure, when he, from the cradle to the grave, must
obey a master's imperious will. It is found expedient, almost necessary, to
remove the slave from these influences, and send him back to the intellectual
stagnation and gloom of the plantation. The slaves in the cities, working
in the midst of the conversation of white men, listen eagerly, and gain some
information. This has alarmed their masters, and they are sending them
off, as fast as possible, to the plantations.

"The cities," said a gentleman to me, "is no place for the niggers. They
get strange notions in their heads, and grow discontented. They ought, every
one of them, to be sent back to the plantations."

The Irish and the Germans seem to do nearly all the work of the streets.
White girls are being also more and more employed in domestic service;
and I think that but a few years will pass away ere nearly all the colored
population will be removed from the *cities* of the South. Indeed, now, New-
Orleans and Mobile seem but little more like slave cities than do Philadelphia
and New-York.

This process is now going on with exceeding rapidity. Even now, a person
may take a tour of the United States, and hardly see any thing of Slavery.
He will see well-dressed servants in the hotels, and petted maid-servants
waiting upon kind mistresses. The miseries of the plantation are remote
from his eye.

The society I meet here is frank and agreeable. Indeed it seems to me
that there must be two classes of Southerners, as different from each other as
light is from darkness. I often wonder if our brethren at the South are
bewildered by the same apparent diversity of character in our Northern
men. The Southerners whom I meet at the South in social intercourse, to
whom I am introduced at hotels, in steamboats, and at the fire-side, are
genial, friendly, courteous—gentlemen in tone, kind and polished in manners, ever recognizing the courtesies of refined society. But there is another
class whom I never meet, whom I seek for in vain, but who are revealed to

LOADING COTTON BALES BY TORCHLIGHT

me in newspaper editorials, in convention speeches, and in Congressional debates. The difference between these two classes is so vast as to excite astonishment. From what I read I should infer that there was a very numerous class at the South, composing the great majority of its population, whose mothers had fed them in infancy on "buttered thunder."

It is difficult to account for the fact that one never meets any of these fierce creatures in his travels. I have not met with a single one. I have seen, of course, some uncultivated men, some poor and debased, some profane men, but I have met with not a single specimen of this kind of character; and I can truly say that almost every Southerner whom I have thus far seen, has seemed to me a courteous, unassuming, kind-hearted gentleman. I expected to have caught a glimpse of some of these creatures, tearing over the hills like a locomotive under an attack of delerium tremens. But thus far I have been disappointed. I have met with many, who were truly genial companions, and whom any gentleman would love as intimate associates and neighbors and friends. Do those fierce men, who utter such terrible menaces, like lions, sleep in their lair by day, and never come out but in the night?

We passed this afternoon one large and beautiful mansion, which would be deemed beautiful anywhere. It occupied a very commanding position, and with its cupola, verandah, white fence, green blinds, and shrubbery, reminded one of those pleasant homes which are seen in countless thousands in the Northern States. It was such a house as with us would cost perhaps ten thousand dollars. The owner was evidently a man of thrift. His plantation was large, piles of cotton-bales were collected on the shore, waiting for a steamer to take them to Mobile. Groups of negroes, of all ages, and both sexes, coarse, soul-less-looking creatures, were scattered around, watching the passage of the boat. This is the only house *I have seen* since leaving Mobile, for a distance of more than two hundred miles, in which I think I would be willing to live.

And yet, this must be a rather gloomy home. There is no church here, no village school, no singing-meeting, no social winter-evening gatherings. The soil is so soft and rich, that for much of the year the roads are quite impassable. The proprietor may find enough to occupy him in the care of his vast estate. But to the sons and daughters, the home must be almost like a cloister. But the whole region is beautiful, very, very, beautiful. It is still eminently a new country, with probably not one tenth of the land as yet under cultivation.

The scenes which we witness at night are often exceedingly wild, and weird-like in the extreme. The boat frequently arrives at some obscure landing. The whistle is blown just before our arrival, which brings a group of half-dressed negroes tumbling down the bank to see what is going on. In a sort of iron frame-work basket, with a long handle, chips of pitch-pine knots are placed, which are set in a blaze, and which instantly produce almost the most brilliant touch imaginable. The forests, the dark flowing river, the barbaric-looking negroes, the boatmen, the shouts, and the lurid flames of the torches, all produce a spectacle, which I never weary of beholding.

Dec. 16.—A dark wet day, and the rain falling in floods. We have spent the whole day ascending the river, which is so tortuous in its course, that, though it is but two hundred miles by land from Mobile to Montgomery, it is four hundred miles by water. And yet the land route is so exceedingly uncomfortable, leading through miry roads, or over corduroy bridges, that nearly all the travel is in the boats. The scenery of the river, from its sameness, ceases to interest. We see nothing but the sweep of the forest, with frequent expanses of cotton fields, now looking dry and dead, and occasional groups of forlorn-looking negro-cabins.

No one can pass through our Southern States, and not be saddened by the aspect of forlorn and decaying villages; wretched cabins, where a degraded race, of more than four millions, live a mere animal existence, in homes which it seems a mockery to call a home. These worn-out fields, these dilapidated dwellings, these poor, degraded white men and women, with no incentive to work, with all their energies paralyzed by those laws, framed exclusively for the benefit of the slave holder, present one of the most oppressive aspects of gloom I have ever witnessed. The poor whites! Slavery seems almost more dreadful in its infliction upon them, than upon the blacks.

Slavery drags the whites with the blacks down into the gulf of ignorance and penury. It is impossible to rescue the poor white man without, at the same time, liberating the negro. But the slave holder seems to watch more carefully to keep the poor white man in subjection than he does to guard the slave. He knows that the slave is powerless, and, in case of insurrection, can soon be shot down. But should the poor whites, begin to get their eyes open, they could not so easily be disposed of.

Dec. 19.—At eight o'clock this morning, I took the cars, and, crossing the turbid flood of the Savannah, entered the State of South-Carolina. It was a warm, unclouded morning, and the sun, that wonderful beautifier, illumined the landscape, and, as we glided along over an undulating country, diversified with groves and streams and wide-expanded cotton fields, warmed and fertilized by a clime so genial, one could not but exclaim, What a favored region has God here provided for man!

But what has man done to develop the resources thus placed at his disposal, and to embellish the garden thus given him to till and to enjoy? Vast regions are in solitude. Many fields are worn out by wasteful culture, and are abandoned. Old plantation-houses, deserted by their former inmates, are tumbling into ruins; and the negro cabins, hardly superior to ordinary pens for pigs, in their rottenness and desolation, harmonize with the whole aspect of decay. Occasionally we pass a mansion which presents some little air of gentility, but even the best of these residences have a lonely and unattractive aspect. But very little taste is expended in their external adornings. The "nigger cabins," in the vicinity, always look repulsive. These residences are widely scattered, remote from society, from schools, churches, shops, libraries, post-offices, and markets.

The cabins of the negroes, when regarded as homes for fathers and mothers, sons and daughters, are miserable indeed. I have not yet been so fortunate as to see one, in which there was a pane of glass, or in which there appeared to be more than a single room. I do not know but that there are plantations where the most tasteful cottages are reared for the negroes. I only speak of what I see along my line of travel. In all these "cabins," a hole cut through the wall, closed, occasionally, by a rough board shutter, affords the only entrance for light, except the door, and the chinks, often very wide and numerous, between the logs, boards or slabs which compose the building. I never see a plot of green grass, a yard, a shrub, or a flower. I have never yet passed through any country so entirely destitute of all picturesque, artistic beauty, *the work of man's hand,* as are our slaveholding States.

It is very rare that I see here any newspapers offered in the cars; there is no aspect of intelligence at the stopping-places, and the poor whites seem as totally destitute of ambition as are the slaves. Let me mention one fact illustrative of this want of intelligence. I heard two young men, over twenty years of age, disputing whether in writing 21, the 2 should come before or after the 1. This seems almost incredible. But when we remember that in benighted South Carolina, there are scores of thousands who can neither read nor write their own names, such ignorance ceases to be remarkable.

In such a community, elevated so slightly in the scale of humanity, a community from which Northern newspapers are excluded, and where not even Southern newspapers can be read, it is easy for unprincipled men to rouse the masses to any violence. We no longer wonder that, in the capital of the State, a mob of three thousand could be collected to wreak the most inhuman barbarity upon a poor Irish stonecutter, merely for expressing the opinion that the institution of Slavery operated to the prejudice of the poor whites. This alarming statement was reported to the vigilance committee, consisting of twelve persons. The poor Irishman was arrested, led through the main street of the city by an immense crowd, hooting and yelling. Two negroes were compelled to drag him through the puddles and muddy places, to the State House yard. A mob of three thousand was assembled around him. He was stripped to the skin; and a stout negro was ordered, with a cow-hide, to lay thirty-nine lashes on his bare back, which should draw blood at every stroke. After enduring the dreadful anguish of this affliction, he was daubed with tar, hair, eye-brows, body and all, and then was covered with feathers and cotton. His pants then were drawn up over his limbs to the waist, and he was thrust into the negro-car, and sent out of the State.

As we rode through Virginia, I was conversing with a Virginian, a very genial, gentlemanly, intelligent man. The cars stopped at Petersburg, where we were to pass across the city, and take another train. A gentleman, portly in figure, well dressed, and with the air of one conscious of authority, stood upon the platform. My companion immediately recognized him, and addressing him, said:

"Well! are you going to dissolve the Union here?"

"Dissolve the Union!" the Petersburg gentleman sneeringly replied. "You cannot dissolve the Union any way you may attempt it. Chief-Justice Marshall said very truly, that the Union would bear a great deal before it would break."

"But I thought," my companion added, "from the noise I heard that the Union was to be dissolved immediately."

"They are acting," the Petersburg gentleman replied, "like crazy people up at Richmond. They don't know what they are talking about. You cannot find two men in the country, who can tell where to draw the dividing line. Where are we to find border States? Virginia, herself, is divided; Western Virginia for freedom, Eastern for Slavery. If neither you nor I die until this Union is dissolved, we shall live to a very old age, I assure you. The thing is impossible, utterly impossible."

So much has been recently said, and so earnestly upon the subject, that I have thought it proper to look at the question seriously. I have, accordingly, availed myself of every opportunity of conversing with intelligent men upon the dissolution of the Union, and of the mode, should that deplorable event occur, by which it is to be accomplished.

It has never yet been my misfortune to meet personally with a man, at the North, in favor of the dissolution of the Union. I am aware that there are a few, a very few, of those who are usually called "ultra-abolitionists," and with whom the North is in but little sympathy, who have proclaimed this desire. But this number is so small that, extensive as is my acquaintance,

I have never yet *met* with the man at the North who advocated disunion.

And here let me make a remark which I am sure will astonish my Northern brethren. On this trip to the South, we had in the steamer which took us from New-York to New-Orleans, one hundred and eighty passengers, who were mostly Southerners. At New-Orleans I spent several days, and was introduced to a large number of friends; I crossed Lake Ponchartrain in a crowded steamer to Mobile; visited friends there; ascended the Alabama four hundred miles to Montgomery in one of the large river-boats, filled with Southern passengers; and thence, in rail-cars, passed through the heart of Alabama, Georgia, South-Carolina, North-Carolina, and Virginia, and during this whole route, in ocean-steamer, river-steamer, rail-car, parlor, and hotel, *I did not meet one single individual who advocated disunion.*

For aught I know, there may have been thousands in that region in favor of disunion, whom I did not meet; but I did not converse with a single one who advocated such views. On the contrary, I met many who spoke in terms of sadness and bitterness of the strife, and who deplored the idea of any separation between the North and the South. As I perused the fierce denunciations in Congress, I was often led to inquire: "Where do these fiery spirits come from? and whom do they represent?"

24

General Sherman Destroys a Civilization, 1864

*D*avid P. Conyngham was born in Ireland in 1840 and emigrated to New *York at an early age. When only twenty-four, he was commissioned by the* New York Herald *to write an on-the-spot record of the war; and, with the*

rank *of captain, he moved with Sherman's army from Chattanooga through*
the Georgia and Carolina campaigns. His observations appeared in book
form as Sherman's March through the South (1865). *After the war his pur-*
suits were almost exclusively literary. He was editor of the New York Tablet
and author of a half-dozen volumes, both of fiction and of fact, dealing with
Ireland and the Irish. The year which saw his last book published, Ireland
Past and Present, *was also the year of his death (1883).*

Portions of Sherman's March *deal with the factual material of the day-by-*
day advance of the army, but mostly his interest centers on pictures of camp
life, incidents in the lives of soldiers, the reaction of war on civilian popula-
tions, and the Negroes. Though given on occasion to a bit of Irish romance,
his account possesses power and a tragic realism. His sympathy was naturally
with the Union army he accompanied, but, nevertheless, it is evident that he
had an abiding hatred for war and an infinite compassion for the helpless
souls caught in the struggle.

THE RED BADGE OF COURAGE

Night had set in. The ground was strewn with the dead and wounded.
Our men slept beside their arms, for the rebel lines were quite close to
them. The living, the dying, and the dead slept beside one another. Rebel
and Union officers and men lay piled together; some transfixed with bayonet
wounds, their faces wearing that fierce, contorted look that marks those who
have suffered agony. Others, who were shot dead, lay with their calm faces
and glassy eyes turned to heaven. One might think they were but sleeping.

Others had their skulls crushed in by the end of a musket, while the
owner of the musket lay stiff beside them, with the death grip tightened on
the piece.

Clinging to one of the guns, with his hand on the spoke, and his body
bent as if drawing it, lay a youth with the top of his head shot off. Another
near him, with his body cut in two, still clung to the ropes.

Men writhing in pain, men stark and cold; broken caissons, rifles, and
bayonets; bloody clothes and torn haversacks, with all the other debris of
war's havoc, were the price we paid for two old cannon.

A battle-field, when the carnage of the day is over; when the angry passions of men have subsided; when the death silence follows the din and roar
of battle; when the victors have returned triumphant to their camps to
celebrate their victory, regardless of the many comrades they have left behind; when the conquered sullenly fall back to a new position, awaiting to

renew the struggle,—is a sad sight. It is hard to listen to the hushed groans and cries of the dying, and to witness the lacerated bodies of your fellow-soldiers strewn around, some with broken limbs, torn and mangled bodies, writhing in agony. How often has some poor fellow besought me to shoot him, and put him out of pain! It would be a mercy to do so, yet I dared not.

Piled up together in a ditch, near a battery which they supported with their lines, I found several rebel dead and wounded. I dragged some of the wounded out under the shelter of the trees.

The ghouls of the army were there before me; they had rifled the pockets of the dead and wounded indiscriminately.

I gave many a poor fellow a reviving drink, amidst silent prayers.

In one place I found a mere boy of about fifteen. His leg was shattered with a piece of shell. I placed his knapsack under his head. Poor child! what stories he told me of his mother, away down in Carolina; and his little sisters, how glad they would be, now that he was wounded, to see him home.

They never saw him home, for he went to the home where the weary are at rest.

I came up to the corpse of a rebel soldier, over whom a huge Kentuckian federal soldier was weeping.

"My man," I exclaimed, "why do you weep over him? Look at your comrades around you."

"True, sir," he replied, wiping his eyes; and pointing to a federal soldier near, he said, "There is my brother; this man shot him: I killed him in return. He was my bosom friend. I loved him as a father loves his child."

Next morning, as we were removing our wounded to hospital, I saw a group collected. I rode up, and found that they were some raw troops jeering and insulting rebel wounded. Veteran troops will never do this, but share their last drink and bite with them. I rated them pretty roundly, and ordered the cowardly sneaks to their regiments. After another battle or two, these very boys would feel indignant at such conduct.

It is an affecting sight to witness the removal of the dead and wounded from a battle-field, and the manner in which the former are interred. In some cases, deep pits are sunk, and, perhaps, a hundred or more bodies are flung promiscuously into it, as if no one owned them, or cared for them.

In other cases, where the bodies had been recognized, they were buried with some semblance of decency. I was once riding with a column over a battle-field, in which the skeletons of the hastily buried dead were partly exposed.

The arm and hand of a man protruded from one of these sunken graves.

I have often met skeletons in the woods, with the bones stretched out, and the old rotten knapsacks under the heads, and the remnants of the clothes still clinging around the bones.

These were poor fellows who got wounded in the heat of battle, and retired to the shelter of the forest. Here they lay; and not being discovered, and being unable to get away, they died, inch by inch, for carrion birds to pick their bodies. What must be the suffering of these poor fellows, with their festering wounds, crawling with maggots, without a hand to tend them, without a drop of water to cool their parched lips, with the ravens and turkey-buzzards croaking around them, watching, until they would be too helpless to defend themselves, to pounce on them, and pluck out their eyes, or drag the quivering flesh from their frames.

I have seen others, particularly at the battle of Chancellorsville, who fell, wounded, out in the woods, and who were burned up when the woods took fire, and whom we could not assist, as the rebel skirmishers and sharp-shooters took down every man who dared to put out his head.

Their shrieks and groans, as they writhed in the fiery furnace, still ring in my ears.

SHERMAN'S MARCH: THE BURNING OF ATLANTA, NOVEMBER 15, 1864

Women and children were dreadfully frightened at the approach of our army. It was almost painful to witness the horror and fear depicted on their features. They were schooled up to this by lying statements of what atrocious murders we were committing.

The country people trembled at our approach, and hid themselves away in woods and caves. I rode out one evening alone to pay a visit to another camp which lay some six miles beyond us. In trying to make a short way through the woods, I lost the road, and rambled on through the forest, trying to recover it. This is no easy matter, as I soon discovered; for I only got deeper and deeper into the forest. I then turned my horse's head down a valley that I knew would lead me out on a camp somewhere.

In riding along this, I thought I saw a woman among the trees. I rode in the direction, and saw her darting like a frighted deer towards a thick copse of tangled briers, wild vines, and underbrush.

Fearing some snare, I followed, with pistol in hand; and heavens, what a sight met my view! In the midst of the thicket, sheltered by a bold bluff, were about a dozen women, as many children, and three old men, almost crazy with fear and excitement.

Some of them screamed when they saw me, and all huddled closer, as if resolved to die together. I tied my horse, and assured them that they had no cause for fear; that I was not going to harm them, but would protect them, if needed. Thus assured, they became somewhat communicative.

They told me that they thought the soldiers would kill them, and that they hid here on our approach. Thinking that we were only passing through, they had brought nothing to eat or to cover them. They were here now near three days, and had nothing but the berries they picked up in the woods. They looked wretched, their features wan and thin, their eyes wild and haggard, and their lips stained from the unripe wild fruit. Some of them were lying down, huddled together to keep themselves warm; their clothes were all saturated from the dew and a heavy shower of rain which fell during the day.

I do not think one could realize so much wretchedness and suffering as that group presented. Some of the women were evidently planters' wives and daughters; their appearance and worn dresses betokened it; others were their servants, or the wives of the farm-laborers.

There were two black women, and some three picaninnies. Under the shelter of a tree, I saw a woman sitting down, rocking her body to and fro, as she wept bitterly.

I went over to her. Beside her was a girl of some fourteen years, lying at full length. As I approached, she looked so pale and statuelike, I exclaimed,—

"What's the matter. Is she in a faint?"

"Yes; in one that she won't waken from," said an old crone near.

"Dead!" I exclaimed.

"Well, stranger, I reckon so; better for her go, poor darling, than have the Yankees cotch her."

It was so. She was dead. I understood she was delicate; and the hunger and cold had killed her. So much were they afraid of being discovered that they had not even a fire lighted.

I inquired my way to the camp, and soon returned with some provisions. The dead body was removed, and the sorrowing group returned to their homes; but some of them had no homes, for the soldiers, on the principle that all abandoned houses belong to rebels, had laid them in ashes.

Many of my readers have not seen a vast army encamped. What a sight it presents! Here are some showy headquarters, with their numerous surroundings of white tents. Look into these and you will find that officers do not fare so badly even in the field. Neat beds are contrived; some are cots; others lithe saplings or frames covered with a cotton tick, and plenty of covering, probably contributed by some plantation house. On one side is a table laden with books, a box of cigars, and most likely a bottle of "commissary." These, with a looking glass and the officers' equipments, compose the furniture of the tent. Four flies form a mess tent; and as the general and staff are going to dine, we will just see what kind of fare they have. It consists of stewed beef, hashed potatoes, and a couple of chickens, which the Georgian housekeepers were kind enough to rear for them, and most likely a few bottles of old rye, which the planters were kind enough to leave in their cellars for our especial benefit—all these flanked by a respectable force of negro waiters.

Officers and orderlies are always lounging or riding about headquarters, which gives it a very gay and stirring appearance. At some distance from these are the less pretentious headquarters of some brigadier general, or colonel, while a little farther on are the modest tents of the rank and file and company officers arranged in streets.

The men around these are collected in groups, listening to long yarns beside the cook fire, or are formed into little parties playing cards, pitch and toss, or a thousand other games, known only in the army; others, are dining, grumbling at their rations while dining on turkey. The cooks are busy around a huge tin caldron, placed on the fire, in which a joint of bacon and some peas are bubbling and bubbling around as if they were patriotic enough to enjoy being eaten for the good of the soldiers. A smaller vessel simmers near it, but as the lid is on it I cannot see its contents—most likely a brace of chickens under the wing of a fat turkey. This is the way our troops lived on Sherman's campaign.

The tents themselves had a very picturesque appearance, scattered over hill and valley, in streets and in clumps, looking like so many canvas villages, or huge gypsy encampments. The groups of soldiers, the lines of soldiers marching to or from picket, the sentries moving stately on their beats, generals and officers gayly dashing about, make a camp scene gorgeously imposing and impressive.

How greatly is the effect of a camp scene improved by night! For miles around you the camp fires glitter and sparkle like the lamps of a city. If standing on a hill, one circle of dancing lights and sparkling fireflies encompasses you; while from the valleys beneath you the fires also glow, and the noise of song and merriment, of the harmony of music, floats around you.

In some places the fire has ignited the tall pines, and envelops them in one sheet of flame, which leaps from limb to limb, and feeds on the resinous trunks, presenting the appearance of thousands of fiery demons, or huge flaming pillars. Then the men crowded around them, gambling and enjoying themselves by their light, look like so many dark imps, keeping up some hellish orgy; and the sentries, walking up and down with their glittering rifles reflected by the fire, add to the sublimity of the scene.

The officers are in their tents reading, telling stories, or enjoying a drink or a cigar. What strong yarns are spun, what a lot of peach brandy is consumed, particularly if a late discovery has been made, and many casks exhumed; if so, all the officers are collected in the mess tent, a huge fire glows in front; around this their servants are collected, all cheered by the peach brandy, and highly amused at the antics of some six young Ethiopian minstrels—servants and camp followers—who are capering about in the most fantastic manner, singing all kinds of negro songs, timing them by clapping their hands together and on their thighs, thus keeping up the most discordant harmony, all agreeing, "dat de day of Jubelon am come."

It was certainly a strange sight to see these poor youths capering and jumping around to the no small amusement of the officers and men, who laughed heartily, and so highly appreciated the fun of the thing, they gave the peach to them so liberally that they soon fell off, one by one. One lad made a vigorous stand to maintain his position. He was a musical genius; could produce all kinds of sounds with his voice; imitate a drum, a piano.

fiddle, and the Lord knows what. He was so appreciated, and filled with vanity like any vain white folk, he struggled on for a time, blending all the harmony of the spheres in the most hissing manner, until at length all his vanity yielded to the potent influence of peach brandy, and he fell down beside his brethren.

Improvident and thoughtless soldiers are full of fun and drollery. Looking upon life as a very uncertain tenure, they try and make the most of it. Their motto is, "Eat, drink, and be merry, for to-morrow we die." You would hear more rich, real stories and incidents of battle-fields, beside a camp fire, from a jolly set of happy dogs, who, perhaps, might be shot the following day, than you would your whole life among your city friends. They will lie like troopers, and, I am afraid, steal and swear like troopers, too; but then they make it all right by fighting like troopers.

The effects of fear, amounting almost to insanity, sometimes developed in action, are very extraordinary. In General Harker's brigade, the men were under orders to advance, when a sergeant retired to his tent, and shot himself through the head. I have known several cases of the kind. It appears strange that a man from fear of going into battle should kill himself. I have often seen men strip themselves stark naked, and run crazy out of a battle-field. I might suspect their sincerity, but I have seen them rush in this manner, under fire, into the rebel lines. This is caused, no doubt, by the stunning effect of shells bursting around them, and killing their comrades. So great is the terror produced by the explosion of several shells, that I have seen a horse that was under a very heavy fire, tremble, the sweat at the same time bursting out of every pore, and then drop down dead, without being touched by ball or shell.

On one occasion General Johnston sent a flag of truce to Sherman, in order to give time to carry off the wounded and bury the dead, who were festering in front of their lines.

A truce followed, and Rebels and Federals freely participated in the work of charity. It was a strange sight to see friends, to see old acquaintances, and in some instances brothers, who had been separated for years, and now pitted in deadly hostility, meet and have a good talk over old times, and home scenes, and connections. They drank together, smoked together, appeared on the best possible terms, though the next day they were sure to meet in deadly conflict again.

Even some of the generals freely mixed with the men, and seemed to view the painful sight with melancholy interest.

An officer, speaking of this sad burial, said, "I witnessed a strange scene yesterday in front of Davis's division. During the burial of the dead, grouped together in seemingly fraternal unity, were officers and men of both contending armies, who, but five minutes before, were engaged in the work of slaughter and death."

Under the shelter of a pine, I noticed a huge gray Kentuckian rebel, with his arm affectionately placed around the neck of a Federal soldier, a mere boy. The bronzed warrior cried and laughed by turns, and then kissed the young Federal.

Attracted by such a strange proceeding, I went over to them, and said to the veteran, "Why, you seem very much taken by that boy; I suppose he is some old friend of yours."

"Old friend, sir! Why, he is my son!"

I have often seen a rebel and a Federal soldier making right for the same rifle-pit, their friends on both sides loudly cheering them on. As they would not have time to fight, they reserved their fire until they got into the pit, then woe betide the laggard, for the other was sure to pop him as soon as he got into cover. Sometimes they got in together, and then came the tug of war; for they fought for possession with their bayonets and closed fists. In some cases however, they made a truce, and took joint possession of it.

It was no unusual thing to see our pickets and skirmishers enjoying themselves very comfortably with the rebels, drinking bad whiskey, smoking and chewing worse tobacco, and trading coffee and other little articles. The rebels had no coffee, and our men plenty, while the rebels had plenty of whiskey; so they very soon came to an understanding. It was strange to see these men, who had been just pitted in deadly conflict, trading, and bantering, and chatting, as if they were the best friends in the world. They discussed a battle with the same gusto they would a cock-fight, or horse-race, and made inquiries about their friends, as to who was killed, and who not, in the respective armies. Friends that have been separated for years have met in this way. Brothers who parted to try their fortune have often met on the picket line, or on the battle-field. I once met a German soldier with the head of a dying rebel on his lap. The stern veteran was weeping, whilst the boy on his knee looked pityingly into his face. They were speaking in German, and from my poor knowledge of the language, all I could make out was, they were brothers; that the elder had come out here several years before; the younger followed him, and being informed that he was in Macon, he went in search of him, and got conscripted; while the elder brother, who was in the north all the time, joined our army. The young boy was scarcely twenty, with light hair, and a soft, fair complexion. The pallor of death on his brow, and the blood was flowing from his breast, and gurgled in his throat and mouth, which the other wiped away with his handkerchief. When he could speak, the dying youth's conversation was of the old home in Germany, of his brothers and sisters, and dear father and mother, who were never to see him again.

In those improvised truces, the best possible faith was observed by the men. These truces were brought about chiefly in the following manner. A rebel, who was heartily tired of his crippled position in his pit, would call out, "I say, Yank!"

"Well, Johnny Reb," would echo from another hole or tree.

"I'm going to put out my head; don't shoot."

"Well, I won't."

The reb would pop up his head; the Yank would do the same.

"Hain't you got any coffee, Johnny?"

"Na'r a bit, but plenty of rot-gut."

"All right; we'll have a trade."

They would meet, while several others would follow the example, until there would be a regular bartering mart established. In some cases the men would come to know each other so well, that they would often call out,—

"Look out, reb; we're going to shoot," or, "Look out, Yank, we're going to shoot," as the case may be.

On one occasion the men were holding a friendly *réunion* of this sort, when a rebel major came down in a great fury, and ordered the men back. As they were going back, he ordered them to fire on the Federals. They refused, as they had made a truce. The major swore and stormed, and in his rage he snatched the gun from one of the men, and fired at a Federal soldier, wounding him. A cry of execration at such a breach of faith rose from all the men, and they called out, "Yanks, we couldn't help it." At night these men deserted into our lines, assigning as a reason, that they could not with honor serve any longer in an army that thus violated private truces.

THE SIEGE OF ATLANTA

From several points along the lines we could plainly see the doomed city, with the smoke of burning houses and bursting shells enveloping it in one black canopy, hanging over it like a funeral pall.

The scene at night was sublimely grand and terrific! The din of artillery rang on the night air. In front of General Geary's headquarters was a prominent hill, from which we had a splendid view of the tragedy enacting before us. One night I sat there with the general and staff, and several other officers, while a group of men sat near us enjoying the scene, and speculating on the effects of the shells. It was a lovely, still night, with the stars twinkling in the sky. The lights from the campfires along the hills and valleys, and from amidst the trees, glimmered like the gas-lights of a city in the distance. We could see the dark forms reclining around them, and mark the solemn tread of the sentinel on his beat. A rattle of musketry rang from some point along the line. It was a false alarm. The men for a moment listened, and then renewed their song and revelry, which was for a while interrupted. The song, and music, and laughter floated to our ears from the city of camps, that dotted the country all round.

Sherman had lately ordered from Chattanooga a battery of four and a half inch rifles, and these were trying their metal on the city.

Several batteries, forts, and bastions joined in the fierce chorus. Shells flew from the batteries, up through the air, whizzing and shrieking, until they reached a point over the devoted city, when down they went, hurling the fragments, and leaving in their train a balloon-shaped cloud of smoke. From right, and left, and centre flew these dread missiles, all converging towards the city. From our commanding position we could see the flash from the guns, then the shells, with their burning fuses, hurtling through the air like flying meteors.

"I hain't no objection to be out of that 'ere place," said a soldier in the group near us, who were also intently looking on.

"Rather hot, I guess," said another.

"A little too much so to be healthy, I reckon," was the response.

"What matter whether one is killed there or here? We must all die when our time comes," said a fatalist.

"I have no objection to wait for my time, and not go meet it half ways," said the general's cook.

"You," said a patriot, with disdain, "you don't feel that it is sweet to die for one's country."

"Be gor, then, as for myself, I'd sooner live for my country, any day, than die for it," replied a wit from the Emerald Isle.

This philosophical conversation might have continued much longer, had not a dark volume of smoke shot up from the city in one vast spiral column; and then came a heavy, dead, rumbling report. One of the aresenals was blown up by a shell. This was followed by a fierce fire, which shot up, almost simultaneously, in different points. A cheer came from our batteries, and was taken up along the whole line.

"War is a cruelty," said the general beside me; "we know not how many innocents are now suffering in this miserable city."

"I'm dog gone if I like it," said a soldier, slapping his brawny hand upon his thigh; "I can fight my weight of rattlesnakes; but this thing of smoking out women and children, darn me if it's fair."

On the night of September 1, Hood blew up all the magazines and ammunition, destroyed all the supplies he could not move, comprising eight locomotives, and near one hundred cars laden with ammunition, small arms, and stores, and then retreated. Our troops, advancing near the city, met with no resistance. Observing that it was evacuated, they entered it about 11 o'clock on the morning of September 2, 1864.

Atlanta was now in our hands, the crowning point of Sherman's great campaign. Hood had been outgeneraled, outmanoeuvred, and outflanked, and was now trying to concentrate his scattered army. On the night of the 1st, when the rebel army was vacating, the stampede was frightful to those engaged, but grandly ludicrous to casual spectators.

Even war has its laughable scenes amidst all its horrors, and the retreat from Atlanta was an illustration of that. Conveyances were bought at fabulous sums, and when all were crowded, those who could not procure any—men, women, and children, old and young—followed the procession, bearing bundles of all contents and sizes. The delicate drawing-room miss, that could never venture half a mile on foot, with her venerable parents, now marched out, joining the solemn procession. Confusion and disorder prevailed in every place, considerably increased by the eighty loads of ammunition now blowing up.

Shrieking, hissing shells rushed into the air, as if a thousand guns were firing off together. We plainly heard the noise at Jonesboro'. How terrifying must it be to the trembling, affrighted fugitives, who rushed to and fro, and believed, with every report, that the Yankees were upon them—to slay, ravage, and destroy them.

But yesterday, they had exultingly gazed upon our abandoned works; to-night, how changed!

The city had suffered much from our projectiles. Several houses had been burned, and several fallen down. In some places the streets were blocked up with the rubbish. The suburbs were in ruins, and few houses escaped without being perforated. Many of the citizens were killed, and many more had hairbreadth escapes. Some shells had passed through the Trout House Hotel, kicking up a regular muss among beds and tables.

One woman pointed out to me where a shell dashed through her house as she was sitting down to dinner. It upset the table and things, passed through the house, and killed her neighbor in the next house.

Several had been killed; some in their houses, others in the streets.

When the rebels were evacuating, in the confusion several of our sick and wounded escaped from the hospitals, and were sheltered by the citizens.

Almost every garden and yard around the city had its cave. These were sunk down with a winding entrance to them, so that pieces of shells could not go in. When dug deep enough, boards were placed on the top, and the earth piled upon them in a conical shape, and deep enough to withstand even a shell. Some of these caves, or bomb-proofs, were fifteen feet deep, and well covered. All along the railroad, around the intrenchments and the bluff near the city, were gopher holes, where soldiers and citizens concealed themselves.

In some cases it happened that our shells burst so as to close up the mouths of the caves, thus burying the inmates in a living tomb.

Sherman's comprehensive mind was already clearing the way for the Georgian campaign. He knew that Atlanta might again be rendered formidable in the hands of the enemy, and had resolved to destroy, or, to use

SHERMAN'S MARCH: THE 14TH AND 20TH CORPS MOVE OUT OF ATLANTA

his own words, "to wipe it out." War is at best a horrid cruelty, and cannot be refined. Expediency and necessity justify acts savage enough to make the angels weep. Friends and foes suffer indiscriminately from its ravages, and too often the innocent suffer, while the guilty escape.

As soon as General Sherman had issued his order, several families prepared to go south at once. The cars taking them down were loaded with a miscellaneous cargo. In some were crowded together tottering old age and maidens in their youthful bloom. The former fretted very much at being thus rudely torn away, root and branch, from the soil on which they grew, and in which they hoped soon to rest their wearied hearts. In addition, the wagons were crowded with a heterogeneous medley of poodle dogs, tabby cats, asthmatic pianos, household furniture, cross old maids, squalling, wondering children, all of which, huddled together, made anything but a pleasant travelling party, which I accompanied.

On Sherman's return to Atlanta he issued an order for its immediate evacuation by all citizens who had not left in compliance with his first order.

The depot presented a scene of confusion and suffering seldom witnessed. Women and children were huddled together, while men, who had lately been millionaires, were now frantically rushing about, trying to procure transportation, and forced to give their last dollar to some exacting conductor or railway official. An order had been issued by General Easton providing all these people with free transportation; but several of his employees could not see it in that light. They saw the thing could be made to pay, and they did make it pay.

The refugees were afraid to complain. Anxious to get off, dishonest employees told them for days that the next train would be the last that would go. In some cases they gave all they had to be let go, and in many cases paid as high as one hundred dollars to conductors, though all the time provided with free passages. In some cases they managed to divide families, so that they could extort the more from the remaining.

I wanted myself to get a poor soldier, who was going home to die, inside one of the cars. Though they were full of strapping, healthy negroes, who were either servants to the extortioners, or had the almighty dollars to pay their way, I could not gain admittance for the poor fellow. A few dollars in a conductor's pocket were of more importance than his comfort or safety. I gave him my blanket and oilcloth, but I have since learned he never reached home, for when taken off the top of the cars at Chattanooga he was found dead.

I simply mention these facts as a caution to generals not to place too much confidence in employees, unless they are well tried and tested. The first fire burst out on the night of Friday, the 11th of November, in a block of wooden tenements on Decatur Street, where eight buildings were destroyed.

Soon after, fires burst out in other parts of the city. These certainly were the works of some of the soldiers, who expected to get some booty under cover of the fires.

The fire engines were about being shipped for Chattanooga, but were soon brought in, and brought to bear on the burning districts.

The patrol guards were doubled, and orders issued to shoot down any person seen firing buildings. Very little effort had been made to rescue the city from the devouring elements, for they knew that the fiat had gone forth consigning it to destruction. Over twenty houses were burned that night, and a dense cloud of smoke, like a funeral pall, hung over the ruins next morning.

General Slocum offered a reward of five hundred dollars for the apprehension of any soldier caught in the act of incendiarism. Though Slocum knew that the city was doomed, according to his just notions of things it should be done officially. No officer or soldier had a right to fire it without orders.

It was hard to restrain the soldiers from burning it down. With that licentiousness that characterizes an army they wanted a bonfire.

On Sunday night a kind of long streak of light, like an aurora, marked the line of march, and the burning stores, depots, and bridges, in the train of the army.

The Michigan engineers had been detailed to destroy the depots and public buildings in Atlanta. Everything in the way of destruction was now considered legalized. The workmen tore up the rails and piled them on the smoking fires. Winship's iron foundery and machine shops were early set on fire. This valuable property was calculated to be worth about half a million of dollars.

An oil refinery near by next got on fire, and was soon in a fierce blaze. Next followed a freight warehouse, in which were stored several bales of cotton. The depot, turning-tables, freight sheds, and stores around, were soon a fiery mass. The heart was burning out of beautiful Atlanta.

The Atlanta Hotel, Washington Hall, and all the square around the railroad depot, were soon in one sheet of flame.

Drug stores, dry goods stores, hotels, negro marts, theatres, and grog shops, were all now feeding the fiery element. Worn-out wagons and camp equipage were piled up in the depot, and added to the fury of the flames.

A stone warehouse was blown up by a mine. Quartermasters ran away, leaving large stores behind. The men plunged into the houses, broke windows and doors with their muskets, dragging out armfuls of clothes, tobacco, and whiskey, which was more welcome than all the rest. The men dressed themselves in new clothes, and then flung the rest into the fire.

The streets were now in one fierce sheet of flame; houses were falling on all sides, and fiery flakes of cinders were whirled about. Occasionally shells exploded, and excited men rushed through the choking atmosphere, and hurried away from the city of ruins.

At a distance the city seemed overshadowed by a cloud of black smoke, through which, now and then, darted a gushing flame of fire, or projectiles hurled from the burning ruin.

The sun looked, through the hazy cloud, like a blood-red ball of fire; and the air, for miles around, felt oppressive and intolerable. The Tyre of the south was laid in ashes, and the "Gate City" was a thing of the past.

ATLANTA TO THE SEA

It was pretty well known that Sherman was going to cut loose from all communications, and to destroy all the factories, founderies, railroads, mills, and all government property, thus preventing the rebels from using them in his rear. After the troops destroyed Rome, Kingston, and Marietta, tore up the track, and set fire to sleepers, railroad depots, and stores, Sherman issued a special field order:

"The army will forage liberally on the country during the march. To this end each brigade commander will organize a good and efficient foraging party, under command of one or more discreet officers. To regular foraging parties must be intrusted the gathering of provisions and forage at any distance from the roads travelled.

"As for horses, mules, wagons, &c., the cavalry and artillery may appropriate freely and without limit. Foraging parties may also take mules or horses to replace the jaded animals of their trains, or to serve as pack-mules for the regiments or brigades."

These orders were all right, if literally carried out; but they were soon converted into licenses for indiscriminate plunder. The followers of an army, in the shape of servants, hangers-on, and bummers, are generally as numerous as the effective force. Every brigade and regiment had its organized, foraging party, which were joined by every officer's servant and idler about the camps.

These, scattered over the country, without any order or discipline, pounced like harpies on the unfortunate inhabitants, stripping them of all provisions, jewelry, and valuables they could discover.

In most instances they burned down houses to cover their depredations, and in some cases took the lives of their victims, as they would not reveal concealed treasures. These gangs spread like locusts over the country. In all cases where the foraging parties were under the command of a respectable officer, they acted with propriety, simply taking what provisions and necessaries they needed. They might as well have stripped the place, though, for soon came the bummers, and commenced a scene of ruin and pillage. Boxes were burst open; clothes dragged about; the finest silks, belonging to the planters' ladies, carried off to adorn some negro wenches around camp; pictures, books, furniture, all tossed about and torn in pieces. Though these wretches were acting against military orders, there was no one to complain. The planter and his family were thankful if they escaped with their lives; and as to their comrades, they were too deep in the pie themselves to complain of a system which was enriching them.

The first day's march was rather slow, in order to give time to sluggard wagons and teams to get into position. The troops were noisy and cheerful; full of hope and excitement. Though all superfluous baggage and trains had been sent to the rear, still our train numbered about two thousand wagons, and would, if stretched out in one line, extend about twenty miles.

"Living off the country" was fast becoming the order. The men knew that Sherman had started with some sixteen days' supplies, and they wished to preserve them if possible; besides, they thought that a change of diet would be good for their health. There was nothing to be got the first two days' march, as the country all around Atlanta had been foraged by Slocum's corps while hemmed in there. Now we were opening on a country where pits of sweet potatoes, yards of poultry and hogs, and cellars of bacon and flour, were making their appearance. A new spirit began to animate the men; they were as busy as so many bees about a honey-pot, and commenced important voyages of discovery, and returned well laden with spoils. Foragers, bummers, and camp followers scattered over the country for miles, and black clouds of smoke showed where they had been. Small lots of cotton were found near most of the plantation houses. These, with the gins and presses, were burned, oftentimes firing the houses and offices. Near Madison we passed some wealthy plantations; one, the property of a Mr. Lane, who was courteous enough to wait to receive us, was full of decrepit, dilapidated negroes, presided over by a few brimstone-looking white ladies. They were viciously rabid, and only wished they could eat us with the same facility that the troops consumed all the edibles on the place, and eloped with plump grunters and indignant roosters, and their families.

The 20th corps encamped near Madison that night. The cavalry had the advance, burned the depot, and cleared out the town pretty well. Madison is situated on the Augusta line, and was a town of near two thousand inhabitants before the war.

Our troops entered the town next morning, and a brigade was detailed to destroy all the works around the depot and railroad track, also to burn a pile of nearly two hundred bales of cotton in a hut near. While this work was being executed, the stragglers, who manage to get to the front when there is plunder in view, and vagabonds of the army, crowded into the town, and the work of pillage went on with a vengeance. Stores were ripped open; goods, valuables, and plate, all suddenly and mysteriously disappeared. I say mysteriously, for if you were to question the men about it, not one of them admitted having a hand in it. Grinning negroes piloted the army, and appeared to be in their element. They called out, "Here, massa; I guess we gwine to get some brandy here." The doors would at once be forced open, the cellars and shelves emptied, and everything tossed about in the utmost confusion. If a good store chanced to be struck, the rush for it was immense. Some of those inside, being satisfied themselves, would fling bales of soft goods, hardware, harness, and other miscellaneous articles, through the windows. I have seen fellows carry off a richly gilt mirror, and when they got tired of it, dash it against the ground. A piano was a much prized article of capture. I have often witnessed the ludicrous sight of a lot of bearded, rough soldiers capering about the room in a rude waltz, while some fellow was thumping away unmercifully at the piano, with another cutting grotesque capers on the top-board. When they got tired of this saturnalia, the piano was consigned to the flames, and most likely the house with it. The wreck of Madison was pretty effective, too. All the stores were gutted, and the contents scattered and broken around. Cellars of rich wine were discovered, and prostrate men gave evidence of its strength, without any revenue test. A milliner's establishment was sacked, and gaudy ribbons and artificial flowers decorated the caps of the pretty fellows that had done it. Their horses and the negro wenches, too, came in for a share of the decorative spoils.

The left wing had destroyed the Augusta line along their march. The right wing had moved by McDonagh to Jackson without encountering an enemy. The rebels were making some little show to the cavalry on our flanks, but did not as yet attempt to give battle. The negroes were joining us in crowds. Near every cross-road and plantation, we would meet groups of old men and women, and young children, who received us with shouts of joy, exclaiming, "Glory be to de Lord; bress de Lord, de day of jubilou is come; dis nigger is off to glory," and fell in with their sable friends in the rear, without even asking where we were going, or what we would do with them. Such was their simple faith that they trudged along, "bressing de Lord, de day of jubilou is come." Many of them had reason to regret their desire for liberty. With them, liberty too often meant plenty to eat and wear, and nothing to do. They found that it meant hardship, hunger, and cold; for many of them perished along the way from fatigue and the hardship of the march.

The country lying between Madison, Covington, and Milledgeville, is a perfect garden; and though not literally teeming with milk and honey, it was teeming with something better—farmyards well stocked with hogs and poultry, stacks of corn fodder, corn-houses, and bins filled with corn and grain. Sweet potatoes and negroes seemed to grow spontaneously. Hogs grunted a welcome on every side—fine, sleek hogs, that strutted about with snobbish dignity; young, petulant hogs, that cocked up their noses in disdain at the Yankees. The Yankees, not to be outdone in politeness, soon cocked up their feet. Poor, timid sheep, and submissive cattle, swinging huge bells, as if tolling a requiem over the desolation around, looked wonderingly upon the foragers as they came down in fell swoop upon the farmyard, and patiently submitted to their fate.

The left column was now closing on Milledgeville. They had struck the Eatonton Branch Railroad, twenty-two miles from Milledgeville.

We revelled in the splendid homes and palatial residences of some of the wealthy planters here. The men, with that free and easy, devil-may-care sort of way, so characteristic of soldiers, made themselves quite as much at home in the fine house of the planter as in the shanty of the poor white trash or the negro. They helped themselves, freely and liberally, to everything they wanted, or did not want. It mattered little which.

It takes an old raider to appreciate how completely and quickly a railroad can be destroyed. At the first start of railroad raids, the rails were simply turned over,—the men ranging themselves at one side, and raising in one huge swath hundreds of yards at a time, and then tossing it over. This only caused some delay, but left the material for use again. We improved on the thing like all other sciences of war. The rails were torn from the sleepers by a kind of drag, with a lever attached for a handle. Then the sleepers were piled up, and set on fire.

The rails were placed on top, and soon became so soft that they could be twisted like a corkscrew, or wound around a tree like an anaconda. Future antiquarians will rack their brains conjecturing how these iron monsters twisted themselves around the trees. I should not wonder if some Barnum of the twenty-fifty century should exhibit an immense rail as the "fungated boa-constrictor found buried in the heart of a huge oak tree, where it must have lain for hundreds of years," with, perhaps, another that has been modelled into a duck of a corkscrew, as "a corkscrew used by the aborigines of America in the days when there were giants upon the earth."

Our campaign all through Central Georgia was one delightful picnic. We had little or no fighting, and good living. The farm-yards, cellars, and cribs of the planters kept ourselves and animals well stored with provisions and forage, besides an occasional stiff horn of something strong and good, which, according to the injunctions of holy writ, we took "for our stomachs' sake."

Indeed, the men were becoming epicures. In passing through the camp one night, I saw a lot of jolly soldiers squatted outside the huts in true gypsy style, and between them a table richly stocked with meats and fowls of different kinds, flanked by several bottles of brandy.

They were a jolly set of scamps—talked, laughed, jested, and cracked jokes and bottles in smashing style.

A planter's house was overrun in a jiffy; boxes, drawers, and escritoirs were ransacked with a laudable zeal, and emptied of their contents. If the spoils were ample, the depredators were satisfied, and went off in peace; if not, everything was torn and destroyed, and most likely the owner was tickled with sharp bayonets into a confession where he had his treasures hid. If he escaped, and was hiding in a thicket, this was *prima facie* evidence that he was a skulking rebel; and most likely some ruffian, in his zeal to get rid of such vipers, gave him a dose of lead, which cured him of his Secesh tendencies. Sorghum barrels were knocked open, bee-hives rifled, while their angry swarms rushed frantically about. Indeed, I have seen a soldier knock a planter down because a bee stung him. Hogs are bayonetted, and then hung in quarters on the bayonets to bleed; chickens, geese, and turkeys are knocked over and hung in garlands from the saddles and around the necks of swarthy negroes; mules and horses are fished out of the swamps; cows and calves, so wretchedly thin that they drop down and perish on the first day's march, are driven along, or, if too weak to travel, are shot, lest they should give aid to the enemy.

Should the house be deserted, the furniture is smashed in pieces, music is pounded out of four hundred dollar pianos with the ends of muskets. Mirrors were wonderfully multiplied, and rich cushions and carpets carried off to adorn teams and war-steeds. After all was cleared out, most likely some set of stragglers wanted to enjoy a good fire, and set the house, debris of furniture, and all the surroundings, in a blaze. This is the way Sherman's army lived on the country. They were not ordered to do so, but I am afraid they were not brought to task for it much either.

We now come to Sherman's last and crowning campaign through the Carolinas.

Sherman's campaign through the Carolinas is not to be judged by hitherto recognized military rules or precedents, for he proved himself not only a great fighter and flanker, but also a great strategist. He inaugurated a new code of tactics, which completely bewildered and defeated the enemy. He discarded the old, effete style of sitting down before natural barriers and fortified places, to take them by assault, or tire them out by siege. Discarding such movements, he swept over the country in separate columns, now throwing one ahead, now another, thus flanking the most formidable positions.

There can be no denial of the assertion that the feeling among the troops was one of extreme bitterness towards the people of the State of South Carolina. It was freely expressed as the column hurried over the bridge at Sister's Ferry, eager to commence the punishment of "original secessionists." Threatening words were heard from soldiers who prided themselves on "conservatism in house-burning" while in Georgia, and officers openly confessed their fears that the coming campaign would be a wicked one. Just or unjust as this feeling was towards the country people of South Carolina, it was universal. I first saw its fruits at Rarysburg, where two or three piles of blackened brick and an acre or so of dying embers marked the site of an old revolutionary town; and this before the column had fairly got its "hand in."

At McBride's plantation, where General Sherman had his headquarters, the out-offices, shanties, and surroundings were all set on fire before he left. I think the fire approaching the dwelling hastened his departure.

If a house was empty, this was *prima facie* evidence that the owners were rebels, and all was sure to be consigned to the flames. If they remained at home, it was taken for granted that every one in South Carolina was a rebel, and the chances were, the place was consumed. In Georgia few houses were burned; here, few escaped; and the country was converted into one vast bonfire. The pine forests were fired, the resin factories were fired, the public buildings and private dwellings were fired. The middle of the finest day looked black and gloomy, for a dense smoke arose on all sides, clouding the very heavens. At night the tall pine trees seemed so many huge pillars of fire. The flames hissed and screeched, as they fed on the fat resin and dry branches, imparting to the forests a most fearful appearance.

Vandalism of this kind, though not encouraged, was seldom punished. True, where every one is guilty alike, there will be no informers; therefore the generals knew little of what was going on. The only cases I knew of theft being punished was on one or two occasions.

The ruined homesteads of the Palmetto State will long be remembered.

The army might safely march the darkest night, the crackling pine woods shooting up their columns of flame, and the burning houses along the way would light it on, while the dark clouds and pillars of smoke would safely cover its rear.

Foragers and bummers heralded the advance of the army, eating up the country like so many locusts. These fellows, mounted on scraggy old mules, or cast-off horses, spread themselves in one vast advance guard, and often-times went twenty miles ahead of the main columns. They returned at night with strings of chickens, bacon, turkeys, and geese, embellishing themselves and their horses, or with a buggy or carriage, which they had borrowed from the owner, well laden with supplies.

Sometimes some adventurous youths, who had gone too far, to have the first haul, got captured, and most likely had their throats cut.

The bummers of different corps sometimes fought among one another about the spoils, and at other times fraternized together, in order to dislodge some troublesome enemy.

The word "bummer" has so often occurred in this work, that I think it well to give an account of the signification of the name. Any man who has seen the object that it applies to will acknowledge that it was admirably selected. Fancy a ragged man, blackened by the smoke of many a pine-knot fire, mounted on a scraggy mule, without a saddle, with a gun, a knapsack, a butcher knife, and a plug hat, stealing his way through the pine forests far out on the flanks of a column, keen on the scent of rebels, or bacon, or silver spoons, or corn, or anything valuable, and you have him in your mind. Think how you would admire him if you were a lone woman, with a family of small children, far from help, when he blandly inquired where you kept your valuables. Think how you would smile when he pried open your chests with his bayonet, or knocked to pieces your tables, pianos, and chairs, tore your bed clothing in three-inch strips, and scattered them about the yard. The bummers say it takes too much time to use keys. Color is no protection from these roughriders. They go through a negro cabin, in search of diamonds and gold watches, with just as much freedom and vivacity as they "loot" the dwelling of a wealthy planter. They appear to be possessed of a spirit of "pure cussedness." One incident of many will illustrate: a bummer stepped into a house and inquired for sorghum. The lady of the house presented a jug, which he said was too heavy; so he merely filled his canteen. Than taking a huge wad of tobacco from his mouth, he thrust it into the jug. The lady inquired, in wonder, why he spoiled that which he did not want. "O, some feller'll come along and taste that sorghum, and think you've poisoned him; then he'll burn your d——d old house." There

are hundreds of these mounted men with the column, and they go everywhere. Some of them are loaded down with silver ware, gold coin, and other
valuables. I hazard nothing in saying that three fifths (in value) of the
personal property of the counties we have passed through were taken by
Sherman's army.

Orangeburg is on the Columbia branch of the South Carolina railroad,
ninety-seven miles from Charleston, and forty-seven from Columbia. It had
been a pretty place before the war, and had a population close on two thousand. It was built upon a rising bluff, one of the first we met since we left
Savannah. It possessed some historic relics of the revolutionary war. It was
formerly looked upon as a healthy, pleasant retreat, and was, therefore,
rather a fashionable little place.

When I reached the city, it was in flames. Our men say that they found
several houses, in which cotton was stored, on fire when they entered it. Be
this as it may, the whole town was soon in flames, and by the following
morning one heap of ashes.

The tasteful churches, with their tall steeples, and about fifty private
houses, alone escaped. A large amount of cotton was also consumed. It was
a sad sight next morning to witness the smoking ruins of the town, the tall,
black chimneys looking down upon it like funeral mutes, and to see old
women and children, hopeless, helpless, almost frenzied, wandering amidst
the desolation.

Our columns were now fast closing in about Columbia.

Early on the morning of the 15th, Major General Hazen threw forward
his skirmishers, and ascertained that the enemy had fallen back behind the
Congaree, burning the fine bridge that spanned the river just on the edge
of Columbia. Hazen had now occupied the front with detachments from his
command. Major Generals Howard, Logan, Blair, and others rode to the
front, to join Hazen and reconnoitre the position, though the rebel battery
was sweeping the road with round shot and canister.

Colonel Ross, chief of artillery, 15th corps, ordered up Captain De Grass's
battery. This splendid battery, under its dashing young captain, took up
position, and silenced the rebel battery that commanded the road. A section
was placed close to the bridge, so as to sweep the streets of the city, which
were crowded with soldiers, citizens, and wagons, clearing out of the town.
We were within five hundred yards of the city, which was situated on a
rising bluff on the other side of the river, so that we could smash it to pieces
in a short time by bringing sufficient artillery to bear on it. It appeared to be
Sherman's intention to shed as little innocent blood as possible.

We expected every moment that the city would be surrendered, for it now lay hopelessly in our power.

It was a lovely sight; the morning sun rose glowing and beautiful, its sparkling rays lighting up the house-tops of the doomed city, and dancing over the bright waters like diamond gems, bathing the river with its silvery rays. The shadows of the forest trees advanced along the sparkling waters as the boats shot over its surface, and the click of the rifle and whir of the bullet echoed around.

As soon as the pontoon was laid, General Sherman, accompanied by several other generals, their staffs and orderlies, forming a brilliant cavalcade, rode into the city amidst a scene of the most enthusiastic excitement. Ladies crowded the windows and balconies, waving banners and handkerchiefs. They were the wives and sisters of the few proscribed Union people of Columbia. As for the rich, haughty secessionists, they had all fled. Negroes were grouped along the streets, cheering, singing, and dancing in the wild exuberance of their newborn freedom. Perhaps the most flattering compliment paid to us was by a negro, whom, with upturned features and clasped hands, I heard exclaim, "At last! at last! our saviours!" Ringing cheers and shouts echoed far and wide, mingled with the martial music of the bands as they played "Hail, Columbia," "Yankee Doodle," and other national airs. It was, indeed, an exciting scene, and one well worth living to witness.

Our march through the city was so orderly that even the southerners began to bless their stars that the reign of terror was over, and that a reign of peace and security, like that at Savannah, was about being inaugurated. Alas that the scenes of the night should mar so auspicious a beginning!

Towards night, crowds of our escaped prisoners, soldiers, and negroes, intoxicated with their new-born liberty, which they looked upon as a license to do as they pleased, were parading the streets in groups.

As soon as night set in there ensued a sad scene indeed. The suburbs were first set on fire, some assert by the burning cotton which the rebels had piled along the streets. Pillaging gangs soon fired the heart of the town, then entered the houses, in many instances carrying off articles of value. The flame soon burst out in all parts of the city, and the streets were quickly crowded with helpless women and children, some in their night-clothes. Agonized mothers, seeking their children, all affrighted and terrified, were rushing on all sides from the raging flames and falling houses. Invalids had to be dragged from their beds, and lay exposed to the flames and smoke that swept the streets, or to the cold of the open air in back yards.

The scene at the convent was a sad one indeed. The flames were fast encompassing the convent, and the sisters, and about sixty terrified young ladies, huddled together on the streets. Some of these had come from the north, previous to the war, for their education, and were not able to return. The superioress of the convent had educated General Sherman's daughter Minnie. He had assigned them a special guard of six men; so they felt secure, and were totally unprepared for the dreadful scene that ensued. Some Christian people formed a guard around this agonized group of ladies, and conducted them to the Park.

I trust I shall never witness such a scene again—drunken soldiers, rushing from house to house, emptying them of their valuables, and then firing them; negroes carrying off piles of booty, and grinning at the good chance, and exulting, like so many demons; officers and men revelling on the wines and liquors, until the burning houses buried them in their drunken orgies.

I was fired at for trying to save an unfortunate man from being murdered.

The frequent shots on every side told that some victim had fallen. Shrieks, groans, and cries of distress resounded from every side. Men, women, and children, some half naked, as they rushed from their beds, were running frantically about, seeking their friends, or trying to escape from the fated town. A troop of cavalry, I think the 29th Missouri, were left to patrol the streets; but I did not once see them interfering with the groups that rushed about to fire and pillage the houses.

True, Generals Sherman, Howard, and others were out giving instructions for putting out a fire in one place, while a hundred fires were lighting all round them.

How much better would it have been had they brought in a division or brigade of sober troops, and cleared out the town, even with steel and bullet!

General Wood's 1st division, 15th corps, occupied Columbia. Colonel Stone's brigade was the first to enter the city and hoist the flag over the capitol—enviable notoriety, had not the drunken, riotous scenes of the night sullied its honor.

This scene continued until near morning, and then the town was cleared out, when there was nothing more to pillage or burn.

In the hospitals were some hundreds of rebel wounded. The agony and terror of the poor, helpless fellows while the fire raged around them were fearful; but, fortunately, the buildings did not catch fire.

While the streets were crowded with murdering groups of demons from all the corps in the army, hundreds of noble-minded officers and civilians were exposing their own lives to save the lives and property of the citizens.

Who is to blame for the burning of Columbia is a subject that will be long disputed. I know the negroes and escaped prisoners were infuriated, and easily incited the inebriated soldiers to join them in their work of Vandalism. Governor McGrath and General Wade Hampton are partly accountable for the destruction of their city. General Beauregard, the mayor, Mr. Goodwin, and others wanted to send a deputation as far as Orangeburg to surrender the city, and, when evacuating, to destroy all the liquors. In both of these wise views they were overruled by the governor and Wade Hampton, the latter stating that he would defend the town from house to house.

On the other hand I must honestly say that I saw nothing to prevent General Wood, who was in command there, from bringing sufficient troops to clear out the place, or his superior generals either from putting a stop to such disgraceful scenes.

The houses of the Prestons, Honystons, and other wealthy secesh were occupied as official quarters, and were preserved. Several soldiers and citizens must have been buried in the ruins of falling houses, or caught by the devouring flames. Next morning I saw a lady, a crazy inmate of the asylum, whose child had been burned during the night.

The 18th of February dawned upon a city of ruins. All the business portions, the main streets, the old capitol, two churches, and several public and private buildings were one pile of rubbish and bricks. Nothing remained but the tall, spectre-looking chimneys. The noble-looking trees that shaded the streets, the flower gardens that graced them, were blasted and withered by fire. The streets were full of rubbish, broken furniture, and groups of crouching, desponding, weeping, helpless women and children.

The Park and Lunatic Asylum, as affording the greatest chance of safety, were crowded with these miserable outcasts. In one place I saw a lady richly dressed, with three pretty little children clinging to her. She was sitting on a mattress, while round her were strewn some rich paintings, works of art, and virtu. It was a picture of hopeless misery surrounded by the trappings of refined taste and wealth. General Sherman ordered six hundred head of cattle and some stores to be left for the nuns and the destitute.

The scene of desolation the city presented next morning was fearful. That long street of rich stores, the fine hotels, the court-houses, the extensive convent buildings, and last the old capitol, where the order of secession was passed, with its fine library and state archives, were all in one heap of unsightly ruins and rubbish. Splendid private residences, lovely cottages, with their beautiful gardens, and the stately rows of shade trees, were all withered into ashes.

The ruins alone, without the evidences of human misery that everywhere met the view, were enough to inspire one with feelings of deep melancholy.

Here was desolation heightened by the agonized misery of human sufferings.

There lay the city wrapped in her own shroud, the tall chimneys and blackened trunks of trees looking like so many sepulchral monuments, and the woe-stricken people, that listlessly wandered about the streets, its pallid mourners.

Old and young moved about seemingly without a purpose. Some mournfully contemplated the piles of rubbish, the only remains of their late happy homesteads.

Old men, women, and children were grouped together. Some had piles of bedding and furniture which they saved from the wreck; others, who were wealthy the night previous, had not now a loaf of bread to break their fast.

Children were crying with fright and hunger; mothers were weeping; strong men, who could not help either them or themselves, sat bowed down, with their heads buried between their hands.

The scenes I witnessed in Columbia—scenes that would have driven Alaric the Goth into frenzied ecstasies, had he witnessed them—made me ponder a little on the horrors of war.

Those who are unacquainted with war cannot realize the fearful sufferings it entails on mankind. They read of it in papers and books, gilded over with all its false glare and strange fascinations, as a splendid game of glorious battles and triumphs, but close their eyes to its bloody horrors. The battle-field is to them a field of honor, a field of glory, where men resign their lives amidst the joys of conquest, which hallow the soldier's gory couch and light up his death-features with a smile. This sounds well in heroic fiction, but how different the reality! Could these fireside heroes but witness a battlefield, with its dead, its dying, and wounded, writhing in agonizing tortures, or witness the poor victims under the scalpel-knife, with the field-hospital clodded with human gore, and full of the maimed bodies and dissected limbs of their fellow-creatures, war would lose its false charms for them. Could many a tender mother see her darling boy, uncared-for, unpitied, without one kind hand to stay the welling blood or wipe the death-damp from his brow, her gentle, loving heart would break in one wail of anguish. War, after all, has horrors even greater than the battlefield presents. The death-wound is mercy compared to the slow torture of languishing in prison-houses—living charnel-houses of slow putrefaction—pale, spiritless, uncared-for, unpitied, gasping and groaning away their lives in hopeless misery. And then think of the sacked and burned city; think of helpless women and children fleeing in terror before the devouring element, without a home to shelter them, without bread to feed them; think of the widows and orphans that water their scant bread with the tears of sorrow; think of all the sufferings, misery, ruin, death, war entails on mankind, and you will curse its authors, and wish that God had otherwise chastised his people. Though war may enrich the Shylock shoddies, paymasters, contractors, and speculative politicians, who sport gorgeous equipages and rich palaces out of the blood of their countrymen, it crushes the people under its wheels, like the car of Juggernaut, and oppresses the millions with taxation.

25

Gone with the Wind: The South after Appomattox, 1865

Though born in Sheffield, Massachusetts, in 1835, the youth and young manhood of Sidney Andrews were spent outside New England. Educated in Illinois and at the University of Michigan, he became a newspaperman, first at Alton, Illinois, and then in Washington, D.C., where he was made a correspondent for the Chicago Tribune. *In 1865 he was commissioned by the* Tribune *and the* Boston Daily Advertiser *to write on the conditions of the war-torn South. His findings were later gathered into book form,* The South since the War, *and published in 1866. The later portion of his life was spent in Boston in various editorial and political capacities. He died in 1880.*

There was a considerable and natural curiosity in the North directly after the close of hostilities for firsthand knowledge about southern conditions.

Many travelers sought to supply this information. Among the earliest, and the best, was the account by Andrews. He traveled through North and South Carolina and Georgia from September to November, 1865. His account is a splendid piece of reporting. Clear and well organized, it covers a wide range of information on political, economic, and social matters—the attitudes of white rebels, the freedmen, state conventions, and race relations. In view of the fact that the passions of war had scarcely subsided, it is amazingly objective. He sometimes expected too much in the way of food, considering the prostrate economic position of the South; and his attitude toward the Negro and race relations reflects his Radical Republicanism. But there is no attitude of "Woe to the Vanquished" or any spirit of vindictiveness.

CHARLESTON HUMBLED, SEPTEMBER, 1865

A city of ruins, of desolation, of vacant houses, of widowed women, of rotting wharves, of deserted warehouses, of weed-wild gardens, of miles of grass-grown streets, of acres of pitiful barrenness,—that is Charleston wherein Rebellion loftily reared its head five years ago. Here is enough of woe and want and ruin and ravage to satisfy the most insatiate heart,—enough of sore humiliation and bitter overthrow to appease the desire of the most vengeful spirit.

We can never again have the Charleston of the decade previous to the war. The beauty and pride of the city are as dead as the glories of Athens. Five millions of dollars could not restore the ruin of these past four years; and that sum is so far beyond the command of the city as to seem the boundless measure of immeasurable wealth. Yet, after all, Charleston was Charleston because of the hearts of its people. Now one marks how few young men there are, how generally the young women are dressed in black. The flower of their proud aristocracy is buried on scores of battle-fields. If it were possible to restore the broad acres of crumbling ruins to their foretime style and uses, there would even then be but the dead body of Charleston.

The Charleston of 1875 will doubtless be proud in wealth and intellect and rich in grace and culture. Let favoring years bring forward such fruitage! Yet the place has not in itself recuperative power for such a result. The material on which to build that fair structure does not here exist, and, as I am told by dozens, cannot be found in the State. If Northern capital and Northern energy do not come here, the ruin, they say, must remain a ruin; and if this time five years finds here a handsome and thriving city, it will be the creation of New England,—not necessarily the pattern of New England, for the influences from thence will be moulded by and interfused with those now existing here; but yet, in the essential fact, the creation of New England.

It was noted on the steamship by which I came from New York that, leaving out the foreign element, our passengers were from Charleston and from Massachusetts. We had nearly as many Boston men as Charleston men. One of the Charleston merchants said to me that when he went North the passengers were also almost equally divided between Massachusetts and South Carolina; and he added, that, in Eastern Massachusetts, where he spent some days, he found many men who were coming to Charleston.

Of Massachusetts men, some are already in business here, and others came on to "see the lay of the land," as one of them said. "That's all right," observed an ex-Rebel captain in one of our after-dinner chats,—"that's all right; let's have Massachusetts and South Carolina brought together, for they are the only two States that amount to anything."

"I hate all you Yankees most heartily in a general sort of way," remarked another of these Southerners; "but I find you clever enough personally, and I expect it'll be a good thing for us to have you come down here with your money, though it'll go against the grain with us pretty badly."

There are many Northern men here already, though one cannot say that there is much Northern society, for the men are either without families or have left them at home. Walking out yesterday with a former Charlestonian, —a man who left here in the first year of the war and returned soon after our occupation of the city,—he pointed out to me the various "Northern houses"; and I shall not exaggerate if I say that this classification appeared to include at least half the stores on each of the principal streets. "The presence of these men," said he, "was at first very distasteful to our people, and they are not liked any too well now; but we know they are doing a good work for the city."

I fell into some talk with him concerning the political situation, and found him of bitter spirit toward what he was pleased to denominate "the infernal radicals." When I asked him what should be done, he answered: "You Northern people are making a great mistake in your treatment of the South. We are thoroughly whipped; we give up slavery forever; and now we want you to quit reproaching us. Let us back into the Union, and then come down here and help us build up the country."

Every little variation from the old order of things excites the comment "Yankee notion," in which there is sometimes good-natured querulousness and sometimes a sharp spice of contempt. Stopping a moment this afternoon in a store where were three or four intelligent men, one of them asked me the use of the "thing" I had in my hand. It was one of the handle-and-straps so common in the North for carrying shawls, cloaks, overcoats, &c. Seeing that none of them had any idea what it was, I explained its use. "Well, now, what a Yankee notion!" "Yes," answered another, "but how handy it is."

To bring here the conveniences and comforts of our Northern civilization, no less than the Northern idea of right and wrong, justice and injustice, humanity and inhumanity, is the work ready for the hand of every New England man and woman who stands waiting. There is much prejudice to overcome, and some of it is bitter and aggravating; but the measure of success won by Northern men already in the field is an earnest of the reward for others. Self-interest is a masterful agent in modern civilization.

Business is reviving slowly, though perhaps the more surely. The resident merchants are mostly at the bottom of the ladder of prosperity. They have idled away the summer in vain regrets for vanished hopes, and most of them are only just now beginning to wake to the new life. Some have already been North for goods, but more are preparing to go; not heeding that, while they vacillate with laggard time, Northern men are springing in with hands swift to catch opportunity. It pains me to see the apathy and indifference that so generally prevails; but the worst feature of the situation is, that so many young men are not only idle, but give no promise of being otherwise in the immediate future.

Many of the stores were more or less injured by the shelling. A few of these have been already repaired, and are now occupied,—very likely by Northern men. A couple of dozen, great and small, are now in process of repair; and scores stand with closed shutters or gaping doors and windows. The doubt as to the title of property, and the wise caution of the President in granting pardons, unquestionably has something to do with the stagnation so painfully apparent; but very much of it is due to the hesitating shiftlessness of even the Southern merchant, who forever lets *I dare not* wait upon *I would*. Rents of eligible storerooms are at least from one fourth to one third higher than before the war, and resident business men say only Northern men who intend staying but a short time can afford to pay present prices. I'm sure I can't see how any one can afford to pay them, but I know the demand is greater than the supply.

I queried of the returning merchants on the steamship how they were received in the North. An Augusta man complained that he could get no credit, and that there was a disposition to be grinding and exacting. One Charleston man said he asked for sixty days, and got it without a word of objection. Another told me that he asked for four months, was given three, and treated like a gentleman everywhere. Another showed me the receipt for a debt of about fifteen hundred dollars contracted before the war, which he had paid in full; and when he asked for four months on a bill of eight thousand dollars, it was readily given. Still another settled his old indebtedness with one third cash and eight and twelve months notes for the balance, while he got ninety days on three fourth of his new bill. One man said he had many friends in the North, and they all knew him for a thorough Rebel; he expected some taunts, but tried to carry himself like a gentleman, and was courteously received, "even in Boston."

It would seem that it is not clearly understood how thoroughly Sherman's army destroyed everything in its line of march,—destroyed it without questioning who suffered by the action. The Rebel leaders were, too, in their way, even more wanton, and just as thorough as our army in destroying property. They did not burn houses and barns and fences as we did; but, during the last three months of the war, they burned immense quantities of cotton and rosin.

The action of the two armies put it out of the power of men to pay their debts. The values and the bases of value were nearly all destroyed. Money lost about everything it had saved. Thousands of men who were honest in purpose have lost everything but honor. The cotton with which they meant to pay their debts has been burned, and they are without other means.

Yet when all this is said in favor of one class of merchants, it must, in good conscience, be added, that by far a larger class is showing itself unworthy of anything but stringent measures. "How do you find the feeling?" said I to a gentleman of national reputation, who is now here settling the affairs of a very large New York house. "Well, there are a good many merchants who don't mean to pay anything more than they are obliged to," said he in reply. I asked of one of the leading merchants this morning, "Are your people generally disposed to settle their accounts?" His answer was, "Those who expect to continue business must of course do so." "How about the others?" I queried. "I'm afraid there isn't so much commercial honor as there should be," he replied. I am told of one firm which represented itself entirely ruined, when subsequent investigation showed that it had five thousand pounds sterling to its credit in Liverpool; and of another which offered only thirty cents on the dollar, when its property in New York alone will cover over seventy cents on the dollar of its entire indebtedness.

The city is under thorough military rule; but the iron hand rests very lightly. Soldiers do police duty, and there is some nine-o'clock regulation; but, so far as I can learn, anybody goes anywhere at all hours of the night without molestation. "There never was such good order here before," said an old colored man to me. The main street is swept twice a week, and all garbage is removed at sunrise. "If the Yankees was to stay here always and keep the city so clean, I don't reckon we'd have 'yellow jack' here any more," was a remark I overheard on the street. "Now is de fust time sence I can 'mem'er when black men was safe in de street af'er night-fall," stated the negro tailor in whose shop I sat an hour yesterday.

On the surface, Charleston is quiet and well behaved; and I do not doubt that the more intelligent citizens are wholly sincere in their expressions of a desire for peace and reunion. The city has been humbled as no other city has been; and I can't see how any man, after spending a few days here, can desire that it shall be further humiliated merely for revenge. Whether it has been humiliated enough for health is another thing. Said one of the Charlestonians on the boat, "You won't see the real sentiment of our people, for we are under military rule; we are whipped, and we are going to make the best of things; but we hate Massachusetts as much as we ever did." This idea of making the best of things is one I have heard from scores of persons. I find very few who hesitate to frankly own that the South has been beaten. "We made the best fight we could, but you were too strong for us, and now we are only anxious to get back into the old Union and live as happily as we can," said a large cotton factor. I find very few who make any special profession of Unionism; but they are almost unanimous in declaring that they have no desire but to live as good and quiet citizens under the laws.

For the first two months of our occupancy of the city scarcely a white woman but those of the poorer classes was seen on the street, and very few were even seen at the windows and doors of the residences. That order of things is now, happily, changed. There doesn't yet appear to be as much freedom of appearance as would be natural; but very many of what are called the "first ladies" are to be seen shopping in the morning and promenading in the evening. They, much more than the men, have contemptuous motions for the negro soldiers; and scorn for Northern men is frequently apparent in the swing of their skirts when passing on the sidewalk.

One doesn't observe so much pleasantness and cheerfulness as would be agreeable; but the general demeanor is quite consonant with the general mourning costume. A stroller at sunset sees not a few pale and pensive-faced young women of exquisite beauty; and a rambler during the evening not unfrequently hears a strain of touching melody from the darkened parlor of some roomy old mansion, with now and then one of the ringing, passionate airs with which the Southern heart has been fired during the war.

Mothers yet teach their children hate of the North, I judge; for when I asked a bright-eyed girl of half a dozen years, with whom I walked on a back street for a block or two, whose girl she was, she promptly answered, "A Rebel mother's girl." Patience, good people who love liberty, patience; this petty woman's spite will bite itself to death in time.

Down in the churchyard of St. Philip's, one of the richest and most aristocratic of churches in this proud city, is a grave which every stranger is curious to see. There are only the four plain panelled brick walls about three feet high, and on them a mottled white marble slab, some nine feet by four in size. At the head of the grave is a single sickly ten-foot-high magnolia tree. At each corner of the foot is a sprawling and tangled damask rose-bush. All around the little plat is a border of myrtle, sweet in its rich greenness, but untrimmed and broken and goat-eaten. It is the grave of the father of the Rebellion, and on the marble slab there is cut the one word,—"CALHOUN."

This churchyard symbolizes the city of Charleston. Children and goats crawl through a convenient hole in the front wall, and play at will among the sunken graves and broken tombstones. There is everywhere a wealth of offal and garbage and beef-bones. A mangy cur was slinking among the stones, and I found a hole three feet deep which he had dug at the foot of one of the graves. Children were quarrelling for flowers over one of the more recent mounds. The whole yard is grown up to weeds and brush, and the place is desolate and dreary as it well can be; more desolate because cruel hands have broken away the corners of the great marble slab of Calhoun,— for mementos, I suppose. Time was when South Carolina guarded this grave as a holy spot. Now it lies in ruin with her chief city. When Northern life shall rebuild and revivify that city, let us pray it may also set chaste and simple beauty around this grave; for there is no need to wish the brave but bad spirit of Calhoun greater punishment than it must have in seeing the woe and waste and mourning which the war has brought the region he loved so well.

YANKEES AND REBELS

From Charleston to Orangeburg Court House is seventy-seven miles. Route, South Carolina Railroad. Time, seven and a half hours. Fare, five dollars. There is one train per day each way. Our train consisted of five freight-cars, the baggage-car, a box freight-car with seats for negroes, and one passenger-coach. The down train, which we met at Branchville,—where Sherman's army was to find its doom,—consisted of seven freight-cars, four of which were filled with troops on the way to Charleston and home, the baggage-car, and two passenger-coaches. Our one car was uncomfortably full when we started; but only eleven of the passengers came through.

"What sort of accommodations can I get at Orangeburg?" I asked of a friend in Charleston.

"You're not going to stop up there? O you can't do it!"

"Well, I shall try it, at all events."

"Don't do it; Orangeburg is just as good as any of these towns; but I advise you to shun all of 'em. The accommodations are awful: push right on to Columbia."

I wasn't to be put down that way, for I had consulted a gazetteer, and learned that "Orangeburg is a pleasant and thriving town on the northeast bank of the north fork of the Edisto River. It is in the midst of a farming district, and is the centre of a large cotton trade. Population two thousand seven hundred." That was before the war, and I knew the place had been partly burned; but I felt confident that my friend exaggerated.

We left the city at seven and a half o'clock in the morning. Twenty miles out, the conductor came through the car, and collected our fares; for no tickets are sold at Charleston. In front of me sat a good-looking young woman, of about twenty-two, I judged. Hearing her very plainly say that she was going to Orangeburg, I determined to ask her about the town and its hotel accommodations.

"Yes, I live there," she said.

"Is there a hotel in the town, or any place at which a person can stop?"

"O yes, there's a hotel," she said; and after a pause, she added, "but it's hardly such a place as a gentleman would choose, I think."

She spoke pleasantly enough, and, having answered my question, might have dropped the conversation; instead of which, she went on to say that persons who had occasion to stop in town for some days frequently took a room at a private house, and were much better suited than at the hotel.

I did the only thing I well could do,—the thing that it was perfectly natural I should do. I asked her if she could mention one or two private houses at which I might ask for accommodations, if the hotel proved unendurable.

I fully expected that she would say her mother sometimes accommodated gentlemen; and I may as well own that I had determined what reply I should make to that announcement.

Instead, however, she turned in her seat so as to face me, and said, with considerable vim, "Are you a Yankee?"

The question surprised me; and I simply answered, "From the North."

"By what right do you presume to speak to me, sir?" she asked, in a clear and snapping tone, that caught the ears and eyes of most of the passengers.

The strangeness of the question, no less than the remarkable change in her manner, coupled with the fact that I knew myself to be under the observation of thirty or more persons of Southern birth and feeling, embarrassed me to such degree that I could only stammer, "By the right which I supposed a gentleman always had to ask a lady a civil question."

"Well, sir, I don't choose to talk with you."

And she settled herself sharply into her seat, jerked her little body into a very upright position, and squared her shoulders in a very positive manner, —while I sat flushed and confused.

What should I do about it? That was a question I asked myself twenty times per hour for the next thirty miles. I was seriously inclined to apologize (though I hardly knew for what; but didn't, for I feared the little Rebel might snub me again, if I gave her an opportunity. In front of her sat a young man who had been a captain in the Rebel army. Him she soon engaged in conversation, and they cheered the slow miles with most lively chat. Surely, thought I, this is beginning the three months' journey unfortunately. I could have borne her indignation quite easily; but each individual in the car soon made me aware that my Yankee baseness was well known and thoroughly appreciated.

The forenoon wore away, and the crazy old engine dragged itself along. Little Miss was vivacious and entertaining; the ex-officer was evidently in a cheerful frame of mind; I sat alternating between repentance and indignation. Finally the whistle sounded for Branchville.

Missy rose in her seat, shook out her skirts, drew on her small thread glove, turned to me,—mind you, not to the ex-officer, but to me,—and asked me if I would be good enough to hand out her basket for her.

Here was another surprise. Queer creatures, these little Rebels, said I to myself, as I followed her out,—carrying the not heavy basket. She didn't stop when we reached the platform of the station-house, but walked on towards its upper end; and I followed, demurely, but wonderingly. Fifteen or twenty yards away from the car, she suddenly stopped, and turned quickly upon me with "Thank you; I want to apologize to you; I was rude."

And here was the greatest surprise of all! It caught me in confusion; but I managed to say something to the effect that perhaps I was too forward in asking the question I did.

"No, you were not. It was right that you should ask it, and I was rude to answer you so uncivilly. But you caught me at a disadvantage; I hadn't spoken to a Federal since Sumter was taken."

"Well, it didn't hurt you very much, did it?" said I. Whereat she laughed and I laughed, and then the engine whistled.

"I'm going to stop here a day or two," she remarked; and then, "You'll shake hands, won't you?" as I started for the car. So we shook hands, and I left her standing on the platform.

I hadn't learned much about my chances for comfort in Orangeburg, however.

We got here at three o'clock in the afternoon. I was determined to stop, let the accommodations be what they would, and firmly said "No" when the stage agent at the depot urged me to take a seat for Columbia.

There were five passengers with baggage. Twenty-five negroes crowded around us, and troubled the hot air with harsh clamor. "Give yer baggage here, sir." "Luf dis yer nig tote yer plun'er, Mass'r." "Have yer balese toted to de hotel, sah?" "Tuk a hack up town, Mass'r?"

I found the "hack" to be a rickety old short-boxed spring wagon, with two rough board seats, on the back one of which was a worn-out cushion, over both being a canvas supported on sticks nailed to each corner of the box. This establishment was drawn by a scrawny lame mule, and we were seventeen minutes in accomplishing the half-mile, which the boy called it, up to the hotel.

I was a little distrustful about the hotel; and learning from the driver that boarders were sometimes taken at another house, I stopped there and asked the white girl of fifteen, whom I found on the piazza, if they could give me meals and lodgings for about three days. She thought they could, but would call her mother. So much of the house and grounds as I could see presented an inviting appearance, and I indulged in visions of a pleasant chamber and many dreamy hours on the broad piazza. Presently "mother" appeared. She was a plump woman of thirty-three, perhaps.

"Yes, sir, we have a couple of rooms, and we sometimes take transient boarders," said she, answering the question I put to the girl.

"I am stopping three or four days in town, and had much rather be at a pleasant private house than at the hotel," I said.

"Are you a Yankee or a Southerner?"

"O, a Yankee, of course," I answered, smiling, though I saw breakers ahead.

"No Yankee stops here! Good day, sir!" And she turned and walked into the house.

The negro boy, who stood with my valise on his head, volunteered the remark, "Haf to go to de hotel, sah"; and I followed him back to the "hack."

At the "hotel" was a negro boy washing the steps from the piazza into the basement. I told him what I wanted. He would call the Missus. She was somewhere in the lower part of the house; and after her head came into sight above the level of the floor on which I stood, she stopped and washed her hands in the dirty water with which the boy had just finished scrubbing the stairway, smoothing her hair with them and wiping them on her apron.

I made known my desires, paid my driver his charge of seventy-five cents, and was shown by Robert, him of the wash-rag and scrubbing-brush, to room No. 8, the figure being at least a foot in length and rudely done in white chalk.

The room is about fourteen feet square, has one window fronting the southeast, and is in the third story. Lath and plaster there are not, on this floor at least. The partitions are of rough unmatched pine, with strips of cloth over the larger cracks, and a cheap wall paper on the boards all round. The ceiling is also of wood, and was once painted white, but is now, like the wall paper, of a smoky yellow. The paper is much broken by the shrinkage of the boards, and large patches of it have been torn off in a dozen places. The walls and ceiling are handsomely decorated with wasp's mud nests and sooty-branched cobwebs. The bed is a dirty cotton mattress in an old-fashioned high-post bedstead. There are no sheets, and in fact nothing but a cotton-stuffed pillow and a calico spread. This establishment is the abode of a numerous and industrious colony of the Improved Order of Red Men, to whom I nightly pay a heavy blood tribute. Beside the bed there is for furnishing of the room one cane-seat chair, a seven-by-ten looking-glass, and a three-foot-square and breast-high plain pine table, on which are a cracked wash-bowl and a handleless and noseless water-pitcher, to which I prevailed on Robert to add a cracked tumbler. In the window are six sound panes of glass, four cracked ones, and the remnants of five panes more. I suppose I should add also to the furniture several very social and handsome mice, and a healthy and lively swarm of uncommonly large mosquitoes.

The house has three stories and a basement dining-room. The first and second floors have broad piazzas on each side of the house. The first floor has four rooms, and the second and third have five each. Robert says mine is the best on the upper floor,—in which fact there is much consolation. Glimpses into the second floor rooms have not bred in me any desire to move down. In the so-called drawing-room there are three old chairs, a round and rickety centre-table, a sort of writing-desk, the wreck of a piano, and several pieces of carpet. In the dining-room are two twelve-foot plain pine tables, and twenty-three chairs of five different patterns. The table-spread of this noon was the same we had on the evening of my arrival, three days ago, and it was horribly filthy then. The dining-room itself is airy and clean.

The hotel grounds consist of a large yard, the gate of which is always open, and within which all the stray stock of the town has free ramble. At the bottom of the broad steps on the upper side of the house is a large mud-puddle, in which dogs and hogs alternately wallow, there being at least five of the former and nine of the latter running about. The dogs are gaunt and wolfish,—the hogs are slab-sided, half-grown, and very long of nose. There is in the yard about everything one can name, except grass and cleanliness,— bits of wood and crockery, scraps of old iron, wisps of straw and fodder, old rags, broken bottles, sticks, stones, bones, hoofs, horns, nails, etc., etc., *ad infinitum*. The barber throws the sweepings of his shop on one side the house, and the cook is equally free with her slops on the other side.

The "Missus" is the head of the house. She is tall and angular, with a complexion sallow to the last degree of sallowness, eyes in which there is neither life nor hope, hair which I am sure has not felt either comb or brush during my stay. Her dress is a greasy calico, of the half-mourning variety, to which she sometimes adds an apron which isn't more repulsive only because it can't be. She is a type of women, thank God, without counterpart in the North. She goes about the house in a shuffling, shambling manner, with the cry "Robert—Robert—Robert," or " 'Manda—'Manda—'Manda," always on her tongue. There is no variety of accent in this cry, but only one of length, as "Robert—Ro-be-rt—R-o-b-e-r-t." During meals she stands at the head of the table, and serves out the allowance of tea or coffee, and sugar and milk, with an unending string of such talk as this: "Robert, tend the hominy"; "Gal, get the gemman's cup and sasser"; " 'Manda, mind the flies"; "Good-ness gracious, nigger, why don't ye pass them biled eggs"; "Now, Robert, do see them flies"; " 'Manda, look arter them squeet pertaterses"; "Now, ye good-for-nuthin' nigger, can't ye brush away them flies?" She complains, in whining, listless fashion, to everybody, about the "niggers," telling how idle, shiftless, and ungrateful they are. She has a husband, who takes special pains to inform everybody that he hasn't anything to do with the hotel; and whose sole occupations, so far as I can see, are smoking, complaining about "the niggers," and doctoring a poor old blind, spavined horse.

The genius of the house is Robert, who stands on his head as well as on his feet; who is trim, pert, wide-awake; who picks out a Northern man with unerring instinct, and is always ready and prompt to serve him; but who is forever out of the way, or very busy when that cry of "Robert—Ro-be-rt— R-o-b-e-r-t" shuffles up through the house. What trick of stealing sugar he hasn't learned isn't worth learning. "*She* talk about the niggers,—bah!" he exclaims, as he goes about his work.

The table is wretched. The tea, eggs, and waffles are the only articles even passably good. Bread and biscuit are alike sour and leaden, and all the meats are swimming in strong fat. The cook is a large and raw-boned negro-woman, who is aided by the "Missus," the boy Robert, and the girl 'Manda.

I suppose Sarah cooks quite to the satisfaction of her mistress; but I doubt if it would be possible for any Northern girl, even with twenty years of training, to make of herself a cook so utterly bad as Sarah is. She certainly exhibits most remarkable ability in spoiling everything in the line of eatables.

The general management of the house, I scarcely need add, is hopelessly miserable. Everything is forever at sixes-and-sevens, and the knowledge of where anything was yesterday gives not the least indication of its present whereabouts. The establishment, not less in its several parts than in its aggregate whole, is an unclean thing. Shiftlessness has here his abode, and there is neither effort nor desire to dispossess him. And the traveller's bill is three dollars and a half per day!

I have not drawn this picture except for a purpose. I hear, already, in this Southern trip, a great deal about the superior civilization of the South. This hotel is a part of its outgrowth. Orangeburg was a place of twenty-five hundred to three thousand inhabitants. It is the county seat. Here is the State Orphan Asylum. The place is midway between Charleston and the capital. Let any one consider what is the character of the only public house in any Northern town of the same size, and similarly situated, and then the quality of this boasted Southern civilization will be apparent. Nor can it be said that the war is responsible for the condition of things here, for the house was full from the beginning, and has not suffered any loss from either army. It could not receive a week's support in any community of any State from Maine to the Rocky Mountains. Yet here it lives on and on, year after year, a witness for Southern civilization. Let us call things by their right names,—then shall we say *Southern barbarism*.

THE DESOLATION OF COLUMBIA

The war was a long time in reaching South Carolina, but there was vengeance in its very breath when it did come,—wrath that blasted everything it touched, and set Desolation on high as the genius of the State. "A brave people never before made such a mistake as we did," said a little woman who sat near me in the cars while coming up from Charleston; "it mortifies me now, every day I live, to think how well the Yankees fought. We had no idea they could fight half so well." In such humiliation as hers is half the lesson of the war for South Carolina.

Columbia is in the heart of Destruction. Being outside of it, you can only get in through one of the roads built by Ruin. Being in it, you can only get out over one of the roads walled by Desolation. You go north thirty-two miles, and find the end of one railroad; southeast thirty miles, and find the end of another; south forty-five miles, and find the end of a third; southwest fifty miles, and meet a fourth; and northwest twenty-nine miles, and find the end of still another. Sherman came in here, the papers used to say, to break up the railroad system of the seaboard States of the Confederacy. He did his work so thoroughly that half a dozen years will nothing more than begin to repair the damage, even in this regard.

The railway section of the route from Charleston lies mostly either in a pine barren or a pine swamp, though after passing Branchville we came into a more open and rolling country, with occasional signs of life. Yet we could not anywhere, after we left the immediate vicinity of the city, see much indication of either work or existence. The trim and handsome railway stations of the North, the little towns strung like beads on an iron string, are things unknown here. In the whole seventy-seven miles there are but two towns that make any impression on the mind of a stranger,—Summerville and George's,—and even these are small and unimportant places. Elsewhere we stopped, as it appeared, whenever the train-men pleased,—the "station" sometimes existing only in the consciousness of the engineer and conductor.

I found the railroad in better condition than I supposed that I should. The rails are very much worn, but the roadbed is in fair order for nearly the entire distance. The freight-cars seemed in passably good repair; but the passenger-coaches were the most wretched I ever saw,—old, filthy, and rickety. On our train was one new feature,—a colored man and his wife, whose duty it was to wait on the passengers.

The "Shermanizing process," as an ex-Rebel colonel jocosely called it, has been complete everywhere. To simply say that the people hate that officer is to put a fact in very mild terms. Butler is, in their estimation, an angel when compared to Sherman. They charge the latter with the entire work and waste of the war so far as their State is concerned,—even claim that Columbia was burned by his express orders. They pronounce his spirit "infernal," "atrocious," "cowardly," "devilish," and would unquestionably use stronger terms if they were to be had. I have been told by dozens of men that he couldn't walk up the main street of Columbia in the daytime without being shot; and three different gentlemen, residing in different parts of the State, declare that Wade Hampton expresses a purpose to shoot him at sight whenever and wherever he meets him. What else the South Carolina mothers forget, they do not seem likely in this generation to forget to teach their children to hate Sherman.

Certain bent rails are the first thing one sees to indicate the advent of his army. I looked at them with curious interest. "It passes my comprehension to tell what became of our railroads," said a travelling acquaintance; "one week we had passably good roads, on which we could reach almost any part of the State, and the next week they were all gone,—not simply broken up, but gone; some of the material was burned, I know, but miles and miles of iron have actually disappeared, gone out of existence."

We rode over the road where the army marched. Now and then we found solitary chimneys, but, on the whole, comparatively few houses were burned, and some of those were fired, it is believed, by persons from the Rebel army or from the neighboring locality. The fences did not escape so well, and most of the planters have had these to build during the summer. This was particularly the case near Columbia. Scarcely a tenth of that destroyed appears to have been rebuilt, and thousands of acres of land of much richness lie open as a common.

There is a great scarcity of stock of all kinds. What was left by the Rebel conscription officers was freely appropriated by Sherman's army, and the people really find considerable difficulty not less in living than in travelling. Milk, formerly an article much in use, can only be had now in limited quantities: even at the hotels we have more meals without than with it. There are more mules than horses, apparently; and the animals, whether mules or horses, are all in ill condition and give evidence of severe overwork.

Columbia was doubtless once the gem of the State. It is as regularly laid out as a checker-board,—the squares being of uniform length and breadth and the streets of uniform width. What with its broad streets, beautiful shade-trees, handsome lawns, extensive gardens, luxuriant shrubbery, and wealth of flowers, I can easily see that it must have been a delightful place of residence. No South-Carolinian with whom I have spoken hesitates an instant in declaring that it was the most beautiful city on the continent; and, as already mentioned, they charge its destruction directly to General Sherman.

It is now a wilderness of ruins. Its heart is but a mass of blackened chimneys and crumbling walls. Two thirds of the buildings in the place were burned, including, without exception, everything in the business portion. Not a store, office, or shop escaped; and for a distance of three fourths of a mile on each of twelve streets there was not a building left. "They destroyed everything which the most infernal Yankee ingenuity could devise means to destroy," said one gentleman to me; "hands, hearts, fire, gunpowder, and behind everything the spirit of hell, were the agencies which they used." I asked him if he wasn't stating the case rather strongly; and he replied that he would make it stronger if he could. The residence portion generally escaped conflagration, though houses were burned in all sections except the extreme northeastern.

Every public building was destroyed, except the new and unfinished state-house. This is situated on the summit of tableland whereon the city is built, and commands an extensive view of the surrounding country, and must have been the first building seen by the victorious and on-marching Union army. From the summit of the ridge, on the opposite side of the river, a mile and a half away, a few shells were thrown at it, apparently by way of reminder, three or four of which struck it, without doing any particular damage. With this exception, it was unharmed, though the workshops, in which were stored many of the architraves, caps, sills, &c., were burned,—the fire, of course, destroying or seriously damaging their contents. The poverty of this people is so deep that there is no probability that it can be finished, according to the original design, during this generation at least.

The ruin here is neither half so eloquent nor touching as that at Charleston. This is but the work of flame, and might have mostly been brought about in time of peace. Those ghostly and crumbling walls and those long-deserted and grass-grown streets show the prostration of a community,—such prostration as only war could bring.

I find a commendable spirit of enterprise, though, of course, it is enterprise on a small scale, and the enterprise of stern necessity. The work of clearing away the ruins is going on, not rapidly or extensively, to be sure, but something is doing, and many small houses of the cheaper sort are going up. Yet, at the best, this generation will not ever again see the beautiful city of a year ago. Old men and despondent men say it can never be rebuilt. "We shall have to give it up to the Yankees, I reckon," said one of two gentlemen conversing near me this morning. "Give it up!" said the other; "they've already moved in and taken possession without asking our leave." I guess the remark is true. I find some Northern men already here, and I hear of more who are coming.

Of course there is very little business doing yet. The city is, as before said, in the heart of the devastated land. I judge that twenty thousand dollars would buy the whole stock of dry goods, groceries, clothing, &c. in store. The small change of the place is made in shinplasters, printed on most miserable paper, and issued by the various business men, "redeemable in United States currency when presented in sums of two dollars and upwards." "Green-backs" and national currency notes pass without question in the city, but are looked upon with suspicion by the country people. "Having lost a great deal by one sort of paper, we propose to be careful now," they say. Occasionally one sees a State bank-note, but they pass for only from twenty-five to sixty or sixty-five cents on the dollar. There is none of the Confederate money in circulation; though I judge, from what I hear, that considerable quantities of it are hoarded up in the belief that things will somehow take such a turn as to one day give it value.

There is a certain air of easy dignity observable among the people that I have not found elsewhere in the State,—not even in Charleston itself. Something of this is probably due to the fact that the capital is located here; but more of it, probably, to the existence of Columbia College. It was before the war a very flourishing institution, but has been closed during the last three years. The old but roomy buildings are in part occupied by the military authorities, partly by the professors and officers of the college, and are partly closed. No indication is given as to the time of reopening the school. It is said by residents that the city contained some of the finest private libraries in the South; but these, with one or two exceptions, were burned.

The women who consider it essential to salvation to snub or insult Union officers and soldiers at every possible opportunity do not seem as numerous as they appeared to be in Charleston; and indeed marriages between soldiers and women of the middle class are not by any means the most uncommon things in the world; while I notice, in a quiet, unobservant manner, as even the dullest traveller may, that at least several very elegant ladies do not seem at all averse to the attentions of the gentlemen of shoulder-straps. Can these things be, and not overcome the latent fire of Rebellion?

BLACK AND WHITE AFTER THE WAR

Recalling how persistently the whites of South Carolina have claimed, for twenty-five years, to be the negro's special friends, and seeing, as the traveller does, how these whites treat this poor black, one cannot help praying that he may be saved from his friends in future. Yet this cannot be. Talk never so plausibly and eloquently as any one may of colonization or deportation, the inexorable fact remains, that the negro is in South Carolina, and must remain here till God pleases to call him away. The problem involved in his future must be met on the soil of which he is native; and any attempt to solve it elsewhere than in the house of these his so-called special friends will be futile.

The work of the North, in respect to South Carolina, is twofold: the white man must be taught what the negro's rights are, and the negro must be taught to wait patiently and wisely for the full recognition of those rights in his own old home. He waited so long in the house of bondage for the birthright of freedom, that waiting is weary work for him now; yet there is nothing else for him and us,—nothing but faith, and labor, and waiting, and, finally, rest in victory.

The city negro and the country negro are as much unlike as two races. So, too, the city white man and the country white man differ much from each other. The latter, however, is just what he chooses to be, while the country negro is just what slavery and his late owners have made him. Tell me what you will derogatory of the country negro, and very likely I shall assent to most of the language you use. He is very often, and perhaps generally, idle, vicious, improvident, negligent, and unfit to care well for his interests. In himself, he is a hard, coarse, unlovely fact, and no amount of idealizing can make him otherwise. Yet, for all that, he is worth quite as much as the average country white.

Everybody talks about the negro, at all hours of the day, and under all circumstances. One might in truth say—using the elegant language of opposition orators in Congress—that "the people have got nigger on the brain." Let conversation begin where it will, it ends with Sambo.

I scarcely talk with any white man who fails to tell me how anxious many of the negroes are to return to their old homes. In coming up from Charleston I heard of not less than eleven in this condition, and mention has been made to me here in Orangeburg of at least a score. The first curious circumstance is, that none of them are allowed to return; and the second is, that I can't find any of those desirous of returning. I presume I have asked over a hundred negroes here and in Charleston if they wanted to go back and live with their old masters as slaves, or if they knew any negro who did desire to return to that condition, and I have yet to find the first one who hesitates an instant in answering "No."

I spoke of this difficulty I have in finding a single negro who loved slavery better than he does freedom to an intelligent gentleman whom I met here last evening,—a member of the Rhett family. "I am surprised to hear that," said he; "but I suppose it's because you are from the North, and the negro don't dare to tell you his real feeling." I asked if the blacks don't generally consider Northern men their friends. "O yes," he answered, "and that's the very reason why you can't find out what they think."

They deserve better treatment than they get at our hands in Orangeburg, at least; and I am told that what I see here is a forecast of what I shall see in all parts of the State. Theoretically, and in the intent of Congress, the Freedmen's Bureau stands as the next friend of the blacks; practically, and in the custom of the country, it appears to stand too often as their next enemy. That General Saxton is their good friend does not need to be asserted. Very likely the district commissioners under him are wise and humane men, and unquestionably the general regulations for the State are meant to secure justice to the freedmen.

The trouble arises from the fact that it is impossible for the State Commissioner or his chief deputies to personally know all, or even half, their various local agents. Take the case right in hand. Head-quarters for this district are thirty miles below here; and the ranking officer of the bureau has, probably, agents in at least forty different towns, the majority of whom are doubtless lieutenants from the volunteer forces of the army. They are detailed for this duty by the military commander of the post or the district,—sometimes after consultation with the district commissioner, but quite generally without. As the post garrisons are constantly changing, there may be a new agent of the bureau once a month in each town of the district; and I need not add, that the probabilities are that half the aggregate number on duty at any given time are wholly unfit for the work intrusted to them.

Again, take the case right in hand. The acting agent here at present is a lieutenant from a New York regiment. He is detailed by the colonel commanding, and has been on duty several weeks. Yet he never has seen the district commissioner of the bureau. His duties are to examine, and approve or disapprove, all contracts between the planters and the negroes, and to hear and determine all cases of complaint of grievance arising between the negroes themselves, or between the whites and the negroes. He treats me courteously, but he has no sympathy with the poor and lowly; and his ideas of justice are of the bar-room order,—might makes right. He doesn't really intend to outrage the rights of the negroes, but he has very little idea that they have any rights except such as the planters choose to give them. His position, of course, is a difficult one; and he brings it to a head more or less muddled with liquor, a rough and coarse manner, a dictatorial and impatient temper, a most remarkable ability for cursing, and a hearty contempt for "the whole d——n pack o' niggers." I speak from the observation of a good deal of time spent in and around his office.

I found Charleston full of country negroes. Whites of all classes concur in saying that there is a general impression throughout the back districts that lands are to be given the freed people on the sea-coast; and this, I am told, renders them uneasy and unreliable as plantation hands. Whites of all classes also concur in saying that they will not work.

"I lost sixteen niggers," said a Charleston gentleman; "but I don't mind it, for they were always a nuisance, and you'll find them so in less than a year." I asked, as usual, what they are now doing. Two or three of the men went into the army, one of the women had gone North as a cook, another is chambermaid on a steamer, and he found three of the men at work on one wharf the other day. "But," said I, laughing, "I thought the free negro wouldn't work." "O, well, this is only a temporary state of affairs, and they'll all be idle before winter; and I don't look for nothing else when cold weather comes but to have them all asking me to take them back; but I sha'n't do it. I wouldn't give ten cents apiece for them."

Many of the private soldiers on duty here tell me that the planters generally overreach the negroes on every possible occasion; and my observation among such as I have seen in town tends to confirm this assertion to a considerable extent.

Coming up in the cars from Charleston I had for seat-mate part of the way one of the delegates to the Convention which meets at Columbia next week. He was a very courteous and agreeable gentleman, past middle age, and late the owner of twenty-two negroes. He was good enough to instruct me at some length in respect to the character of the negro. "You Northern people are utterly mistaken in supposing anything can be done with these negroes in a free condition. They can't be governed except with the whip. Now on my plantation there wasn't much whipping, say once a fortnight; but the negroes knew they would be whipped if they didn't behave themselves, and the fear of the lash kept them in good order." He went on to explain what a good home they always had; laying stress on the fact that they never were obliged to think for themselves, but were always tenderly cared for, both in health and sickness; "and yet these niggers all left me the day after the Federals got into Charleston!" I asked where they now are; and he replied that he hadn't seen anybody but his old cook since they ran away; but he believed they were all at work except two, who had died. Yet I am told constantly that these ungrateful wretches, the negroes, cannot possibly live as free people.

Yesterday morning while I sat in the office of the agent of the Freedmen's Bureau there came in, with a score of other men, a planter living in this district, but some sixteen miles from town. He had a woful tale of an assault upon himself by one of his "niggers,"—"a boy who I broughten up, and who's allers had a good home down ter my place." While the boy was coming in from the street the man turned to me and explained, "It never don't do no good to show favor to a nigger, for they's the most ongratefullest creeturs in the world." The dreadful assault consisted in throwing a hatchet at the white man by one of a crowd of negroes who were having a dispute among themselves, and suddenly discovered, in the early evening, somebody sneaking along by the fence. The boy said it wasn't a hatchet, but a bit of brick; and added, that the man was so far away that no one could tell whether he was white or black, and that he didn't throw the brick till after he called out and told the man to go away. I followed the negro out after he had received his lecture from the officer, and had some talk with him. "D——n him," said he, referring to his employer, "he never done nufin all his d——n life but beat me and kick me and knock me down; an' I hopes I git eben with him some day."

Riding with an ex-Confederate major, we stopped at a house for water. The owner of the property, which was a very handsome one, was absent; and it was in charge of a dozen negroes, former slaves of the proprietor.

"Now here," said the late officer, "here is a place where the negroes always had the pleasantest sort of a home,—everything to eat and drink and wear, and a most kind master and mistress."

Pompey, aged about twelve, came to bring us the water.

"Pompey," said the Major, "Pompey, how do you like your freedom?"

He hung his head, and answered, "Dun know, mawssa."

"O, well, speak right out; don't be afraid; tell us just how it is now," said he again.

Whereupon Pompey: "Likes to be free man, sah; but we's all workin' on yer like we did afore."

"That's right, Pompey," said I; "keep on working; don't be a lazy boy."

"It won't do," said the Major; "he'll grow up idle and impudent and worthless, like all the rest."

"No, sah," answered Pompey, "I's free nigger now, and I's goin' to work."

There is much talk among the country people about a rising of the blacks. A planter who stopped here last night, and who lives twelve miles to the west, told me that it was believed in his neighborhood that they had guns and pistols hid in the timber, and were organizing to use them. His ideas were not very clear about the matter; but he appeared to think they would make serious trouble after the crops are gathered. Another man, living in Union district, told the company, with evident pleasure, that they'd been able to keep control of the niggers up to his section till 'bout three weeks ago; he 'lowed thar'd bin some lickin', but no more'n was good fur the fellows. Now the Federals had come in, and the negroes were in a state of glad excitement, and everybody feared there would be bloody business right away.

A thing that much shocks me is the prevalent indifference to the negro's fate and life. It is a sad, but solemn fact, that three fourths of the native whites consider him a nuisance, and would gladly be rid of his presence, even at the expense of his existence. And this in face of the fact that all the planters are complaining about the insufficiency of labor. Thus, in Charleston, a merchant told me, with relishing detail, a story to the effect that, soon after the promulgation of the order against wearing Confederate buttons, a negro soldier doing duty in the city halted a young man, informed him of the regulations, and told him that if he was seen on the street again wearing the obnoxious buttons, he would probably be arrested; whereupon the hopeful scion of the Charleston aristocracy whipped out a large knife, seized the negro by the beard, and cut his throat. The soldier died in about a week; but nothing had been done with the man who killed him. So, too, a man who seems to be acting as stage-agent here says "a d——d big black buck nigger" was shot near Lewisville about three weeks ago; and the citizens all shield the man who shot him, and sanction his course. All the talk of men about the hotel indicates that it is held to be an evidence of smartness, rather than otherwise, to kill a freedman; and I have not found a man here who seems to believe that it is a sin against Divine law.

The white man and the negro do not understand each other, and consequently do not work together so harmoniously as it is desirable that they should. It would seem that, one party having work to do and the other needing work, there would be such community of interest as leads to unity of purpose and action; but the fact is, that each party distrusts the other, and therefrom results bickering and antagonism.

That there are many kind-hearted planters—men who made slavery in very truth a sort of patriarchal institution, and who are now endeavoring in all sincerity and earnestness to make the negro's situation not only tolerable, but comfortable—is as true as it is that there are many negroes who cling to the old places and the old customs, and are doing their work just as faithfully and unselfishly as ever. These men, on either side, are, I am convinced, the exceptions.

The fault unquestionably, it appears to me, lies with the white man. He is of the ruling race, and might, I feel very certain, have established a different order of things if he had pleased to do so, and had exercised good common sense in the beginning. That there are some planters who find the free negroes honest and faithful is positive proof that there might have been many more, and if many more, then without number.

Most of them began by assuming, however, that it was right to keep the negro in slavery just as long as possible, and by adding thereto the assumption that the free negro would not work. Military power has compelled the recognition of his freedom in every district, I believe, though in some of them not till within the last six weeks; but this almost universal belief that he will not work is doing a good deal to prove that he will not; and troubles which are dimly foreshadowed will come from this cause alone,—the brutal assumption that the negro cannot be controlled except by fear of the lash.

There is among the plantation negroes a widely spread idea that land is to be given them by the government, and this idea is at the bottom of much idleness and discontent. At Orangeburg and at Columbia, country negroes with whom I conversed asked me, "When is de land goin' fur to be de-wided?" Some of them believe the land which they are to have is on the coast; others believe the plantations on which they have lived are to be divided among themselves.

As I have already intimated, the negroes are drifting down toward the coast in great numbers. In the night of travel between Orangeburg and Columbia, we met scores of them trudging along with their whole earthly possession in a bundle on the head. Walking in the bright moonlight seventy or eighty rods ahead of the hack, I spoke with many. They had but few words; "Goin' to Char'ston," was often their only reply. Whether talkative or taciturn, there was a firm foot and an unruffled voice for the coast. "What are you going to do there?" I asked,—only to get for my answer, "Dun know." I never shall forget the scenes of that two or three miles' walk between one and two o'clock in the morning of that 11th of September. There had recently been some robberies of travellers on that road, and guerillas suggested themselves with every outline seen in the sheeny distance. Yet it was only the exodus of the negroes, going out ignorantly and mistakenly, yet seeking nothing less noble and worthy than freedom.

Despite the fact that nearly everybody tells me the free negro will not work, the experience of some of the better class of planters convinces me that he will work, if he is treated like a man. He is unquestionably sensitive about his freedom,—it is the only thing he has that he can call his own.

Some of the blacks are working along as heretofore, under private arrangements with their former masters; but in most cases there is a written contract between the employer and the employed,—one copy in the hands of the planter and the other at the Freedmen's Bureau office. I hear of very few cases in which the compensation is in money; in nearly all instances it is a part of the crop. The laborer's share ranges from one tenth to one half; on some small farms, where special privileges are given the negroes in the way of clothing, use of land, use of team, use of time, the share may not be over one sixth to one tenth of the regular crop; in the lower part of the State, where most of the labor is done by hand, and where there are no special privileges, the share is from one third to one half; in the upper part of the State, where horses or mules are more in use, the share is from one fourth to one third. The contracts generally expire at New Year's.

It is beyond question that but little work has been done in the State this season. The free negro is the scapegoat on which the whites lay the burden of this wrong, of course; but it seems to me that the disturbed condition of the country in the early summer and through all the spring is extenuation enough.

It is, however, true that the lately freed negro has not generally been made to comprehend that there are six laboring days in each week. The railroad companies complain that they can get but three or four day's work per week from the blacks engaged in rebuilding the roads; and the contract officers of the Freedmen's Bureau quite universally concur in the statement that five days make a plantation negro's week for work. Instances in which the contract officers have been called on to go out into the country and convince the negroes that work must be done on Saturday as well as on other days are not at all rare.

The indifference which so many of the people feel and express as to the fate of the negro is shocking and to the last degree revolting to me. He is actually to many of them nothing but a troublesome animal; not a human being, with hopes and longings and feelings, but a mere animal, valuable, but altogether unlovable. "I would shoot one just as soon as I would a dog," said a man to me yesterday on the cars. And I saw one shot at in Columbia as if he had been only a dog,—shot at from the door of a store, and at midday! "If I can only git shet of 'em I don't care what becomes of 'em," said one of my two stage companions in the ride from Columbia to Winnsboro, while speaking of the seventy negroes on his plantation. Of course he means to "git shet of 'em" as soon as possible. There are others who will follow his example.

There has been much talk to the effect that the planters are, now that the main work of the season is over, turning the negroes adrift. It will not be easy to do this on any large scale, nor can I believe that many employers will attempt it. Indifference most heartless is one thing,—downright active cruelty is quite another. The one may prevail; but, aside from all other considerations, fear of the military will prevent the other. The facility with which the negro can bring his late master before the provost-marshal is something not wholly unpleasant to see.

The whole labor system of the State is in an utterly demoralized condition. How soon it can be thoroughly reorganized, and on just what basis that reorganization will take place, are questions of no easy answering. The labor question, and not reconstruction, is the main question among intelligent thinking men of the State. Scarcely one in a dozen of the best of them have any faith in the negro. "The experiment of free negro labor is bound to be a failure; and you of the North may as well prepare for it first as last," is substantially the language of hundreds. And thereafter follow questions of, "What shall then be done with the negro?" and, "Where shall we then get our labor?"

Look at the figures for a few districts. In Sumter there were, in 1860, of whites, 6,857, and of negroes, 17,012; in Fairfield, 6,373 whites, and 15,736 negroes; in Colleton, 9,255 whites, and 32,661 negroes; in Beaufort, 6,714 whites, and 33,339 negroes; and in Georgetown, 3,013 whites, and 18,292 negroes. Is it any wonder that the white population of these districts is nervously sensitive about the negro? The proportion of blacks is even greater now than these figures indicate; for war has taken out the whites and brought in the negroes to such an extent that one delegate told me there were in his parish but twenty-two voters and over two thousand negroes. What is to come of such a condition of affairs?

INDEX

Index

Index

Date Due

DATE DUE

Demco, Inc. 38-293